Praise for *Anatomy of a Champion*

"Dic   leveloping great players, supportii   ...ucavors, and forging great teams is unsurpassed in NCAA tennis history. His book gives insights into his holistic approach, and we can all learn, whatever our profession, from this outstanding coach and exceptional man."

Condoleezza Rice
Provost, Stanford University (1993–1999)
Secretary of State (2005–2009)
Director, Hoover Institution

"Most books on leadership are written by highly successful leaders who have taken their own experiences, converted them into a set of principles that guided their behavior, and recommended them to the reader. Dick Gould, the most successful men's tennis coach in NCAA history, has turned this formula upside down. Instead of building a guiding framework of leadership relying on his own experiences, he synthesized the views of 166 players he coached over thirty-eight years of leading the Stanford tennis program and created a powerful picture of what it took to build and guide an enduring, high-performing organization. Loaded with lots of direct quotes from his players, Gould presents so many pearls of wisdom in this book that I highly recommend it as an excellent resource for anyone interested in leadership—from parents to coaches to those aspiring for leadership positions in any enterprise and at any level."

Jerry Porras
Lane Professor of Organizational Behavior and Change, Emeritus
Graduate School of Business, Stanford University
Coauthor, *Built to Last*
Faculty Athletics
Representative to the PAC-10 and the NCAA (1988–2001)

"Although I wasn't privileged to know Coach Gould as a tennis coach, I have been honored to collaborate with him on his visionary youth concussion education work with TeachAids. Dick is passionate, purposeful, full of humor and grace, and cares deeply about our youth. Dick reminds us that first and foremost, a coach is an educator who cares. This critical trait reverberates from his player's comments throughout *Anatomy of a Champion*."

Brian Hainline, MD
NCAA Chief Medical Officer
Clinical Professor of Neurology
NYU Grossman School of Medicine

"*Anatomy of a Champion* is a fantastic book! I appreciate the 'reverse engineering' format of asking the players to provide much of the content, followed by Dick's insightful coaching interpretation and contextualization of their comments. It very much feels like an ongoing discussion (fireside chat) throughout the decades. Masterfully done! The balance of the conceptual, and also sometimes chronological, approach keeps the reader engaged throughout. As a pure tennis coach, player, or fan, this is a must read. However, I wholeheartedly believe that this book also provides great information for business leaders, educators, and sports administrators who will derive tremendous benefits from reading this book."

Paul Roetert
Managing Director
USTA-U; National Campus

"We just watched in awe each day how Coach worked to transform Stanford tennis in that tiny wood shack. It was nothing more than a woodshed, but with DG inside it was like the 'temple of college tennis.' You walked inside the place and his unbridled enthusiasm was infectious. You just knew that being around this guy was going to be worth the ride. And oh, what a great ride it was."

John Corse
Stanford Tennis Team, '82

"When you joined the team, you automatically felt like you were there to do your job and that was to help win an NCAA championship. Coach magnified this sense of pride and purpose each and every day. Coach Gould had an aura that demanded respect, and he had all the attributes that made it easy for players to put their faith in him. He was always prepared and knew what to say. You could see that he cared deeply about his role and was extremely driven to succeed. You could see that he knew the formula of what it took to be a championship team, so there was no reason to resist it. There was never doubt in his eyes, and he always confidently executed his plan. It was nice to be able to trust that this man could guide the team and in turn help every member reach his full potential."

Mike Bryan
Stanford Tennis Team, '00
Pro: All-Time World Doubles #1
NCAA Doubles Champ

"It is critical to understand that the results that Dick Gould had are truly the by-product of his personal greatness. His pursuit of constant and relentless improvement. His pursuit of fulfilling and executing the value systems of work ethic, attention to detail, perseverance, determination, a willingness to take chances to do and be special, never letting his competitors see him down or discouraged, his amazing recruiting skills and optimism. If I were to summarize it all up, it would be that Dick had and has a profound understanding that life is about the journey and for God sakes make the most of it! This is the profound example that Dick Gould has passed on to me. Dick's example has been so relentless and consistent that it has left an indelible impression on me in my life. Life is a journey, a blessing, an opportunity, so don't waste today and make the most of it! The results are truly the by-products of an incredibly powerful and positive philosophy of life! That is the true legacy."

Nick Saviano
Stanford Tennis Team, '73
Pro: Singles #48
Former USTA Director of Coaching & Coaching Education

Anatomy of a Champion

Bianca —

With THANX for being such a good "new" friend. Your attitude is so refreshing. It is contagious. Looking forward to working with you. THANX for your support — All my best,

Sid Gould

6/5/23

Anatomy of a Champion

Building and Sustaining Success in Sport, Business, and Life

As shared by 166 CEOs, entrepreneurs, coaches and world champions

Dick Gould
with
Tim Troupe Noonan

Waterside Productions
Cardiff-by-the-Sea, California

Printed in the United States of America
First Printing, 2022

ISBN-13: 978-1-957807-89-8 print edition
ISBN-13: 978-1-957807-90-4 e-book edition

Waterside Productions
2055 Oxford Ave
Cardiff, CA 92007
www.waterside.com

Anatomy of a Champion is dedicated to the memory and great times spent together with "my guys" who contributed to this book but who passed during the five years it took to complete:

Craig Baise, '68
Chris Bradley, '72
Scot Love, '79
John Corse, '82

EPIGRAPH

COACHING IN ANY ARENA IS A SACRED RESPONSIBILITY

—Dick Gould

TABLE OF CONTENTS

Foreword

MY TIME AT STANFORD

John McEnroe

John McEnroe: NCAA Singles Champion; World Singles and Doubles #1

My time at Stanford was short as I decided to pursue a professional tennis career after my freshman year. But what an education it was, not the least of which was my relationship with Coach Gould!

Dick was the perfect "life coach" for me at the time, even more than he was as a tennis coach. Hell, he never said a word to me about tennis. He didn't need to—I was ranked twenty-one in the world when I got there! What I did see him do, however, was navigate what could have been a very tricky team situation into an undefeated team that I believe (yes, I'm biased!) was the best team Stanford ever had.

Maybe that's for a different book, but I watched as he was able to bring out the best in us individually, simultaneously make us better as a team, and, oh yeah, provide a couple of life lessons along the way. That is what to me leadership is all about, and you will read in this book about numerous other teams with whom he was able to work his "magic," eventually retiring with one of the great coaching résumés in college history.

By the way, this book is not intended to be a "History of Stanford Tennis" and the seventeen NCAA tennis championships over those thirty-eight years. Rather, Coach Gould sought out comments from all his former players as to what impacted them most in their Stanford tennis experience. The answers provide a unique insight into why Coach became one of the most successful leaders and managers ever, as measured by those he led and managed—his players.

This book is packed with quotes from 166 players—83 percent of all those who played over a thirty-eight-year period—and ranging from world champions to those barely on the team, addressing key management topics. These personal experiences are what sets it apart from other "how-to" books on leadership and management. Anyone in a position of leadership in sports or otherwise will both enjoy and learn from this fast-moving book.

Congrats, Coach, on a job well done and a life well lived!

PREFACE

THE SECRET SAUCE

In August of 2004, I retired after thirty-eight years serving as Stanford University's men's tennis coach, during which time my teams won seventeen NCAA team championships. After I left coaching, I served fourteen more years as director of tennis and finally retired from Stanford athletics in January of 2018. With the combined fifty-two years, I was, and still am, Stanford athletics' longest-serving employee.

The seeds for this book were planted early in my career, when I had the great pleasure of serving as a founding board member of a renowned nonprofit, the East Palo Alto Tennis and Tutoring Program, alongside a man who became a valued friend, Jack Gifford. Jack was one of Silicon Valley's tech giants and the founder and CEO of Maxim Integrated Products, as well as a couple of other companies.

As a business leader, Jack had a great interest in both management styles and formulas for success. One day, after we had won about ten NCAA men's team titles at Stanford, Jack asked me how we won so much for so long.

"I get the best players," I answered. Jack being Jack, his question was not casual, and he wasn't interested in my off-the-cuff, cavalier response. Jack is in the UCLA Athletic Hall of Fame as a baseball player, and he wanted a serious answer. "A lot of coaches have great players and never win," he responded, deliberately pushing me.

He was right. More often than not, teams with great players fail to win consistently—"consistently" being the operative word. Our Stanford men's tennis team, by contrast, won national titles year after year for almost four decades with several generations of players. I am proud of the fact that every player who played for me for thirty-four years, from 1970 to 2003, owns at least one national championship ring. Paul Goldstein, Charles Hoeveler and Misha Palecek own four!

To Jack's point, this had gone on so long that none of the players on our last championship team in 2000 had even been born when we won our first championship in 1973. I have so much respect for the handful of coaches in Division I athletics who have been able to attain similar program successes—North Carolina Women's Soccer under Anson Dorrance, Arkansas Indoor Track and Field under John McDonnell, UCLA Volleyball under Al Scates, and Iowa Wrestling under Dan Gable, all of whom have joined me in winning at least seventeen national team championships. It's not easy to win even one championship, let alone the numbers of titles these great coaches have achieved!

I certainly wasn't alone in being asked over the years about our success. My players also fielded this question from time to time, and sometimes they came from surprising quarters. Roman Sydorak, '93, remembers the time he and a Stanford football player happened to be having lunch with me and my friend, former San Francisco 49er and then Stanford football coach Bill Walsh, who is of course recognized as one of the greatest coaches of all time in any sport: *"During the lunch, Coach Walsh asked me how Coach guided our team to so many titles. I didn't have the answer."*

It was the same question Jack had asked me, and I didn't have the answer either. I could not articulate for Jack or Bill or anybody else the "secret sauce" of our success. As we added national title after national title for almost forty years, Jack's question gnawed at me and continued to chafe, even after I retired. And to "ice" the question, the year I retired, Baylor's great coach, Matt Knoll—whose teams my teams had never beaten—asked me how many times we had won when we were in the final match playing for championships. I did not have the answer, and I had to review the record book. The answer was "all but two!"

Ultimately, instead of trying to analyze my own career and methodologies, I decided the right thing to do was to let the answers come from the players themselves. It was their shots and their competitiveness that won those seventeen national titles, so it seemed logical that their thoughts and reflections, not mine, tell the tale. I sent a list of twenty challenging questions about many aspects of their team experience to two hundred former players. I was elated when 166—83 percent—returned the questionnaire, particularly since a full response took at least two hours to complete. I hoped that, among other things, I would be able to coax the formula we used to win for thirty-eight years from these hundreds of extraordinary and eye-opening insights and revelations.

This, then, is my players' book. I trust no one will be offended that it happens to be written by a male coach for a team composed of all males. The intent is to only use this as a factual example of what transpired. The lessons learned and offered are meant to pertain to a leader or "team" of any gender.

Just like always, my job has been to prepare and organize and create the opportunity for them to succeed; once again, they have done so. In this book, it is the players who have the stage, this time not to compete, but to reflect collectively on their experiences and why they had been able to win so much and so consistently, for so long. And, with class and integrity.

In the process of assembling all this information, I had a nice surprise. In the words of young—and now some not-so-young!—men who have since their Stanford days demonstrated personal and professional success far beyond the tennis court, their thoughts turn out to be as much about leadership and management as

**My book walls, where I compiled the thousands of
comments from thirty-eight years of players.**

coaching. The lessons they took from our time together transcend
sport, extending in time to business, public service, the military,
and very often, family and parenting. What they value from their
college tennis careers seems not to be the championship rings, as
much as, I am happy to say, life lessons.

This book is full of life lessons as described by the players themselves. These lessons and values extend into examples of how one
might build any successful team—not only in sports, but business
and life. One of my original goals was to see if there was a "secret
sauce" to our success. These guys describe in their own words
what they thought it was that allowed us all to win together for so
many years.

So Jack, here, finally, is the serious answer to the question you
asked so long ago. Thanks to 166 players for helping me answer it.

Introduction

EARLY YEARS ON THE FARM

Prior to the arrival of Coach Gould, the Stanford tennis team was a loose collection of tennis players without a sense of "team."

—Craig Baise, '67
A senior on my first team

Building a successful team in any endeavor that endures over time is not a simple undertaking, and I am convinced there is no magic formula. A leader must be prepared to face many obstacles and challenges along the way—those that emanate from within one's own team, as well those from the outside. And if the top is reached, to stay there, which is not easy. Fortunately, these lessons learned on team building are transferable to most situations. Here is some background on how this all started in our example, that of the men's tennis team at Stanford University. I began at Stanford in the fall of 1966 with a reasonably good group of players, but none of whom were world-class. As Charlie Herlands, '68, a junior that first year, says, *"Coach inherited an odd assortment. . . . Most of us were math, physics, or pre-med majors with labs and seminars that sometimes conflicted with practices and matches. We were really there because of the academics and had no expectation that we would have any professional careers in tennis. A few of us spent more time studying together than we did playing tennis together."*

I also was able to retain three decent freshmen recruited by my predecessor: Rob Rippner, John Spiegel, and Ron Kahn—all experienced tennis players, but none of whom had attained an especially high junior ranking. I immediately contacted each of them to ensure they would still be enrolling in the fall. My enthusiasm turned out to be key.

"I was undecided until I met Dick Gould at the National Junior Hardcourt Championships in Burlingame in June 1966," remembers John Spiegel, '70. *"He convinced me that he was going to build a great program at Stanford, so I came! It was one of the best decisions I have ever made."*

When I caught up with Rob Rippner, '70, that summer at an 18s tournament in Beverly Hills, he was planning on attending one of the Los Angeles schools, so I went to work on him. Rob writes, *"His enthusiasm and personable nature were key in my decision to joining him in his new endeavor."*

It was obvious that this group of great guys was not going to win a national championship, but I nevertheless tried to establish a championship mindset from the start. *"Dick created a special culture when he arrived,"* Bill Closs, '69, says. *"His total commitment and inspirational leadership were the keys that opened the door to excellence for Stanford tennis."*

His classmate, Brad Cornell, '69, adds what this would in general look like. *"What makes a great tennis team is the environment— the enthusiasm and the sense of camaraderie."*

This sounds easy, but it was a different era. Open tennis, which would give players a chance to earn prize money, would not begin for another two years. Unless a player was truly exceptional, there was no realistic option of playing as a professional.

The disparity between this reality and my dreams was itself a teacher, demonstrating to me that a leader who is ultimately responsible for his team's success or failure often envisions things the rest of the team cannot yet see. I had a lot of confidence in my teaching, but I found that particular hard truth a real challenge: How could my team—most of whom had never heard of me—buy into what only I believed to be possible?

Still, I believed in the dream, and I was young and brash and dumb enough to think I knew it all. But obviously I did not, which made for an incredibly steep learning curve. I quickly learned that what I hoped to do could not be accomplished overnight and that "listening" to my players was critically important . . . perhaps the very first step on the road to that dream. Listening was also important as a balance to my brash boldness, but it did not come easily for me.

"Coach was an absolute natural when it came to recruiting players," says Chuck Alloo, '69, a sophomore when I arrived. He's blunt about my initial shortcomings in this regard. *"He was a natural when it came to selling Stanford. He was a natural when it came to promoting events or causes. He was a natural at organizing people. However, my experience in the early days was that 'listening' was a challenge for him."*

Rob Rippner, '70, helped teach me to listen by explaining to me that my goals, which were just too far out there at that point for the guys to understand, let alone embrace, were not necessarily the team's goals. He says, *"One afternoon in spring of 1967, after a particularly productive practice, we sat together on the steps of court one talking about the future of Stanford tennis. It was here that I first heard Coach declare, 'One day, I am going to lead Stanford men's tennis to a national championship.'*

"Given the ragtag team Coach had in those early days, this was a bold—and improbable—statement! In my wisdom, I rolled my eyes and declared, 'Sorry to burst your bubble, Coach, but there is no way that's going to happen here. We are a group of

individualists more committed to academics than tennis. It simply will never happen!'"

It was a message delivered in the way only a sarcastic eighteen-year-old can!

Initially, Rob was right. We staggered along in that first year as I got to know my players and they got to know me. I kept trying to listen and adhere to the lessons I had already learned—going after what I wanted, being persistent, making things exciting, having enthusiasm, being myself, putting the team first—and ever so slowly things began to come around. Craig Baise, '67, adds, *"Coach Gould came in with a love for Stanford, a love for tennis, an infectious personality, and the desire to make the tennis team a force in intercollegiate tennis."*

I gave it my all every day, and slowly the players recognized that I was completely dedicated to getting Stanford tennis to the next level and that I truly believed this could be accomplished. We did so much together, especially when it came to interfacing with the community. In so doing, they learned about me on different levels than simply "coaching their team." As an example, the team helped me as "teaching assistants" for approximately one hundred community members with Saturday morning lessons in return for a couple of pennies. Here is an observation from one of the team player "teachers" in this situation.

"Everyone at all times got Coach's best," recalls team captain Paul Marienthal, '71. *"What was most important was how much he loved teaching and how much he loved seeing people learn. I think he also had a magical connection to beginners. This is an extraordinary thing, to be able to work with experts at the top of their games, and also be utterly committed to ten-year-olds who can't even make contact with the ball. What an extraordinary asset that is."*

It means a lot to me today that a lesson I hadn't even realized I was imparting apparently helped Paul in his career. *"As a col-*

lege professor at Bard College, it always has served me well as a model. Bring my A game. Always bring my A game. To everyone, all the time."

If the leader of a team deems it relevant to promote themselves to the public, the team or business must be accessible and relatable to others. These weekly lessons gave the public a chance to meet and know the team. This emphatically reinforced the importance of my guys mixing personally with our community and the value of the personal interest it created in our players. People would say things like, "Today I returned Roscoe Tanner's serve," and so on. This interest ended up bringing much-needed support to our program over the years.

I found other challenges I did not expect. In the beginning, I was not only the coach for the varsity, but also the JV and freshmen teams, as freshman were not eligible to play on the varsity in those days. Each of these teams had their own match schedules. In addition, I taught a beginning PE class, and a class for PE majors who might be assigned to teach or coach tennis someday. This was all before assistant coaches in tennis had come about. I was a full-time coach, and yet I barely had time to focus on the team! How could I be a really good coach when I had thirty players each day to herd around, plus classes to teach?

A Rocky Start

My six years of experience as a schoolteacher, high school football coach, and high school and junior college tennis coach prior to coming to work at Stanford helped me cope with this myriad of duties. But the mountain was steep. In my first season, and for the first time ever, a Stanford tennis team ended the season outside of the top ten at number sixteen.

With freshmen still not eligible, my 1967–68 team dropped even farther, finishing thirty-third in the country, marking Stanford's second consecutive year out of the top ten. I didn't even know that many universities had tennis teams, and now we were looking up at all of them! The assurances I had made to everyone, including athletic director Chuck Taylor, at my hiring that I expected our team to win a national championship began to sound hollow. I could almost hear Mr. Taylor drumming his fingers on his desk.

Through this rough time, my guys were great. I was only in my late twenties, so we all literally grew up together, and they really pitched in on the recruiting process. With their help, we attracted better recruits, and the "far-out" ambition of a national championship began to seem a slightly more realistic goal.

A Dream Achieved

Things got worse before they got better. In 1969, my third year, we won just nine dual matches and lost twelve—an ignominious and embarrassing losing record. When it came time to select the team for the NCAA championships, we were helped by a new NCAA rule that permitted freshmen to play for the national title.

"I became part of his first significant recruiting class," team captain Rick Evans, '72, recalls. *"Dick made the momentous decision that this group was the core of his future teams and elected to take an all-freshman team to the 1968 NCAA tournament. The next recruiting class, which included Roscoe Tanner, was exceptionally strong, and Stanford tennis was off and running."*

Because we had successfully recruited better and better players, the team I selected for the championships that year consisted of all freshmen—Paul Gerken, Mac Claflin, John Wright, Chris Chapin, and Rick Evans—none of whom had played in a varsity match. Gerken and Claflin had been top ten US juniors, and the rest were all ranked nationally, so they brought a lot of firepower the older guys frankly didn't have. Our all-freshman team finished back in the top ten at number eight.

"I sometimes tell the story that as a freshman, it was the final year in the NCAAs when freshmen were not eligible to play varsity,"

remembers Wayne Leiser, '72. *"We had a sensational class of freshmen. Nine were ranked number one in our states, regions, etc., with some ranked nationally, and two were on the Jr. Davis Cup National Team (Paul Gerken and Mac Claflin). I think I was the worst of the nine. However, I took pride in the fact that our freshmen could beat our varsity!"*

In 1970, with superstar freshman Roscoe Tanner from Tennessee now in the lineup, we finished fifth in the country. Rob Rippner nearly proved his earlier prediction wrong by reaching the final of the NCAA doubles as a senior with Roscoe. The next year, 1971, with the addition of Sandy Mayer, another top five junior, we were fifth again and finished with a 20–3 dual meet record.

But a lot of negativism and pessimism had developed within the Stanford community, including among some coaches. Stanford's lack of athletic success for so long provided much room for excuses such as: Stanford cannot attract the best athletes; top academics and top athletics do not mix; the top athletes are not admittable to Stanford; and on and on.

But other Stanford sports were also starting to make a mark on the national level. In 1967, men's swimming won Stanford's first national championship in any sport since men's golf in 1953. Football had had a 0–10 record in 1960 during my last year as a student, but it changed with the arrival of the most positive person I have ever met, football coach John Ralston, who proceeded to lead his teams to back-to-back wins in the Rose Bowl in 1971 and 1972. Excuses were becoming a thing of the past!

Dick Gould and football coach John Ralston sparked a vew era in Stanford Athletics

Sanford's First NCAA Champions Since 1942:

Roscoe Tanner: NCAA Singles Finalist (Twice), NCAA Doubles Champion; World Singles #5, World Doubles #10

Alex "Sandy" Mayer: NCAA Singles Champion; NCAA Doubles Champion; World Singles #7, World Doubles #3

Dreaming big was about to pay off for all Stanford sports. Perhaps John Ralston and I both played a part in turning the negativism of Stanford athletics around! Stanford has not looked back since.

Meanwhile, Stanford athletics really stepped up to support tennis and provided eight full scholarships. In 1972, we finished a close second to Trinity University, and Roscoe Tanner and Sandy Mayer won the NCAA doubles title, the first time any Stanford tennis player had won a championship since Ted Schroeder won the singles, and with Larry Dee, the doubles title thirty years earlier in 1942.

Finally, in 1973, seven years after my arrival and my audacious promises to Chuck Taylor, players Sandy Mayer, Rick Fisher, and Jim Delaney led us to our first national championship. In 1974, headed by John Whitlinger, James

Stanford's first Men's NCAA Championship tennis team–1973

"Chico" Hagey, and Jim Delaney, and without Roscoe and Sandy, we did it again. Stanford tennis had truly arrived!

What I learned during forty-four years of coaching, and in particular, the last thirty-eight at Stanford University, make up the substance of this book. I certainly don't "know it all," and I continue to learn each day. I know I was a much better coach in the '70s than I was in the '60s, better in the '80s than in the '70s, better in the '90s than in the '80s, and even better in the '00s than in the '90s. But it all seemed to work for me. During this period, we won seventeen national titles. We lost only twice when reaching the final championship match: an excruciatingly close 5–4 loss to UCLA in 1984 and a similar 4–3 loss to USC in 1994.

For the 2004–05 season, I ceded the head coaching position to our 1974 NCAA singles and doubles champion and my longtime assistant, John Whitlinger. I became director of tennis, where my job description, which I wrote, was to further enhance the facilities and program. In this capacity, and when I finally retired from Stanford, we had completely endowed the program financially, set up an incredible live streaming system on all our courts, and hosted two NCAA championships—something I had not wanted to do while I was coaching—including the first NCAA championships with men and women playing at the same site. In addition, we achieved many other accomplishments of which I am proud because they helped ensure that the facilities and supporting aspects of the Stanford tennis program represented the gold standard.

In January 2018, I retired fully. Unable to sit still, I have assumed the extremely rewarding role of vice chairman of TeachAids, a nonprofit spin-off from Stanford University that creates breakthrough educational programs addressing persistent problems in health education around the world. Initially, the focus was on HIV education, and now it is on concussion education.

It has only been since "retiring" that I have finally had a chance to ask my players what it was that worked. And what it was that didn't! The rest of this book is their answer. There was success to be sure, and a lot of it, but all success is a road paved with errors and missteps. I made more than my share . . . even after I should have known better . . . and these guys are nothing if not blunt. All that is in here too. The term "warts and all" comes to mind. As I've said, I long ago learned to be myself, and at this point, these guys—a family in a very real sense—weren't about to let me be anyone else. I continued to listen and learn and was able to become a better team leader and *improve* myself as a coach with each passing year. In providing perspective on the entire ride, "my guys" have been eloquent on all counts! And what an exhilarating ride it was!

Chapter One

FUNDAMENTALS OF LEADERSHIP

In the bestselling management book Good to Great, the author, Jim Collins set up an extensive analysis of what leads certain companies to consistently outperform others in the marketplace. The most important was having a "Level 5" leader. Collins identifies the key characteristics of a Level 5 leader as "humility, will, ferocious resolve, and the tendency to give credit to others while assigning blame to themselves." Coach Gould embodies all these key characteristics.

—Vijay Sekhon, '00

Vijay quotes from a great book. In an earlier book, *Built to Last*, coauthors Jim Collins and a longtime and respected friend, Jerry Porras, stress that one of the criteria used to determine truly "great" companies is longevity. Companies included have great vision, are able to adapt to market demands, and have great leadership as well as succession leadership plans that enable them to successfully "exist" for over one hundred years, and so forth. We didn't make it that long, but seventeen national team championships within a twenty-eight-year period is not bad in the sports world.

There are a thousand strategies and "best practices" that go into coaching in any sport or leading in any field, from recruiting and hiring, to motivating and inspiring; from technical proficiency to simply learning how to compete; or how to close a deal. There is no "One Way to Lead and to Manage." But long before you get to the court or the playing field or the office where you must lead your team into competition, there are a fundamental set of attitudes, values, and practices each successful leader or coach implicitly possesses which underwrite all the others.

I emphasize, there is no universal answer. Every leader is a different person. Each has a different management style. Each coach has his or her own fundamental truths. Though these truths differ, many are shared. For instance, styles and even ethics may vary widely, but it is difficult to imagine a good leader who does not have passion for his sport or field, or who does not possess a strong work ethic. Beyond a few basics, though, the mix of possible fundamentals is a kaleidoscope of values, beliefs, opinions, principles, and practices. Everyone's foundation will look a little different, based on their own values, personalities, and backgrounds.

Robert Franklin, '96 states, *"I have spent seven years of my career at Amazon learning from Jeff Bezos and his team. Coach's style reminds me so much of Jeff Bezos:*

1. Coach recruits the best.
2. He sets big/lofty goals for the team.
3. He provides a platform for them to be successful.
4. He hires great assistant coaches (Whit) who complement his skills.
5. He leads through example."

The funny thing is, as I have already explained, before I sent out the extensive questionnaire to my players, I could have probably only articulated—and then only vaguely—a few of the beliefs and practices that made up my own foundation. They came to be second nature to me, and I really did not think much about them.

That's why I deflected questions about the secret to our success with throwaway answers about getting the best players. The truth was that I had never really given it a lot of thought. For thirty-eight years, I was just being myself.

It fell to my players much later who kept referring to a core group of principles that they clearly felt were always there, even down to the background music we played during our final preparations for the national championships. By virtue of a preponderance of them remembering these aspects of our time together so vividly, they've organically selected the list of fundamental principles below. I certainly didn't come up with them. I've just organized them here. Upon reflection, though, I think they are the right ones; indeed, they are the rudders I used to guide my ship.

Interestingly, the player's observations over time—which player from which era said what—also revealed to me how my own learning curves manifested themselves over my coaching career. I certainly didn't arrive in 1966 equipped with all these practical and motivational tools. In fact, some of the stories the players have related emphasize that I hadn't discovered something then that later I would come to believe was critically important.

There is an important codicil that is worth mentioning again. For better or for worse, the guys articulated the set of ideals and values that were true for me. Other coaches would be different. The one thing I believe is absolutely true for every good leader is that one must be oneself.

Below, therefore, as revealed by my players, are the six fundamentals representing the foundation for our success. As with elsewhere in this book, I have let their words make the point, and I have simply added some perspective. The six are:

1. Personal Responsibility: The Power of Example
2. Core Values: Class, Humility, Respect, and Integrity
3. Outlook: Enthusiasm and Positivity

PERSONAL RESPONSIBILITY
The Power of Example

We just watched in awe each day how Coach worked to transform Stanford tennis in that tiny wood shack. It was nothing more than a woodshed, but with DG inside it was like the "temple of college tennis." You walked inside the place and his unbridled enthusiasm was infectious. You just knew that being around this guy was going to be worth the ride. And oh, what a great ride it was! Many of us went on to careers outside of tennis in business, law, medicine, real estate, and public service, and much of that success is undoubtedly due to what we witnessed.

—John Corse, '82

The Tennis Office (Shack) from 1966 to 1983

Words are cheap; actions are golden. A team is invariably a mirror image of its coach in terms of personality and values. You can tell a great deal about a coach or leader simply by watching how the team competes under pressure. The values—or lack thereof—will be readily apparent. *"Coach expected nothing from his team that he wasn't willing to do himself,"* says Craig Johnson, '76. *"And he never stopped setting an example for exactly what that meant."*

The question for any leader becomes how to instill the team with his or her values. It's difficult, if not impossible, to impose values upon others by fiat. You can preach values all day long, but I quickly learned nothing was more powerful than example. If you aren't willing to set the example, if you don't demonstrate your values by personal action <u>and then accept the responsibility for your actions</u>, then you will not be able to lead effectively.

Why? Because players and employees are not willing to follow blowhards and phonies. How, for instance, could I expect my team to work hard if they saw me being lazy or content to "just get by"? I had to model what I wanted from them. Very simple. Paul Goldstein, '98, an NCAA finalist and world singles #58, reflects on my impact in this regard. *"Lead by example:* TOTAL *commitment to continuous improvement.* TOTAL *commitment to be willing to change and adapt.* TOTAL *commitment to doing it the right way.* TOTAL *commitment to caring for those around you and lifting others up.* TOTAL *commitment to communicating."*

Please don't get me wrong—I certainly wasn't perfect in setting examples. Who is? Even being genuinely myself, my sense for what to say and when and how to say it had to be developed over the years. I learned this when I started working in my first job out of college as a high school teacher and coach of the ninth to tenth grade JV football team. In a particular one-on-one tackling drill and with the entire team looking on, my player was slipping and falling away just when he was supposed to be making contact. After three halfhearted attempts to try to make the tackle and with a frustrated response, I leaned over the fallen player and yelled every swear word I could think of as he was lying on his back. In response, he lay there and quietly listened until I had finished ranting, and then he looked up, flipped me off with his middle finger, and yelled back, "F**k you, Mr. Gould!" I quickly realized I was *not* a tough guy like my idol Vince Lombardi, so why was I trying to emulate what I thought he was like? For better or worse, I was Dick Gould. I learned then and there that there are many ways to coach, to manage, and to lead. But the lesson was clear—as a leader, one must be true to oneself and one's values. A coach cannot try to be who he or she is not!

But I learned quickly enough that my players responded well. As Jim Grabb, '86, an NCAA semifinalist, world doubles #1 and #24 singles says, *"Coach was an incredible role model. He didn't just talk about it. He was the first to raise his hand and claim responsibility."*

Jim goes on to provide an example that would certainly, given that it decided a national championship, stick with anyone. It occurred during the final point of the last match of the NCAA finals with UCLA in 1985. With the team score tied 4–4 and playing UCLA's great team of Michael Kures and Mark Basham, Jim Grabb and John Letts were at 4–5 in the third set on Jim Grabb's serve. Match point and "hold" point in no-ad (no advantage) scoring. I told Jim to serve to Michael's forehand, his strength, hoping to catch him by surprise. *"In one of the biggest matches of my college career, on the last point of the match, after much discussion, I served a ball that our opponent smoked by partner John Letts and me to win the match and the national team championship. My vague recollection has always been that it was my decision to serve it into the strength, but Coach was always taking responsibility for that 'fateful' decision."*

This was my decision. I felt UCLA's Michael Kures, who had the biggest forehand in college tennis at the time, would *never* expect a ball to be served to his strength on a key point . . . so that's where I called for Jim to serve it. (Plus, the net was lower, and the receiver had less of an angle at which to hit his return.)

As it turned out, it was almost as if Michael knew exactly what we would do. The ball came back twice as hard as Jim's serve—unreturnable—and secured the championship for UCLA.

Later that evening, I bought Michael a congratulatory beer and asked him about that point. His answer floored me. *"Coach, I have played against you too many times. I absolutely knew you would call that serve at that moment!"*

Wow! I was stunned. My guys had worked their butts off all year to put themselves in a position to be national champions, and my call cost us the championship! It was worse than being out-coached; I'd been outsmarted by an opposing player!

Needless to say, I felt horrible about this for years. In nineteen NCAA final appearances, we only lost twice, and this one was my fault. Over thirty years later, though, Jim released me from my purgatory over this matter with his broader perspective. *"Coach's attitude around taking responsibility is one of the most valuable takeaways for me, and something for which I'm extremely grateful. It had an impact on me in terms of my tennis career, my career in business, and on my interpersonal relationships, including the way I am as a parent."*

Because I was willing to lead by example, my players were willing to follow; they knew I was putting myself on the line right alongside them. Because I was willing to take responsibility for my actions, even when things didn't turn out the way I wanted in something as important as a national championship, my players learned to take responsibility for their actions as well. At some point, it was just something we did. I didn't have to talk about it, and it was not by design. I just did it. Much more powerful!

I also understood from the very beginning, and at a visceral level, that I couldn't make up a set of values that were not my own. First, simple honesty is fundamental to good leadership. Second, it would have been impossible for me to exemplify a set of values—to lead by example—day after day if the ideals I was modeling were something I had simply adopted out of convenience, or because I thought they would bring success. Again, my players would have sniffed out the phoniness in seconds. Being genuine is critical. I had to lead by example, but I had to do it while being true to my own beliefs.

"'The fences surrounding the tennis court define my hallowed ground—my living room!'" Rob Franklin, '96, remembers me saying. *"'Once one enters this area, I expect it to be treated and respected as such.' This was perpetuated by Coach Gould. You did not spit on his courts, you did not throw your racket, you did not hit the net, slam balls or yell, Coach called the complex our 'house'—and you do not act like that in our house. I was trying out for the team my first year and during a challenge match, I slammed the net in frustration. From five courts away I heard: 'Bobby . . . that is not how we act here.' From that moment on, I never let out a whisper in frustration."*

CORE VALUES
Class, Humility, Respect, Integrity

We exhibited the ultimate example of the proper spirit of competition. We worked hard, played hard and played competitively, but did so with class and integrity. We competed in a manner that earned the respect of our teammates and our opponents.

—Paul Goldstein, '98
Current Stanford coach

So, what core values did I want my team to exhibit and reflect? More important, as a coach, what values did I want to pass along to these young men or, for that matter, my own children? A coach or parent is, after all, first and foremost a teacher.

I didn't think much about it at the time, but the players listed four core values that I hammered home to them as representative of the foundation of the team I wanted to build, and of the young men who played on it. I didn't have to think about these, though, because they were simply my own values—traits I admired most highly and to which I aspired myself. That's why the players' comments seem right again.

In brief, they were class, humility, respect, and integrity. There's nothing magic about those values and virtues.

Those words and the ideas they represent are so rich and so deep. An entire book could be written on each. I will simply say here that I consider them core values because they exceed winning in importance. They point out my belief in the old maxim that "it's not whether you win or lose, but how you play the game." I firmly believe in winning, or losing, with class, respect, integrity, and humility! This belief clearly had a big impact on my players and how they carried themselves both in victory and defeat, on the court and off.

In delivering this message, I always endeavored to lead by example.

Leading by example did not, however, mean that I refrained from expressing my expectations verbally and often. As Chico Hagey, '75, an NCAA singles finalist and world singles #72, comments, *"'Class' was a word Coach often used. I interpreted it as respect toward our opponents, honesty, not giving up, and accepting occasional defeat without a lot of whining. John Wooden's former players say he imparted the same message."* There's a comparison I'll take as a big compliment!

Davis Cup and Olympic team captain and world doubles #3 Patrick McEnroe, '88, echoes Chico. *"Most of all, have class. That was a crucial part of being at Stanford."* And Martin Blackman, '91, world singles #158 and later director of US Player Development, remembers, *"My biggest takeaway was that although winning was very important, representing the team, Stanford, and ourselves with integrity and class was always more important."*

Martin's words bring out a good point about delivering the message. It would have been a little tiresome to go on and on about "class and integrity" day after day (though I probably did), so I had some shorthand phrases that have apparently survived as code among my players for years.

"I learned my most valuable lessons from Coach beyond the courts—that is, how to conduct yourself with class and integrity," says Geordie McKee, '86. *"Some of the players from my era still jokingly coin the phrase, which was one of Coach's favorites, 'Remember who you are and what you represent.'"*

Given that Geordie remembers this phrase thirty years later, I seem to have made my point! And I'm glad because it's a good reminder that you are rarely just representing yourself, but also your family, your teammates, your company, your school, the sport . . . whatever it may be.

The important thing, of course, is not to simply communicate an idea, whether by example, words, or metaphor, but to have the idea manifest itself in action. Class, respect, integrity, and humility aren't just concepts: they require certain behaviors. Don't cheat. Compete within the spirit of the rules. Be a good winner. Be a good loser. Always respect your opponent.

When translating values into behavior, experience is always the greatest teacher. Greg Hing, '81, team captain, relates one experience that has stuck with him all these years. *"One time after one of us had behaved badly on the court, Coach sat us all down in the bleachers and said, 'You should behave on the court as if your son or daughter was in the stands. What behavior would you want him/her to see?' That has stuck with me all these years and is something I have often quoted to kids."*

It is incredibly satisfying to hear that certain lessons are being played out decades later to subsequent generations. But back to exhibiting the values in the here and now, I'll let Geordie have the final word on how class, respect, integrity, and humility can be borne out with one simple practice: *"All kidding aside, this embodies how Coach conducted himself and the expectation he had for each and every one of us: win, lose, or draw, and no matter how disappointing a loss we may have taken, Coach always was gracious to the opponent."*

OUTLOOK
Enthusiasm and Positivity

The number one factor in our success was Coach's contagious optimism. It lifted everyone's play. I imagine I'm not alone among his former players in trying to retain and apply the outlook to my non-tennis activities. Certainly, in my case, his confidence helped me infinitely more than any comments he made about mechanics or court tactics.

—Chico Hagey, '75
All-American; world singles #72

I love the song from the Walt Disney movie, *Song of the South.* I sometimes get out of my morning shower "singing" (and I can't sing):

> Zip-A-Dee-Doo-Dah; Zip-A-Dee-A
> My oh my what a wonderful day
> Plenty of sunshine headed my way
> Zip-A-Dee-Doo-Dah; Zip-A-Dee-A

In other words, I am a naturally positive and upbeat person. Because this is honestly who I am, enthusiasm naturally underlies my coaching. Positivity and enthusiasm also lead to optimism, which can spread sunshine throughout an entire room, even on a rainy day or in the most trying of circumstances.

This applies to everyone, including beyond my teams. *"Coach was so good with people, whether it was with a rival coach, a billionaire, or an underprivileged kid from East Palo Alto,"* Alex Kim, '01, an NCAA singles champ and world singles #106, writes. *"I can't recall hearing Coach ever talking bad about someone else. He seemed to be able to communicate with his eyes. He was a 'players' coach,' but he was STILL 'Coach.'"*

Positivity, enthusiasm, and optimism are all contagious and can make us all feel better. My players have told me this was a critical aspect of their experience on the team. Team captain Brian Leck, '67, refers to an *"infectious enthusiasm in the culture,"* and John Corse, '82, says nearly the same thing. *"Coach's unbridled enthusiasm was infectious. You just knew that being around this guy was going to be worth the ride."*

And again, Paul Marienthal, '71, is particularly eloquent about this. *"Coach was always in 'let's go' mode. His fundamental enthusiasm cannot be overstated. Showing up every day with that kind of energy is extraordinary."*

I relish being around people who think this way as well, and so it's not surprising I tended to recruit enthusiastic guys. But this approach had a much more practical aspect than simply creating an upbeat atmosphere.

"Coach was always so, so upbeat," Wimbledon semifinalist and world #14 Pat DuPré, '76, adds. *"He saw the positive and never dwelled on the negative. That allowed us to be more self-confident and brought out our best."*

That is of course ultimately what any coach or leader wants to do—bring out the best in one's team. Bruce Dines, '76, relates *"The culture was one of encouragement. Coach said, 'You know, Bruce, you are a good tennis player now—but you could be great!' It meant a lot to me."*

I believe that if you see the glass at least half full, with well-directed hard work and resolve, you can fill it up 99 percent of the time. But this task is up to us and our attitude! At worst, we have the opportunity to make any situation better than it is. Enthusiasm also translates easily into positive reinforcement, which is a very powerful tool.

"Coach's strengths were his positive attitude and demand for excellence. He was always positive," says team captain David Martin, '03, an NCAA doubles finalist.

I appreciate David's perspective because I don't believe there is ever any place for negativism. All it does is bring not just oneself down, but everyone else as well. There is always something to be thankful for and feel good about, although it is true that sometimes we have to look a little harder to find it!

It is another hard truth that 99.9 percent of the time an athletic season involves losses, which must be dealt with. And sometimes, there are even more traumatic situations, personal or family issues team members inevitably face. Minor or major challenges can threaten a player's self-worth, so it is always best to start with positive conversations and remain as positive as possible. Negativity just doesn't help. When in doubt, always err on the side of positivity.

CRITICAL FIRST STEPS
Preparation and Organization

I probably learned most from Coach the value of organization and management skills

—Roman Sydorak, '93

Athletic contests and business opportunities are won or lost in the hours of detailed preparation and practice leading up to the event. This is a critical first step that increases the chances that all the hard work will pay off. We approached everything with the same thorough thought and preparation as we would improvement of a skill or preparation for a match! Why? Because success is often determined by the behind-the-scenes work. Simply trying to compete or execute well are not enough without thorough preparation.

This starts with basic things like being on time for practice or work. Staying positive even if having a bad day, and then being able to change your focus if necessary, is also important. In tennis, it can flow into mechanical techniques and then tactics. In business, it might be the preparation of a legal brief or a change of emphasis on the activity scheduled for the day or week.

As an essential skill for an effective leader, preparation begins with clarity in defining the job at hand and expectations associated with the end result. As a coach, I had to prepare my team for most anything that could happen and to play all styles of opponents. In this sense, I often had to expect the worst and prepare to adapt to it. *"Coach was always prepared. He always had a plan,"* says Martin Blackman, '91. He's right. I did.

Preparation, though, will still not get the job done; it must be paired with organization. Michael Flanagan, '94, an NCAA doubles finalist, adds, *"Coach is one of the most organized individuals I have ever been around. Coach always got the most out of every minute of every practice session; constantly writing down notes on his 5 x 7-inch note cards."*

I was that way because I learned that an organized person is better able to prioritize responsibilities and then address them one at a time without getting sidetracked. Otherwise, the enormity of a challenge or project can be overwhelming. There are always so many things to attend to and to get done that we often can feel overwhelmed. We get lost in the forest. This can paralyze us into nonaction. Focus on and finish A, then move on to B. As a leader, give members of your team clear priorities for finishing assigned tasks.

Organization often involves a routine that is helpful to players. *"Coach Gould gave the team confidence by establishing routines both in practice and how we went about our practices,"* recalls All-American John Letts, '86. *"He was always on time, always organized, and always had a plan for our practice. The sheer expectation of repetition and routine was comforting and gave us confidence."*

Simplicity is also an important aspect of organization. Things must be so efficiently done that it is easy for the player or team member to see progress, and more important, build confidence in the end result. To accomplish this, coaches must cut to the chase with their team; they must simplify and define the method of attacking the problem one step at a time! Define step one, decide how best to address it, complete the task, and then move to step two. This simplicity gives the players clarity and leaves them free to focus on that day's task.

Scott Bondurant, '82, team captain and All-American adds:

"Coach was unbelievably organized. All we had to do was show up and give our best effort. Any player/employee wants to be free of obstacles/impediments and be allowed to focus on getting the important stuff done. He always cared and did everything he could to help us win. Coach made every practice important; every road trip was organized, and we always knew that he lived and died inside in every match we played. When your players or employees know that the coach/manager is 110 percent committed, they feel compelled to give 110 percent as well."

Being prepared, being organized, and relying on simple routines served me well. A lot of time and effort can be wasted in trying to get better, but preparation and organization maximize the value of the work that follows.

WORK ETHIC

No Shortcuts!

Hidden beneath Coach's congeniality resides a combustible mix of ambition and work ethic. How could there not be? No one coaches to seventeen national championships without an inextinguishable fire within. . . . Resting on laurels isn't part of his DNA. . . . In his calculus, there's more to achieve, more to do, more to offer.

—David Wheaton, '91

As important as all the foregoing principles and strategies are, without a strong work ethic, success doesn't happen.

It's no secret that a great work ethic is almost always present among the best teams and performers. I have rarely seen a top team or individual compete at the highest level day in and day out by expending just enough energy to get by. We were no different. I was happy to see Brian Leck, '67, reference our team's *"incredible work ethic."*

Robert Devens, '94, tells a story that underscores how the players are always watching their leader, particularly when it comes to work. *"Coach was a tireless worker. There was never a plane flight wasted. It was a great lesson for me watching him in the last row of every plane flight grind away with a very small golf pencil on his notecards. . . . Road trips were meant to expand the network."*

Part of a strong work ethic involves high expectations. *"Coach displayed 24-7 efforts to set the bar personally for each of us at the absolute highest levels, and on so many more levels of life than just the tennis courts,"* says Craig Johnson, '76.

Another part of the equation emanates from a burning desire to always get better and to improve. It cannot be turned on and off. It absolutely must be present in every practice, when preparing for matches and when promoting the program. It's an all day, every day thing, not just during competition. Never stop trying to improve.

"As a coach and manager, I also saw and learned how one can't sit on one's laurels," states Mihir Mankad, '95. *"And how one needs to consistently work, and not shirk. In an academic institution myself now, I see that there are many opportunities to cut corners. To get a bit lazy as you age."*

The coach bears the burden of setting the example in this regard to counteract natural human tendencies of laziness, shortcuts, rationalizations, and procrastinations. I am pleased that Robert Devens, '94, takes my example to heart. *"I think hard work was one of Coach's secret weapons. He was a tireless worker. I remember calling the office one morning my freshman year at 7:00 a.m. to leave a v-mail. Coach picked up on the first ring—that left an impression: be action-oriented, move the ball forward, and tirelessly work in pursuit of your goals."*

Hard work does not mean to never relax, but the decision to do such must be purposeful and planned. One can and should allow time for relaxation. That's important to help stay fresh and help prevent burnout. But I felt we could never sit back and rest on what we may have accomplished—because we could always continue to achieve and do more!

Hard work provides a framework for goal setting. There can be no shortcuts.

PERSONAL ACCOUNTABILITY
No Excuses!

*Coach's strengths were his positive attitude
and demand for excellence. He . . . never
allowed us to make excuses. If the weather
was windy or the courts in poor condition,
he never dwelled on it or let us dwell on it.
His attitude was essentially 'deal with it.'
It wasn't insensitive or demeaning. Those
were simply the conditions and he challenged us to rise above them.*

—David Martin, '03

If there are no shortcuts, there are also no excuses. Ricky Becker,
'96, puts it another way. *"We always tried to deal with the cards
we were dealt. This was a mantra Coach used to use that I try to
impress on the people I care about to this day."*

And Rich Andrews, '70, references my common plea to my players to "let your racket do the talking," saying, *"To me that meant
that you need to earn what you get—no alibis."*

Rich had my meaning pretty dead-on. Although I was never one
to make excuses, and many other coaches weren't either, I found
a particular kindred spirit in football coach John Ralston, who
took Stanford to the Rose Bowl in 1971 and 1972. John was
not only relentlessly positive, but strident about never offering
an alibi or making an excuse. I felt I was setting a standard not
only for the tennis team, but also all of athletics. It was nice to

know that the highest-profile coach at Stanford was setting the same expectation.

There is one time I remember making an "excuse." In 1974, during our Los Angeles swing to play USC on Friday and UCLA on Saturday, we had an invitation to play at the Playboy Mansion on our day off, Sunday. Unfortunately, we got a late start playing UCLA on Friday due to wet courts, and because they had no lights, the match was halted when it got too dark with Stanford leading 3–1 in singles. With USC on tap for Saturday, we would normally have finished the UCLA match on Sunday, but with a dozen college guys looking forward (to put it mildly!) to the Playboy Mansion visit, there was no way this was going to happen. The only thing I could do was offer my athletic director a very feeble excuse for not being able to complete the UCLA match. I felt kind of bad about it, but in today's jargon, maybe it could be partially justified by saying it promoted "student athlete wellbeing." Had we canceled the mansion visit, at best there would have been angry and disinterested players risking a loss, and at worst a full-on mutiny! Occasionally, I guess there's an exception to every rule.

However, with this one exception, when confronted with a challenge, there is no better slogan than Nike's "Just do it!" And with no alibis! Pretty simple concept. Nothing more needs to be said.

In summary, regarding leadership, Peter Morris, '80, says, *"Dick has high-level CEO attributes. He recruits talent and provides the resources for the players, and the team to succeed. He is an outstanding manager, administrator and fundraiser, all things a great CEO needs. He has infinite positive energy and enthusiasm, and it is infectious."*

Chapter Two

RESPECT FOR ALL PEOPLE

I never once saw Coach interact with anyone in a manner that was discourteous, disrespectful, or unkind. And I saw him interact with a lot of people from every demographic and walk of life—ushers, maintenance workers, players, other coaches, students, parents, teachers and plain strangers. . . . I've tried to bring this quality to my personal and professional relationships. Coach set a great example of how to treat others.

—Steve Winterbauer, '83

Leadership is directly affected by how one treats those around him/her. *All* people matter—not just one's stars, but also those on the periphery of any team. This chapter will address three key areas:

- Respect

- Caring for Players and Families

- Feelings of Relevance

RESPECT

What was most special to me was the lack
of hierarchy and how Coach Gould treated
everyone with respect. Coach Gould and
the players had a bond that was based in
mutual respect. Coach treated everyone
the same, which did not go unnoticed. I
strive to do the same in my business.

—Adam Ross, '95

Respect is earned based on how one treats others—all people at
all times. It is of course particularly critical to how members of
a team feel they are being treated—both on and off court. Doug
Dey, '70, son of Bennett Dey, who was the 1936 national intercollegiate doubles champion at Stanford,[1] was on my first team. He
echoes Adam and goes further, attributing much of our success to
this culture of respect. *"Dick's incredible success was reflected in*
all his interactions with all the other human beings with whom he
interacted. This was especially true with his players, regardless
of whether they were top ranked or of infinitesimal importance to
the tennis program."

As a matter of perspective, any coach and any team are only part
of a much larger program within the school or organization. For
me, I was not only a coach, but I was a team member in Stanford
athletics along with the coaches in the other sports. In addition
to trying to win championships, we all sought to represent the

---

[1]   Doug's daughter, Dena Dey Evans, was a three-time All-American and MVP of the track
teams and member of the soccer team at Stanford. She later successfully served as the
national championship Stanford women's cross-country coach in 2003.

school well and teach our players about their sport and life. We respected one another in our shared endeavor.

As it turned out, I benefited greatly from this larger culture of respect, of which the director of athletics was the leader. One time when the position of director of athletics opened, the provost of the university asked if I would serve as the interim director. I was extremely flattered by this sign of respect, but we were in the process of completing a couple of big projects for the tennis program—including the hosting of the first combined men's and women's NCAA championships. I felt this role would have diverted my attention. Consequently, I recommended Bill Walsh, who was not in the best of health at the time, and yet was still overseeing the construction of a new football stadium. Bill accepted anyway, and Stanford came out way ahead, but I will always have great appreciation for the show of respect and trust extended to me by our provost!

The point is that respect for each other was unquestionably a critical element in our success over the decades. What experience and the players' answers reveal, though, is that respect extends down from the top six players to the bottom six and even to the other teams on campus, as well as upward to the athletic administration and the university as a whole, and outward to all those who support the team in any way.

"Be kind and respectful to everyone," sums up Steve Winterbauer, '83. *"This really should be the number one lesson. I have had the opportunity to see that its value transcends context and applies with equal force on stages large and small."*

CARING FOR PLAYERS AND FAMILIES

So, it is late here in Colorado on a Wednesday night, and I have a brief due tomorrow. I should have spent this time working on the brief, but when I saw Coach's email, it took priority. Why? Because he would have done the same for any of his players—not because they were stars and helped win titles, but because he cared about all of us as people.

—Rich Young, '69

Occasionally, we hear in sports of situations where members of a team feel they are only cogs in a wheel. This can also be true for teams outside of athletics. Yet, even if they perceive they are treated poorly, as long as the team wins, everything seems to work out.

That was never my philosophy, and it is, I believe as Rich Young suggested, the reason so many players responded to the questionnaire. Stanford tennis is a family, and membership does not expire at graduation.

Gene Mayer: World Singles #4; World Doubles #5

"No one has compiled the record that Coach has since no one was

as uniquely suited to the task," states former world singles #4 and doubles #5 Gene Mayer, '76. *"Coach Gould cared about every player regardless of ranking and made us feel like we belonged. Coach Gould was more about the man himself than his role as a coach."*

Creating a family dynamic, a dynamic of caring, begins on the court but extends to off-court situations and experiences. Putting together trips and distractions and educational opportunities off court or out of office is a small example of truly caring for the welfare of the individual (see chapter 9). The bonding of off-court experiences like team trips or team retreats can help to create an atmosphere in which trust can grow. Building this trust is critical for conveying to the player that you care about him or her, and for creating an environment of being receptive to your concerns and advice.

Caring includes all areas of the athletes' lives, not just their athletic lives, as it does for other types of teams as well. An effective leader must show this compassion. In its heyday, one of the original Silicon Valley giants, the Hewlett- Packard company, coined their approach to business as "The HP Way." It was a powerful statement, and the first tenant emphasized trust and respect for the individuals on the team. As Paul Goldstein, '98, says, *"One thing I think I valued the most: Coach always, always, always, always made me feel that he had all the time in the world for me and my concerns. His door was always open, his phone was always on, his ear was always willing to lend. It was incredible."*

Ideally, a player should be able to share just about anything. It is impossible for me to imagine a lasting legacy of greatness where this is lacking. I am convinced a major component of sustained success is whether the vast majority of members of any team feel the coach or leader truly cares about them personally.

"Coach was always focused on winning with the goal being to be at our best come the big matches and NCAAs," says Craig Johnson, '76. *"But that focus never excluded the humanity he always*

showed for the people in his life. For me, what I may have learned from Coach more than anything was the way he made each and every person he encountered feel as if they were the only person on the planet that mattered at the time he was with them."

NCAA singles champ and world singles #7 Tim Mayotte, '82, agrees:

"It is complicated and daunting to try to express what I have been lucky enough to witness and take part in over these years. Coach as an individual, the many circles of friends that he has held, and holds together, through his deep caring have been central in me believing that there is reason to be optimistic about the world. I tend to be cynical, but Coach's gentle and kind insistence toward all of us, to stick it out together helps keep me on the hopeful side of things. I think Coach recognizes correctly that people get lost in their own worlds and minds, but he insists on bringing us back to this larger group. That he invites us without making us feel guilty is perhaps his greatest strength. Coach always welcomes us back. And when we are back, we see the goodness in being together. Those events keep us connected to our memories, and histories."

Tim Mayotte: Team Captain;
NCAA Singles Champion;
World Singles #7

As inferred, this caring extends well beyond years of competition. The first example I offer is from Phil Heimlich, '75, whose father, Henry, invented what became known as the "Heimlich Maneuver." In short, I used it to save the life of my stepfather, who was choking in my home due to a piece of chicken wedged securely in his throat. According to Phil, *"I was only a JV player, but Coach Gould always made me feel of value,"* wrote Phil. *"My most touching experience with him was about twenty-five years after I graduated—he learned that I had been given a position at a prominent law firm in Cincinnati and took the time to call and congratulate me. I'll never forget that."*

Paul Galichia, '96, remembers:

"When my first film was in the theaters, I was featured in the Stanford *Magazine which was really cool and a great honor. But by far the best thing was getting a personal note from Coach Gould saying that he saw the article and was proud of me. I certainly didn't expect it but in retrospect it would have been out of character for him NOT to send something, even though I was a pretty insignificant piece of the program, ultimately. Doesn't matter. He made me feel like one of 'his' guys. To this day, I'm so appreciative of the man. He's just the best that ever was."*

Neither Phil nor Paul were stars, or even starters, but they were no less "my guys." My philosophy is that once any person joins my team, he and his family are members of my team (and my family) for a lifetime!

I had a relationship with Chris Bradley, '72, that preceded either of our careers. I coached him as a young boy at Fremont Hills Country Club. He reminisces, *"So important is Coach's caring about myself and my family. I had a very eventful 18–21 (and further) year-old time. He stuck by me through thick and thin and was always supportive of my whole family. Coach's visiting my son, Matthew, in the hospital when he was real sick meant so much to me and to him. Coach's interest and caring for me was like the father I never had. He was and still is my mentor, and I can't thank him enough."* Like Phil and Paul, Chris was never a starter. He became a highly respected teaching professional, who never stopped supporting his former tennis team. We remained close friends until he succumbed this past year to cancer.

Chip Fisher, '75, a pastor and chaplain, explains, *"Dick modeled respect and a deep loyalty. Dick cared about things more important than another win: he also cared what kind of men we were each becoming. I have a huge respect for Coach Gould as a man and as a coach. Well after we Fishers were graduated, when there was nothing more we could possibly do for him, Dick Gould continued privately to visit my mother Sue Fisher for years—even after she drifted downward into dementia and eventually terminal Alzheimer's disease. Nobody saw Dick make these visits and Sue could not register her gratitude, but our family will always appreciate this faithfulness."*

(As an aside, three of the "Fisher boys" earned championship rings—two as starters and one as team manager).

Often team members need special care and help during the season. How a coach responds is critical in terms of building respect and creating loyalty, which works both ways. This is especially true if an injury or illness sidelines a player, either permanently or temporarily.

David Wheaton, '91, an All-American and world singles #12, has his own story to tell:

"During first semester exam week in December, I was doing what any responsible student would do—rollerblading. I had just left Coach's office where he had stated, 'Get off those things—you'll break your neck.' I skated back to a dormmate's window where I could see him doing what I should have been doing—studying—and knocked on the glass. Whether I didn't gauge my momentum or the glass was brittle (it was an ice-cold day), I'll never know, but the window imploded all over my friend. Momentarily stunned, I looked down to see drips of blood splashing on the ground. I turned my left hand over to check for the source of the blood and almost fainted upon discovering the gaping hole in my wrist. My dormmate was outside in a flash, taking his shirt off to tourniquet the wound and hold my arm aloft until the ambulance arrived. And then he called Coach Gould. I wish I could have

heard Coach's response to the news that I had severed two tendons and partially a nerve requiring delicate surgery, and that it would be months before I would be able to hit two-handed backhands again. My dormmate said, 'He laughed and swore at what he thought was a prank call and hung up.' It wasn't long before Coach was at my bedside at Stanford Hospital. He would be there every step of the way on the months-long road to recovery—never condemning, often joking, always positive. Just another midseason setback to navigate on the way to another national title."

After the "trouble" David had given me upon leaving my office, I *did* think the first call was a joke. After making a caustic comment, I hung up. However, I received a second call from a friend who was on duty serving as a volunteer "Pink Lady" at the hospital. She said that I had better get over there right away because one of my players was severely injured. I was there in five minutes!

Fortunately, as far as tennis was concerned, this was David's left wrist and the only part of his game it really affected was his two-handed backhand. By late winter, he began to chip one-handed backhands, including his serve return. He improved to the point where, although severely limited, he could play in the NCAA team championships. His heroic comeback win over the great Scott Melville preserved the team win in the finals against USC! He went on to attain a world #12 singles ranking.

When a player is injured and can't practice, it is easy to overlook him. But this is when he needs support the most. Regular check-ins, even if he is out for the season, are critical!

Parents

You must convey by your actions to the parents that your players are the most important thing to you in the world. You must show you care about their kids and their overall welfare as much as they do. This almost always overrides a parent's concern about where their son or daughter is playing or even if he or she is ever getting a chance to play. It starts with the player knowing that you care about him or her. If the player is OK, the parent will be as well.

I was so very fortunate in that parents seemed to respect me in this role and that I *never* had a parent interfere, either with what I was doing on the court with their young man, or off the court.

I did face two potential challenges, however, in this regard. My first test was when Alex Mayer Sr. asked if he could work with his sons when he showed up during spring break. My immediate solution was to give him full access to his sons, Sandy and Gene, even during regular team practice. Both later would attain singles and doubles rankings in world's top ten. Dr. Mayer handled this beautifully and never interfered with the practice itself nor other players. He was a great coach, and I closely watched what he did and how he did it. In fact, his teaching had probably the biggest impact of all on my own coaching—he provided a great laboratory for me! I am proud to say I am an Alex Mayer Sr. disciple. All of our other local parents simply avoided our practices.

Another potentially touchy situation occurred when David Wheaton, soon to reach the semifinals of Wimbledon and earn a world singles #12 ranking, enrolled. David was one of America's top junior players the same year as Pete Sampras, Jim Courier, Andre Agassi, and Michael Chang. I received a note in the months prior to the start of school from David's parents asking me if I would send along the faculty/staff "newsletters." I thought nothing of it at the time, but as it turned out, they were looking for a faculty home on campus to rent during a time that some professor might be on a sabbatical leave. On the first day of practice, they were present—several courts away from David—but there! I tend to swear on occasion, and they were a most devout Christian family. I managed to hold all in check that day. Then they were present the next day . . .

After the first week, I just ignored their presence, and became my normal self. I did ask when they were going home, and to my surprise, they replied they would be at Stanford all year. Further, David's sister, Marne, had obtained a job helping to teach the Stanford tennis physical education classes. *Ouch!* Now what? As it turned out, at least one of David's parents attended some part of every practice throughout the entire year—always inconspicuously sitting far away from David. *Never* did they ask me things like, "How is David doing?" "What do you think if he tried this?" "What position in the lineup is he going to play?" and so on. Rarely have I respected or admired any parents more.

I have a responsibility to be certain, in attempting to be the best, that values and high standards are *never* sacrificed. We had our moments, but I was so very proud overall of how our teams represented themselves, their families, their teammates, our university, and our sport—both on the court and off. We set the bar high in showing how to win with humility and lose with grace. This to me was as important as any win or loss, and I think my players understood this and became better people because of it. In the end, it is neither the win nor the loss but the process of it all that has made the attempt worthwhile. I truly believe that our opposing players and coaches—although they wanted to beat the heck out of us because, frankly, we were the gold standard—had the utmost of respect for how we competed.

All-American Scott Humphries, '98, summarizes:

"The coaching staff put the responsibility back on the players to hold each other accountable, which is one of the reasons I think the teams for decades were so strong. Unselfishness, respect for the program, sportsmanship. With all the guys that have come through the program my feeling was that all of them were able to put the team goals over their own. I think this was just the culture. The sportsmanship piece is tied into the respect for the program because Coach stressed that we were representing the university, the team and ourselves, and the teams always did it in a classy way."

FEELING RELEVANT

The biggest lesson Coach taught us had nothing to do with tennis. He "is the greatest example I've ever met of making people feel important." Not even Dale Carnegie could match him. And there is no more important lesson.

—Chico Hagey, '75

Another way to show respect is to do all one can to make every member of the team feel relevant. This stems initially from simply caring about your players as people. Caring about people makes them feel good about themselves and each other and underscores to them that they are relevant. Fortunately, we had some success in this area. *"Coach is the best I've known at making a person feel like they're the most important person in the room when he is talking to them," says* John Wright, '72, a longtime physician in San Diego.

I also made some huge mistakes before I learned that simple caring was not enough. For instance, in the early years, I failed to award *all* team members a championship ring when a national championship was won. This was at my personal discretion because budgets were really tight in those days, and our department did not provide championship rings to other than our lettermen, which was usually our starting six and maybe one or two others. In retrospect, I have deep regret that I failed to approach a donor or two for funding to be sure all team members received a ring! Later, an endowment was started by our department to rightfully fund rings for all team members when a national championship was won. This reinforced that we truly won or lost as a team!

The lesson for me was that sustaining success would be dependent not only upon caring for each team member, but upon *all* members of the team feeling a part of the effort to do something special. I also learned that making everyone on the team—not just the stars—feel relevant is easier said than done. And it's more difficult with college tennis than most other sports because the hard fact is that six players on the team "start," six others do not, and some might never play in a match. In other words, half of the team is relegated to "sitting on the bench" during dual meet competitions. Unlike most other sports, there aren't any "in-game" substitutions! If you don't start, you don't play! In addition, pre-college, these players had competed in tournaments as individuals and not as a part of a team, so not all had a sense of what it was like to be a part of a team.

These challenges must be overcome because keeping everyone—all twelve players—involved on a day-to-day basis, making the "second six" feel relevant, is critical to the morale of any team and its short-term and long-term success. *"I was never a top player,"* says Eduardo Cardoso, '04, *"but I NEVER felt irrelevant. I always felt PART of the team and an integral member of the team. Coach made us all feel relevant, and that we all contributed to the team."*

It takes extra time, in terms of planning practice, mixing practice partners, and planning off-court activities, but I really worked hard to try to make Eduardo and the other guys who were not starters understand how important they were to the team. I committed a lot of effort and planning to include them with other and better teammates in drill rotations and all team activities. *"Coach did an amazing job of making everyone feeling relevant,"* adds team captain Ali Ansari, '01, who worked two years to become a starter. *"He made sure in every practice that everyone would play with a different teammate. The bottom of the team would play with the number one on the team and vice versa."*

I worked on treating the second six the same way I treated my stars, both on the court and off, especially so early in the season. *"Making players feel relevant was a tremendous strength of Coach's,"* states Glen Garrison, '69. *"In fact, it is the only reason I have taken the time to respond to these questions. I am always proud to say I played on the Stanford tennis team."*

In the end, though, the extra effort is part of the secret, because making people feel cared for and relevant in turn builds loyalty to each other, toward the coach, and toward the program.

Piers Henwood, '95, another one of the guys who played lower on the ladder, has his own take. *"Coach was very inclusive and welcoming. This was a key trait of the program's culture. Although the Stanford men's tennis program was one of the most elite in the country, he didn't make it feel like an exclusive club, nor a hierarchical one. He found ways to invite people into the circle. This sense of inclusion was a core driver of culture and values around the program. Coach treated his players as human beings first and foremost."*

Practices are important, but there is nothing like playing in an actual match to make a player feel relevant, so I also tried to put the second six into matches whenever possible. Fortunately, we were deep enough that the second six players could win tough matches against the top six at other schools, so we were able to play them frequently against lesser opponents. That was a big help.

Robert Devens, '94, surmises:

"I think a secret talent of Coach's was to recruit and retain guys who were lower in the lineup at Stanford, but who could have been number one players at other schools. It was part of the Stanford/Dick Gould mystique, and Dick Gould was able to effectively communicate it in recruiting and running the team—'every starter over 34 years earned at least one championship ring!' And

I would say, Coach's focus on detail, hard work, leaving no stone unturned in the recruiting process paid off, because these number five and six players probably were more important in winning championships than almost any other position on the team."

Though it's not just about ladder rankings. In tennis, where only about one-third of the Division I players are receiving athletic financial aid due to NCAA rules limitations, the non-scholarship player must feel as if they are treated just as well as the scholarship player. In addition, our athletic department had strict requirements to meet in terms of who on the team could receive a "letter" at season's end. One year, we had held out our top players in favor of playing the lower guys on the ladder so often that near the end of the season, we realized that our top two players, Roscoe Tanner and Sandy Mayer, were in danger of not lettering. For a brief while, the running joke among some of the players was that Stanford was so tough that Roscoe Tanner couldn't even letter! Ultimately, we were forced to add a couple of dual matches at the end of the season so that Roscoe and Sandy could qualify to get their letters.

Lloyd Bourne, '80, NCAA doubles finalist and world singles #71, comments, *"A great team needs all its individual members to believe in themselves singularly and to believe in the greatness of the team as a whole. Coach helped us attain that belief by conveying to each player that he believed in them individually. His ability to form good personal relationships with the individual players was a strength. This created the desire to not only win for oneself, but for Coach and the team."*

An important part of our philosophy was that the importance of keeping people engaged and "feeling an integral and important part" of the tennis family extends well beyond the team itself to the person who prepares meals, the custodian who cleans the toilets, the person who delivers mail and packages, the office staff and secretaries, and of course the fans who support the team on a regular basis.

"Enthusiasm. Optimism. Friendliness," is how Brandon Badger, '99, describes it. *"I think that these attributes really pulled it all together and brought in great talent and community support is how Coach Gould made everyone feel like a long-lost friend. I saw similar enthusiasm and energy from Coach Harbaugh as he turned the football program around."*

The first step in implementing this involved making sure that my own office door was rarely closed. It remained open to anyone and everyone—*all* the time! Second, I made it a regular habit to create a pass-by visit to the general athletic offices, which were next door to the tennis stadium, at least once a day. Usually this was for a meeting or to pick up or drop off my mail or something else. On every visit, I would make it a point to "touch" as many people with contact as possible. I would walk through the café and greet the cooks, walk by desks of the secretaries and other staff, say hello and share a smile, try to exchange a quick greeting to as many coaches I might be able to pass near, and the same for our equipment person, our athletic trainer, our medical staff, and so on. All of these people, including myself, were a part of the larger team, and they were truly important to me.

"Coach gave me one piece of advice I never forgot when he was addressing our team for the first time my freshman year in '74," says Perry Wright, '78, team captain, All-American and NCAA doubles semifinalist. *"He said essentially (and it had nothing to do with tennis) that when you are walking the halls or the quad or whatever, to engage with people . . . say 'Hi' . . . be open to interacting. That has worked well for me over the years, and I never forgot it. I have imparted this to my kids and others over the years."*

I felt this helped them feel I cared about someone beyond simply my own program and the players for whom I was directly responsible. As a coach, it was up to me to carry myself in this manner; to set this standard of behavior of treatment toward others because it would demonstrate that each of us was part of a greater team than just our individual selves. I think everyone appreciated this and felt more relevant because they knew I cared about them. It worked both ways!

Dave Larson, '78, concludes:

"My takeaway is that everyone has something to offer, and if you see the potential of someone and give them hope and a chance, good things happen. After I graduated I spent the next twenty-five years in the sporting industry, half the time in tennis. I had to create footwear and apparel lines, promotions and contracts with influential players, many of whom played at Stanford. I made a career out of tennis—the business of it—all because of my positive experience on Stanford's tennis team. I have great memories of how I was treated when I was a low man on the team totem pole."

Chapter Three

TRUST

*I remember Coach saying, "You don't have
to like each other, but you do have to trust
each other." Trust was huge on the team
as well as respect for your teammates. I
recall being on a team in which the number one and two players did not like each
other. But in the big matches, they were
rooting hard for one another and trusted
each other to give 100 percent when the
chips were down.*

—Robert Devens, '94

I grew up at a time when a handshake or one's word was as good
as gold. This may explain why I trust people and tend to give
them the benefit of the doubt. It's a trait that has served me well;
only very rarely have I been disappointed or let down by people
I trusted.

Since trust was a characteristic I had mostly taken for granted,
it was almost an afterthought when I asked my guys, "What's
the importance of trust in developing successful teams?" The
depth of their replies attesting to the importance of trust has had
a significant impact on me. I am now certain that trust was a major factor in our success. The following examples are offered in
the context of the athletic world, but they have at least as much

relevance for non-sport teams, such as a business team, a family team or beyond.

Because a team is a complex social compact, I have broken the subject of trust down into three categories:

- Trust of the teammates in each other
- Trust of the players in their coach
- Trust of the coach in his players
- Trust violated: Coach at his angriest

TRUST OF TEAMMATES IN EACH OTHER

We had to be able to trust every guy on the roster to do their job, including trusting the coaches to have the team ready and the best lineup to win. I think it was developed from the get-go with the past success but then also from the upperclassmen.

—Scott Humphries, '98

The most poignant example of the importance of mutual trust came in a very challenging 1998 season. In retrospect, this was perhaps the critical factor in our eventual success that year.

The challenge lay in the fact that I had four players I sincerely felt could play number one, and I had two others almost as good. In fact, one of them, Alex Kim, would win the NCAA singles championship a couple of years later. In 1998, though, future NCAA doubles champion and all-time world doubles #1 Mike Bryan, '00, was one of the four competing for the number one position. *"Coach would always be fair and award the top spots on the team to those who were playing the best in practice and the tournaments. During our sophomore year, Paul Goldstein, Ryan Wolters, Bob Bryan, and I were all at about the same level. We all had the potential to be at the top spot."*

I had rarely faced such an embarrassment of riches before, but it is easy to see, on a personal level, how sticky it made setting a lineup. No one wanted to play ladder (intrasquad) matches against each other, so just before the dual meet season began,

I sat the whole team down on the court to discuss things. As a practical matter, it didn't help solve the problem, but much more valuable was the fact that it demonstrated to me the respect these guys had for another and the selflessness with which they were prepared to face the season. In essence, the discussion went something like this:

Bob started it off by saying, "Ryan just won the All-American championship and should be number one."

Ryan deferred, saying that "Mike is playing better than any of us right now."

Mike pushed it in yet another direction. "Paul had a great year last year and is the only junior player in history to have won in succession the national boy's 16s, and two national boy's 18s."

In keeping with the previous trio, Paul responded with, "Bob had the best summer of all of us, and he deserves the chance to play number one."[2]

Now what was I to do?

I thought about it that night and realized we had a total of twenty-four dual matches leading up to the NCAAs. The next day, I sat them down on the court again to present my plan, which I had talked over in-depth with my great associate coach, John Whitlinger.

I had decided to suggest that we play each of my top four players in an equal number of matches (six each) at numbers one through four respectively. Coach Whit had made out the match schedule, and so I went even further by passing out to them a sheet stating what number they would be playing for each match the remainder of the year. I did the same at numbers five and six, alternating Geoff Abrams and Alex Kim for an equal number of matches. It's still incredible to think back that this team was so strong that the guy who played number six for part of that year (Alex Kim) would win the NCAA singles championship two years later.

---

2   Bob defeated Paul in the NCAA singles title later that year.

I asked them all if they could support this plan for the entire season, no matter what happened as the year progressed. This was important because in two or three months, when one player would be scheduled to play number one, it was inevitable at least one of the other three would be playing better at that specific moment. In other words, my question was: "Can each of you handle playing two or three or four if you know you are in fact playing better than the guys playing ahead of you that day?" I also told them that I was retaining the right, once the twenty-four-match, dual meet season was over, to choose the order in which they would play in the NCAA championship.

Every one of them emphatically agreed to all of this. *"Coach knew he had four guys that all wanted this,"* explains Mike. *"But he found a way to make us okay with taking a backseat and playing lower in the lineup. He came up with a very smart plan to rotate the four of us in the top four spots and thus give us all an equal chance to play number one."*

The result was incredible. In 164 total singles matches (including twenty-four in the NCAA championships), the top six collectively lost only two matches all season. Numbers one and two doubles also rotated according to a preplanned schedule, and we only lost one doubles point all year. Because these guys all trusted each other, they proved themselves to be the most selfless team I ever have had the pleasure to coach!

Their teammate and captain Scotty (Hugh) Scott, '01, speaks about the closeness of this arrangement and what the subsequent trust and respect that came out of it meant for the culture:

"Our values were centered around being a family," he says. *"While Coach was the father of our program . . . it was through the sharing of leadership responsibilities that we all became the family that supported our brothers, were the first ones to pick them up when they were down, and a group that always put team success way before individual success."*

The point is that an effective and well-oiled team has absolutely no place for selfishness or petty jealousy. To me, "selfishness" partly means "self-promotion." It is not unusual in an organization for individuals to try place their agendas ahead of the team agenda—and even to minimize the achievements of a team in order to maximize the importance of their own part or to try to draw attention to themselves as if saying, "See how great I am!" Mark Jacobson, '87, sums up my own feelings well. *"A great team not only wins, but its players trust and respect each other and act with humility, regardless of their position."*

Creating this kind of culture of trust is not smoke and mirrors or some arcane art form. There are in fact certain keys to it. First, it is critical to counter the tendency toward selfishness by using the word "we" as opposed to "I"! Second, the coach must offer earned praise to the team in front of everyone. Third, and more specifically, those individuals who lack confidence or outright achievement, but are really trying, can be acknowledged for exceptional effort. One must never lose sight of the end goal and the central truth that it can rarely be reached unless all are working together to achieve it. According to Gene Mayer, '76, *"Trust stands out as the most important to me. We believed that each teammate had done his best to contribute to the overall success. There was no star system."*

Even when these principles are applied, there will always be challenges along the way. Jared Palmer, '93, one of the best athletes I ever had, could have been a collegiate quarterback, but he went on to win the NCAA singles (1991) and Wimbledon doubles (2001) titles and attain a world doubles #1 and world singles #35 ranking. During his time on the Farm, he was also on teams that faced a variety of challenges, and he remarks on the importance of handling these in such a manner as to not lose sight of the goal. Again, somewhat to my surprise, it came down to trust. *"I think one of the biggest things I learned was that when you have a goal you're trying to reach, which in our case was always an NCAA title, there can be craziness and chaos and bad luck along the way,"* says Jared. *"But if you don't panic and you have trust in the people around you, then it can still somehow all come together at the right time."*

Jared Palmer: NCAA Singles Champion, NCAA Doubles Finalist; World Singles #35; World Doubles #1 (with Coach)

What I learned from this culture we all built together was that every person has the best opportunity to succeed individually when this trust is built upon respect for one another—on one another's effort and preparation in sticking with a problem and dealing with it head-on without excuses or alibis. It is built on the knowledge that a teammate will keep fighting to the very end to not let the team down, doing whatever it takes within the rules and spirit of competition and unwritten ethical and moral rules to succeed! This is a great mantra for any team.

TRUST OF THE PLAYERS IN THE COACH

Coach Gould had an aura that demanded respect, and he had all the attributes that made it easy for players to put their faith in him. He was always prepared and knew what to say. You could see that he cared deeply about his role and was extremely driven to succeed. You could see that he knew the formula for what it took to be a championship team, so there was no reason to resist it. There was never doubt in his eyes, and he always confidently executed his plan. It was nice to be able to trust that this man could guide the team and in turn help every member reach his full potential.

—Mike Bryan, '00

Building this kind of trust is not always an easy thing to do. It builds over time, every year, and often through those challenges that Jared referenced. It builds when, as in 1998 with six top players, they are handled with respect for everyone involved. It's not, as Adam Ross, '95, points out *"a one-time thing. Trust and respect are earned over years, in good times and in bad."*

And there were many tough times over the years, and respect and calmness were key every time. All-American Jeff Arons, '83, says, *"Watching Coach handle any team discord with grace and poise enhanced his team's confidence in him. We understood that he did not rattle easily and made good decisions under stress. By the time the NCAA tournament started, we all believed Coach Gould would lead us to another title."*

There are multiple factors that go into this. First, as in everything else, one must be genuine and real, as opposed to political or duplicitous in any way. One cannot pretend. And it can't be for one day a week. It must be evident every minute of every day! And finally, once again, it's the coach or team leader who sets the tone. *"Dick was a 'player whisperer.' Everyone felt Coach had their backs,"* reflects Marcos Manqueros, '78. *"I could see he was stern when he had to be, but led more out of respect than fear. Trust and fear do not fit on the same page."*

If the coach cannot establish an environment of complete trust from their team, both in terms of their vision for the team as well as in their personal interest in each member of the team, the chances for success of the team are greatly diminished. My cherished values of humility and respect are examples. Mark Jacobson, '87, emphasizes this. *"Coach set the example for humility and respect."* This credibility must be earned. It will not be attained if any part of the process or relationship is judged to be fake!

Second, I believe "listening" is a big part of both earning and fostering trust and respect. Coaches are used to directing, as they must do, but it is a true talent if the coach can listen well enough that a team understands they themselves are an integral part of the leadership process. This could relate to things as simple as practice, to social events, to actual philosophy, and even to the point of helping to set team goals. If this can be achieved, great things can be accomplished.

"Coach listened to me and really instilled in me trust in the game, trust in the match, trust in Stanford, trust in my individual abilities against my opponent, and to not overcomplicate things," is how Jimmy Gurfein, '81, NCAA singles finalist and world singles #72 describes our relationship then. *"He was very calm and collected, and I trusted in his coaching."*

If I were going to share with the players my thinking about practice, upcoming matches, the season, community relations, or what was best for the entire program, as opposed to simply dictating what I wanted to happen and then listen to their ideas, opinions, and feedback, I had to make the third step and take their ideas seriously. The fact is that they had a lot to say about what was best for them, as individuals, and as they were all smart guys, I was sincere about soliciting their points of view. In the words of Garry Tyran, '75, *"Coach empowered his players to do their best and made everyone feel special. This resulted in the team having confidence and the will to win. There was overall a wonderful camaraderie among the team. This was due to Coach trusting his players, listening to them and making everyone feel special!"*

The rewards are often immediate, as Jimmy Gurfein, '81, goes on to note. *"In the NCAA team finals match, that calm, firm reassurance from Coach and the other players helped me win the final singles match and even the team score at 3–all. We then came back to win the doubles and the team championship. One year later, it helped me reach the NCAA singles finals."*

That 1981 individual final, by the way, was against his teammate, Tim Mayotte.

And third, another big example of where trust in their coach consistently came into play was when I "asked" a player to push beyond his comfort level, perhaps suggesting (strongly!) he be more aggressive, especially on a critical point. This was particularly true if I felt a player was holding back and waiting for something to happen. We spent endless hours working on executing these skills in practice, but the guys certainly weren't going to listen to me or anyone else telling them to take more risks in the heat of battle unless they trusted the individual giving the advice!

"Trust is the most important thing," as K. J. Hippensteel, '02, All-American, NCAA doubles champ and singles semifinalist and world singles #150, puts it. *"Once trust is lost, respect is lost. We have a saying in the Navy. It takes a lifetime to build trust and*

respect and just a second to lose it. Coach developed my trust by letting me work on my game in huge matches (UCLA/USC, etc.). By forcing me to come to net when I literally was looking at him saying, 'I don't feel comfortable' given the stakes of the point/ match. But Coach said, 'Go, go!'"

The more players saw that this system worked, the more of their trust I earned. Over the years, this philosophy became accepted and commonplace for our team. It was also practical. *"Trust is an extremely important element of successful teams because it allows you to just focus on execution,"* is how Michael Flanagan, '94, sees the dynamic. *"When Coach told me to serve and volley on a big point, even if I didn't feel like that was the right play, I would do it because I knew that he truly believed it was the best idea at that time, and I knew that he had more experience than me at critical junctures because of the success of his past teams."*

Happily, the trust and respect, fired though the years of competition with every player, has in many cases lasted decades. For me this has been the ultimate gift. *"My trust in Dick Gould has continued to grow over the years,"* adds All-American and world singles #48 Nick Saviano, '76. *"Dick has been a true friend and mentor, and someone I could always turn to for good advice and/ or help. His friendship and counsel and support has made Dick one of the most important people in my life. There is and always will be an unbreakable trust and bond."*

These comments matter greatly to me because I believe that one of the greatest compliments a person can receive is for others to say, "You can really trust that guy!" Once this is earned, then teaching, achieving, and succeeding are greatly facilitated. You must not let it go. *"The reciprocal trust that Coach built, whether he did it intentionally or whether it was just subliminal or subconscious, worked,"* says team captain and world singles #100 Jeff Salzenstein, '96. *"By the way he showed up, he was a leader, and he helped us in that way. We trusted Coach, because he had brought us in, and in the way he was going about things we trusted him to lead us."*

Looking deeper, a big part of trust, I think, is first, "being there" when people most need you, and second, "being there" the rest of the time, even when there is no crisis. *"It has to start at the top with the coach,"* concludes Eduardo Cardoso, '04. *"I shared things with Coach that I didn't share with my family. Trust was everything."*

TRUST OF THE COACH IN HIS OR HER TEAM

I think with all the different personalities, Coach trusting us that we would come up big in the clutch, well, that was huge! He showed belief in us and our abilities.

Jeff Salzenstein, '96

It is important to remember that trust must flow in both directions. As important as it is that the team trust the coach, at some point the coach must show he trusts his team. This can pose an interesting dichotomy. In terms of coaching technique and strategy, I became stronger and stronger in my methods and beliefs. But there are other aspects of leadership where a more flexible approach must be considered or implemented. The coach must realize that to get the best results, different personalities may need to be treated differently in different situations.

This can be a problem for one who micromanages everything. In fact, this has been a difficult process for me to learn because I know exactly what my vision is for everything I do, and in many cases I think I can do it better than anyone else. Of course, I may or may not be right in this belief, but when I turn over an "assignment," I often have it so well defined, there is no room left for out-of-the-box thinking. To meet my expectations, one must first do 1, then 1a, 1b, and so on. For example, in 2006 when we hosted the first-ever mixed men's and women's NCAA championships, I had detailed outlines of exactly what I expected from each of twenty-plus committees to accomplish, as well as specific examples of how to get things done.

How much better would that undertaking, or others, have been if I had given more reign to each person with whom I was working? I will never know. Obviously, in the above example, I really did not allow much room for this. In other ways, I did a better job because I also believe creativity is one tenant of a strong team. But how can creativity be developed if the team members have not learned to think for themselves? The team must feel confident that their ideas or methods will be listened to by their leader.

"When a coach creates an environment in which an athlete can let his skill run free, unencumbered by anxiety of outcome, his performance is enhanced," John DeVincenzo, '84, explains. *"The culture that Coach Gould created at Stanford was just such an environment. When I became a professor of medicine, I practiced it on my medical students, and they reinforced this wisdom. Treat people fairly, give them responsibility, and expect much from them. If you do, they will rise to the occasion."*

As another way to think about the dangers of micromanagement, consider your relationship with your family team and especially your own children. Too often, kids are not allowed to think for themselves. Too often, everything is organized and planned out for them by their "helicopter parents." They may not have had the chance to be creative with things as simple as how to use their own time. How seldom nowadays are they simply told to "go play," without being given instructions? We must have and show trust in them by letting them make decisions, even if we know they may on occasion fail!

I thus would argue that we must let our children make more of their own choices. We must place more trust on the values and sense of right and wrong we have taught them, encourage their participation, and then support their interests that develop from this participation. We must all let our children find their own ways.

As coaches, we have to trust and support our players, their choices, and their instincts. If we don't, the senior won't have any better sense of his own mind, or how to make a choice, or how to handle a sticky situation on court or off, than he did as a freshman because he will not have had experience doing so. And he will desperately need that experience and the life skills it teaches when he graduates.

"Coach remained pleasantly hands-off in regard to specific matches but did share strategies regarding lineups with us and included our input on such decisions (with himself retaining final decision-making)," says David Siegler, '83, and world singles #137. *"Thank you, Coach, for your confidence in your players and how you allowed us to have significant input into our destiny and your respect for us to avoid micromanagement!"*

I found that the best way for me to learn this was to remember what a great teacher "failure" is. We all must learn how to deal with failure, learn from it and then move on. Sports in particular remain a great teacher of the learning potential in failure. As a coach, this meant allowing players the freedom to make mistakes. Jared Palmer, '93, goes further. *"I think Coach Gould did a great job of treating his players, even the young ones, like young men and not like kids. He was good at giving them a sense of responsibility and of accountability for their actions."*

I also found the best way to do this was to have essentially no team rules. If I was treating them like men and not boys, then I had to trust them to set their own limits for the good of the team, even while realizing they were young men who would make mistakes. This will not apply for all coaches because it isn't everyone's style. In my own mind, the downsides of an autocratic rule were far greater than the downsides of the occasional error in judgment, which could also present yet another teaching and learning moment.

John Letts, '86, refers to this as *"a calm confidence and laissez-faire attitude. . . . Many people have asked me over the years about Coach Gould's approach toward discipline of his players, curfews, making sure there were no late nights, etc. The simple answer was there was none. Coach Gould had a complete 'laissez-*

faire' approach to his players. There were no curfews, demands of 'no drinking' or girls, etc." And he points out the benefits we reaped as a team from this approach. *"Coach Gould's own utter enjoyment and relaxed attitude was mesmerizing to his young athletes. This was a fun, stress-free zone. We came to Athens, Georgia for the NCAA championship to enjoy all it had to offer, even though the underlying mission was never forgotten. Stifled with strict curfews and early wake-up calls, other teams were deeply envious of the freedom Coach Gould granted his players to enjoy the nightlife."*

This approach is not without challenges of its own. If you are going to trust the players and let them make their own decisions, you also have to be prepared for bumps in the road, particularly on life outside the team. For example, we all know that young people think they are bulletproof, so asking them to take it easy if they choose to participate in other sports—skiing, skateboarding, and so forth—is a challenge for all coaches. Each year, I spoke to my team about my feelings regarding participation in intramurals representing their residential groups. I had played intramural football and basketball for my fraternity through college and absolutely loved the experience. How could I deny this opportunity to my players? I decided I would leave it up to their judgment. *"Many other coaches would never let their players take part in IM sports,"* explains Jared Palmer, '93. *"But Coach said 'you do what you want but if you get hurt, I'll kill you.'"*

In other words, not having rules was not the same as not having expectations and standards!

Nick Saviano had been a high school basketball star and called me late at night from his intramural game representing his college fraternity to say he had badly hurt his ankle. I don't remember saying a negative word on the phone that night, but when guys came to practice the next day, they found two tennis balls dangling on strings above the door to my office in the shack. One ball had been cut in half. The sign above the display simply read: "Nick's."

In the end, trusting the players comes down not to keeping track of successes and failures, or even errors and transgressions, but rather to giving unqualified and universal positive support whether they win a great match or make a bonehead mistake off court or on . . . whether they are an NCAA champion or the last guy on the ladder struggling to get into his first match. As Scott Matheson, '75, sees it, *"Coach firmly believes in the potential of each individual. Not everyone can be the best athlete, but everyone can be a better one, and he was there to help make that happen. He gave his players unqualified support—everyone wanted to do their very best because Coach believed in them."*

As parents and coaches, we have responsibilities far broader than managing a particular situation; we are in fact in the position of managing our children or our players' involvement in their sport. And I believe that too often parents insist on their child's participation in the sport they played, or that all their time be spent with this one sport only. If we mismanage them, force them into a sport in which they have little interest, or drive them into burnout or injuries, then they will—and rightly so—lose trust in us. My own children all started pretty much with tennis. But I encouraged them to participate in as many sports as realistic and to delay participation in any one sport for as long as possible. For most of them, their interest shifted to sports other than tennis. One (Sue) did play tennis at Princeton for a year, and three others were team captains in college: women's volleyball (Kim—Harvard), women's swimming (Karin—University of Southern California), and men's swimming (Rick—Stanford) respectively.

How sorry I am for young people, who because of pressure from a parent, a school coach, or more recently a club coach, feel they must devote all their time to a single sport, with no real "time off" during the year! In addition, the threat of overtraining in each practice session is ever present. No wonder so many sports injuries are now being attributed to overuse! No wonder so many young people burn out and leave organized sports at an early age! Fun activities must accompany their efforts as well.

In recent decades, this phenomenon has extended well beyond sports (although one of the silver linings of the pandemic may have been it forced people to take their foot off the pedal a bit). For example, in our business world of start-ups, "overuse" has always been a problem, as we tend to burn out our workforce. Medical schools have gradually reduced the rigors related to the concept that one hundred hours a week of internship or residency training makes one a better doctor. Sure, success doesn't just happen; success is based on a solid premise and achieved by hard work. But there is a limit.

I was always wary of player burnout and felt for my college guys that two-and-a-half hours on court five days a week, plus a thirty-minute strength/conditioning program, was plenty . . . *if* we used our time well. This was critically important both for the health of the players and the team, but also for the fostering of trust, because a coach, like any leader, must never forget the importance of bringing balance to the workplace, field, or court. If he or she does not, any success will likely be unsustainable, and the team will lose trust in the leader.

Trust Violated: Coach at His Angriest

I place a lot of trust in my athletes. I am usually pretty mellow and patient. It takes a lot to get me upset. But if I feel that this trust has been violated so that it reflects negatively on our team, I quickly address the issue. No team leader is impervious to all situations. Some can be very stressful. For me, those usually involved behavioral issues. I have no patience for poor behavior, alibis, procrastination, or lack of effort. I give a lot, but don't ever let me feel you have taken advantage of me! In addition, I give my guys a lot of freedom, but I expect them to be ready to play. And as far as performance is concerned, I expect them to play to win and never "not to lose."

The following truly occurred just as Paul Goldstein, '98, remembers. *"We won the 1995 national team indoor title in Louisville and traveled back to the Bay Area after the match. As a team, we had a bit too much fun on the journey back. About seven days after we got back from the trip, Coach sat us all down at the beginning of practice—didn't say a word, just pulled out a piece of paper and read: 'Dear Mr. Leland (AD at the time), I had the pleasure of watching your men's tennis team compete in Louisville last week at the national team indoors. They competed hard, they competed with class, etc. . . . you should be very proud. Sincerely, so-and-so.'*

"*After reading the letter, he didn't say a word. Rather, he just pulled out another letter. 'Dear Mr. Leland, my name is so-and-so. I had the misfortune of traveling with your men's tennis team to the Bay Area from Louisville recently. There were several young men who appeared to be intoxicated and underage. Moreover, they kept referring to a gentleman as 'Coach' who made no effort to curtail their behavior. Finally, one of the young men ultimately spilled tobacco juice on me. It was a disgrace. Sincerely . . .'After reading that letter, Coach told Ricky Becker that he would be sitting next to him for every flight the remainder of the year. What was so special about that experience is he built us up with that first letter and then humbled us with the second letter.*

"*I would characterize this story as another time when I saw Coach the angriest with our team. The year was 1998. Our team this particular season was arguably the most dominant relative to the competition in the history of all collegiate tennis. During the course of the season, we outscored our opponents in singles 162–2. What was perhaps more noteworthy about this team was the incredible team chemistry we had throughout the year. I share this background because it gives some context for the story. Because we were so successful on court and because there seemed to be relatively little off-court drama (at least to me), it strikes me that Coach had fewer opportunities to get mad at the team than perhaps in years prior (or in years future).*

"*In the middle of the PAC-12 season, we headed to Tempe to play at Arizona State. The date of the match happened to coincide with*

Stanford's first NCAA Final Four appearance in men's hoops in many, many years. Coach had to put up with several of us imploring him to reschedule the ASU match so that we could attend the Final Four in San Antonio. Nevertheless, the match was not rescheduled, and the team somewhat begrudgingly went out to play the Sun Devils. We lost the doubles point—this was the first (and only) doubles point we surrendered all year and only the third point we had surrendered the entire season. In the ten minutes between singles and doubles, Coach lit the team up like a Christmas tree.

"I distinctly remember Coach telling me, 'Paul if I hear you question another line call, I'm yanking you from the match immediately.' It was certainly a wake-up call for me and my teammates. I bet if Coach checked the scores of the singles matches that day, he would see the most competitive singles match (of the six played) must have been something like 2 and 2 as we won the overall dual match 6–1. We were all convincingly out of there in forty-five minutes or less. We then went on as a team to watch the Final Four game at a local Tempe restaurant that evening and had a blast, despite the overtime loss for the Cardinals to Kentucky."

Here are a couple of examples that occurred during our NCAA championship runs. Aleem Choudhry, '99, recalls, *"It was NCAAs in Georgia and I think some of the guys had invited the Bryan brothers to come out with them for a drink on a night before one of our matches. The next morning I think was by far the angriest I'd ever seen Coach lecturing the team. I'm talking orders of magnitude angrier than I had ever seen him. It was a good lesson though about not doing anything to compromise our chances of winning when we had done so much work the entire year to get to that point."*

As a coach, I also detest playing "not to lose" almost as much as I do a lack of effort! When Michael Flanagan, '94, began playing "not to lose" against UCLA in the semifinals of the 1992 NCAA championship, I felt it required fairly drastic action to snap him out of it. Michael picks up the story. *"Coach was a gifted psychologist and often knew how to get the best out of me whether I liked his methods or not. One time in particular occurred in the semifinals of NCAAs when we were playing UCLA. I was playing #2 singles against Billy Barber, who was at least nine inches taller than I, and whom I had never beaten before. Not to mention, I had lost my singles matches the previous two days in the round of sixteen and quarters. Despite that, I was playing well and won the first set, but had faltered and lost the second. When I walked to the changeover after losing the second set, I looked at the big scoreboard in Athens to see whether my teammates were winning and if they would bail me out in case I lost my own match. Coach did not wait for me to reach the bench. There was smoke coming out of his ears as he reached forward to pull my head away from looking at the scoreboard, essentially slapping me across the face to attention. He told me to focus on my own court (with a few colorful expletives thrown in) and focus on the aspects of the match that helped me win the first set.*

"The slap and the tone in his voice got my attention, and I knew he meant business. I had never seen him that pissed and that focused before. His strategy, whether it was intended or not, worked, as I was more scared of Coach for the rest of that match than I was of losing. Afraid that he would hit me again, I never sat down at the changeover for the rest of the match, choosing to cross the net on the opposite side of Coach rather than feel his wrath. I didn't dare look at the large scoreboard again, and I had no idea how any of my teammates were doing when I ended up winning the third set of my match."

In today's world, I would have lost my job if I did this. But in reality, I did not think we could have won Mike's match and then the championship without such drastic action. I felt he needed it to be able to focus completely on the task at hand.

The competitive season for which I am responsible lasts essentially the entire school year. The calendar now is filled with individual events in the fall, followed by the dual match season beginning the first of the year—it never stops! It is easy to be mentally ready to practice before an important event or prior to play in a big match. But what if the match seems to mean little?

Rarely have I been angrier than I was with Roscoe Tanner at UCLA when we were playing for third place in the Pac-8 championship. Now nobody likes to play for third place, but I took great pride in having *never* lost such a match. I really felt I was at my best getting my guys to rise back up and respond positively to this kind of challenge. However, on this day we were playing a good Washington team, led by the great Dick Knight. Dick was certainly capable of beating Roscoe. Roscoe was just going through the motions, and he was getting kicked. I never care if one loses a match if he has prepared well and is giving his best effort. On the other hand, the opposite could just not be tolerated! As Roscoe changed sides walked toward the back fence to pick up a ball to serve, he must have felt a maniac was attacking him! Right

in front of a large crowd, I bear-hugged him from behind and threw him up against the fence and "whispered" clearly and loudly exactly what I thought of his effort, and that if he didn't get with it immediately, I was going to pull him from the match. (I can't print here what I *actually* said.) The point is, he—and the entire team—snapped out of it, regrouped, and played well enough to win against a quality opponent.

Roscoe Tanner: NCAA Singles Finalist (twice), NCAA Doubles Champion; World Singles #4; World Doubles #14

Roscoe Tanner, '73, a two-time NCAA singles finalist, NCAA doubles finalist, Wimbledon finalist, Australian Open winner and pro singles #4 and doubles #14 continues, *"We were playing the Pac-8 tournament in LA at UCLA. We had lost to USC the day before, and we were playing Washington for third place. After losing in the semifinals, we didn't care. We had beaten Washington easily during the season. However, the whole team wasn't concentrating and the whole team was losing. Coach came to my court first and grabbed me by the shoulders, pushed me to the fence, and said, 'The whole team is losing.' With that we woke up, and all six players won. He was mad!"*

Again, times were different in the early '70s than nowadays.

But there are other times in practice or even for matches where one is not prepared to perform. The same situation can occur in any group setting. Remember, a lot is going on in the personal lives of your team's members, and certainly this was the case in the lives of college students. My challenge was to be sure that when a player on my team walked through the gates and onto the tennis court for practice or a match, he knew he was in now a separate and special world. My job as the leader of the team was to be certain that my player's mind was now focused totally on the challenge ahead. I was pretty good at conveying how I valued this trait and getting the result I expected.

I can put up with a lot of things, but *never* misbehavior nor lack of effort. *Rarely* would I ever think about calling a player out in front of his teammates. If I did, it was calculated and contained, by example, a lesson for all. Usually, I would prefer a "direct" but "soft" approach—at least the first time around. If I came across as mad, I was *really* mad!

Team captain Carter Morris, '03, remembers my "pipe and a bag" speech in Hawaii. *"This was when someone smoked weed on the Hawaii trip. I think Coach was pretty good at handling these issues 'directly.'"*

When I first started coaching, the on-campus Vietnam War protests got pretty hostile. When they reached "my turf," I erupted.

The "long hair" episode was another sign of the times, which I got over pretty quickly. Bill Rompf, '72, describes the time this way.

> *In the Spring of '72 I participated in a sit-in at the ROTC building on the Stanford campus. Most of the athletic offices were also in this building. I was sitting in the doorway and when Coach Gould walked through on the way to get his daily mail, I got the most hateful look of my life.*

> *At another time, one day at practice he took us all up into the stands and went crazy about RESPECT. He was right, but in the early years, he had to earn respect, and he wasn't "Dick Gould, Tennis God" yet! And then he looked at Mac (Claflin) and me and went berserk about our long hair. No one had ever seen him so mad! His face was red, and he was spitting out his words. It looked like his head was going to explode. We could not wait for that day of practice to end!*

I thought the timing of the on-court behavior incidents described below was incredible. I am glad I didn't miss these opportunities. These moments to lighten the mood in the "workplace" and still address the problem in a way that obviously made an impression. *"I was at practice one afternoon, neither playing nor behaving very well,"* remembers Jim Hodges, '80. *"After I threw my racket in anger against the fence, I looked up and saw Coach smiling at me. 'Jimmy,' he called, 'come on over for a minute.'*

"I trudged over and calmly, with a smile on his face, Dick said 'Jimmy, I would like you to meet Stanford's new athletic director, Andy Geiger.' I, deservedly, felt about two inches tall and Dick was able to teach me a lesson that I have never ever forgotten!"

Throwing a racket in practice when a player gets frustrated is a fairly common occurrence, but one that can quickly get out of hand if others start to join in. *"One memorable example was at a practice when everyone was seemingly in a bad mood, and there was a lot of racket throwing and yelling,"* reminisces Jason Yee, '91, an All-American and NCAA doubles finalist. *"Coach made us stop practice, keep our rackets and follow him to Angel Field, our home for track and field. Then he made everyone throw his racket on his command as far as he could; he had us go get them and stay there until he told us to throw them back! This went on for several rounds. We must have gotten it out of our systems, for there were no more rackets thrown for a while."*

Practice may start out fine, but if one person is a little off for whatever reason, his behavior can become suspect. Throwing a racket is one example. Swearing is another—remember, the court is my "living room." When one person yells out, it is like a cancer and it spreads, in this case to everyone. Here is an example of how I handled this situation one day. Adds Robert Devens, '94, *"One day we had a lot of complaining, swearing and temper fits in practice. Coach took us behind the courts and got us all together on this field. 'Guys, a lot of moaning and groaning out there. Let's get it all out and go around the circle. I'll start . . .'And he let loose yelling at the top of his voice such a torrent of swear words I could not believe it. We all sheepishly followed suit. I thought it was a perfect example of Coach using his sense of humor, unity and putting himself out there first to bring the team together and deal with an unfortunate circumstance. These were the tools Coach often used."*

Once I heard a talk from the Positive Coaching Alliance by Mike Legarza, a great coach and teacher of life lessons. He talked about "flushing" the negative out of one's system and then moving on. I found a perfect time to use it to make a point after something negative happened on the practice court. I had the guys follow me into the public restroom. *"One time there was a bad practice and guys were in a foul mood,"* recounts Anthony Flores, '01. *"Coach took us all into the bathroom, had everyone take the flush handle of a urinal or a toilet, and on his command, we 'flushed it all' down the drain. To make a point, we were letting it go. Another time during a match, Coach called an 'unsportsmanlike conduct' penalty on our own player to make a point it was unacceptable and never to be tolerated again."*

Chapter Four

"WINNING" IN PERSPECTIVE

My experience is that Coach always wanted the best for the player, wherever that might go.

—Peter Morris, '80

Our democratic system is largely based on free enterprise, which encourages competition, but our society sometimes gets so caught up in the importance of winning that competition often gets blown way out of perspective. Above all, I did not want to win at the expense of my players' welfare. I always wanted the best for them, just as I did for my own children, and in neither case did it always involve winning. Team members, and especially young people, must understand you care about them as people, both in the present and beyond.

It is gratifying to hear that Carlos Moravek, '86, feels I followed through on that promise. *"Coach has been willing to help any player at any time, even many years later. He has an interest in the player being successful in tennis, school, and his personal life. If he has been able to assist in any way in regard to tennis or other areas, he's been quickly supportive and effective as an advocate."*

Daryl Lee, '87, goes on to say, *"I think his most meaningful legacy is how much he helped his players in their lives after they graduated."*

I am not alone in that approach by any means. Many coaches adopt a role as life mentor to their team members, but the ability to care beyond the performance on the court, and beyond a player's four years on the team, is often crowded out by an overemphasis on winning, which puts incredible stress on both participants and coaches. Coaches sometimes demand their better players—even at a young age—participate only in their sport year-round, and no other. This is often not in the best interests of the player, either as a person, who can get sick of his or her sport or activity, or as an athlete, who can suffer burnout or injuries from overwork of the same muscle groups.

Unfortunately, we are currently overrun by overzealous coaches—including parents and others—who continually emphasize winning over anything else. In the worst-case scenario, it can lead to bending the rules and cheating. This win-at-all-costs attitude can take the pure fun and enjoyment out of sport or any other activity. It then no longer becomes a great experience for many youths. And it makes it easier to see why approximately two-thirds of young people leave sports by age fourteen. When a nine-year-old youth soccer player comes off the field at the end of a game in tears because her team lost the game . . . when a fourteen-year-old tennis player leaves the court with his racket freshly smashed in frustration . . . or when a parent yells at her son that he should have done better to the point the child feels worthless, then the positive values of sport are lost.

The unintended consequence is that a bad experience at a young age often drives young people from physical activity altogether to more sedentary lifestyles. Enter e-sports video gaming, which is taking our nation by storm. E-sports are not a bad thing in and of themselves, but when they are played to the exclusion of more traditional physical activity, it only reinforces an increasingly sedentary national lifestyle, a dynamic that is a very real threat to our public health.

I offer you a challenge: when your child calls you in the evening to check in from a competition, I challenge you to *never* during this five-minute conversation ask, "Did you win?" Instead, engage with questions like, "Did you make any new friends? Did you enjoy your competition? How are your teammates doing? What might you have done better today?" Regardless of the outcome of the game or match, remember these magical words, "I am proud of you! I love to watch you play!" And most important, always finish with, "I love you!"

Ricky Becker, '86, finds this personal approach to have been central to his Stanford experience. *"This is important! We never felt like we were winning for Coach. I can honestly say I sometimes felt like personally he didn't care if we won or lost, and it didn't feel like his acceptance of us as people or tennis players hinged on whether we won or lost."*

If we orient our response to the positivity of the experience and the effort expended, it's my hope that we can get away from an overemphasis on results, which only adds to the incredible pressure placed on our young people. Thankfully, great organizations like Positive Coaching Alliance, Coaching Corps, and others are helping both parents and coaches approach coaching constructively. Games are meant to be fun, and we all have a responsibility to ensure that they remain so. My hat is also off to those coaches who offer uniforms to all who want to play, and who have a "no-cut" philosophy for their teams.

At the same time, one of the values of sport can be to help teach us to perform under pressure, a quality that all good managers try to install in their teams. As leaders, we must constantly try to find the right and most effective balance—to make the experience as positive as possible, and to teach our team members to look forward to meeting the challenge at hand.

I learned a great deal about differing and changing goals in the 1980s. The great Swedish player, Mats Wilander, rose quickly in the professional ranks beginning in 1980 to the top five in 1983, where he remained until 1988. When he won the US Open in 1988 in September, he finally attained the world's #1 ranking. But he retained this ranking only until January, and then his ranking started to plummet. People noticed, and finally someone asked him, "Mats, your ranking is dropping. Are you concerned? What's your problem?"

Essentially, Mats responded, "What is *your* problem? My goal was to become #1, and with much work, I reached my goal. This is no longer what I live for. I can still play tennis and enjoy it without the pressure of having to win." This reminds me of the great 1969 Peggy Lee classic song in which she asks after several important life experiences, "Is that all there is?" In summarizing "Winning in Perspective," a coach must realize there are times when it is not so important for all people all the time. My first teams often reflected this, much to my chagrin!

There are four pillars to this perspective process: the process itself, focus, motivation, and communication.

PROCESS

In today's jargon, it was about the "process" or the "journey" rather than the "result" or the "destination."

—Patrick DuPré, '76

Make no mistake, my goal from day one, like that of essentially every coach of a fairly good college team in any sport, was to win the national championship. If I were running a business, it would have been to make it the best. But once we won our first championship, I became a much better coach. I stopped putting so much pressure on my players to win, win, win. The goal became unspoken. As Jake Warde, '76, says, *"The goals were mostly implicit."*

The ultimate goal became unspoken or implicit because, once again, athletics should bring joy not simply by wins, but by the process! It must be a rewarding journey! This—not wins—is how success in sports should be measured. This journey can still be enjoyed with reasonable goals and by dedicated work to reaching them. But the value of each participant must be consistently celebrated independent of wins and losses! Measurable improvement and fun are the result. Note: this may be more difficult in a business situation where outcome is evaluated by investors, but coaches can be fired for the same reason too. I believe it is possible to not only enjoy the process but to be successful as well. If the two are combined, the result can be powerful!

My process usually consisted of incremental goals because I realized my guys played better when I set stepping-stone improvement goals, such as earlier preparation on the forehand, a higher toss on the serve, more consistency from the backcourt, more firmness on the backhand volley, better transition footwork on the serve and volley, and so on. Each player of course had a different challenge according to their game, and they could do better in each practice by improving one single part of their game, which in turn made them feel better and gain more confidence. As Jake Warde, '76, describes it, *"Coach focused mostly on being attentive to individuals on the team and offered them what they needed, when they needed it."*

Amazingly, when I stopped talking about the necessity to win— we won! *"There was never talk about winning the title. Emphasis was put on controlling everything you could control,"* says Mike Bryan, '00, the partner with his brother of the winningest doubles team of all time.

We won again and again by focusing on process instead of winning.

Martin Blackman, '91, eloquently explains better than I could why more often than not the best way we found to win was, oddly enough, to take the focus off winning:

"Winning is a by-product of commitment to process and excellence. Coach was very process focused. I don't remember him ever talking about winning before a match—only about what we needed to do, about our opponents' strengths and weakness, etc. He never put pressure on us to win, only to play our best. As much as possible, Coach tried to have us focus on the process, work on our weaknesses and enjoy the battle. He forced me to work on my weaknesses and made me accountable for the things that were in my control, like preparation, punctuality and attitude. That is a winning formula. I think all great team cultures are process focused."

I'm proud that a guy with this perspective became head of US Tennis Player and Coach Development!

Unfortunately, the fact is that even though we may focus on incremental adjustments, it's difficult in tennis to measure improvement except in the wrong terms. In swimming, for example, you might never win a race, but if you better your existing time, you have obviously gotten better and can feel better about yourself. In track, not only do you have times, but you have inches and feet—you might finish last in the meet, but pole vault a half inch higher than you ever have before and thus still feel good about yourself. The ability to feel good is aided by the measurable!

In tennis, we tend to measure improvement by a ranking or by what number we play on the team, both of which can be misleading. For example, a player might vastly improve his forehand, but it's difficult for him to accept a coach's sincere compliment on that when the next thing he hears is, "Today I'm going to move you from number three to number four." The results in the long run are what really matter. My players like All-American Jim Grabb, '86, who reached number one in the world in doubles in three different years, understood that *"sacrificing individual rankings and short-term payoffs for more solid long-term success was definitely part of the sauce."*

The same focus on rankings and numbers happens on a team level as well. As a team, we may feel we have regressed if during the season our team ranking drops from number three to number five. In business, it may be from failing to meet our quarterly goals. As team members or as leaders, we too often get obsessed with the result and it becomes the most important thing to us. The real problem, since results come and go, is that this can create a negativity that affects both behavior, enjoyment, and outcomes; if a team member is completely result-oriented, they just end up putting too much pressure on themselves to have the freedom to function at the highest level! One must let the results go for minor improvements and focus on the process; the results will then take care of themselves.

One of my favorite essays is a short piece by Robert Hastings called "The Station," which I read for the first time in 1981 in the "Dear Abby" column of a newspaper. It's about life's journey as opposed to the end result. One paragraph read, "However, sooner or later we must realize there is no one station, no one place to arrive at once and for all. The true joy of life is the trip. The station is only a dream. It constantly outdistances us." (See item V in the appendix for the complete essay.)

Another is the poem "If—" by Rudyard Kipling. His words are full of great life values and present the best example of words to live by that I have ever seen. In fact, the following words are above the players' entrance to the center court at Wimbledon: "If you can meet with triumph and disaster and treat those two impostors just the same, then you'll be a man my son." (Also see item V in the appendix for the complete poem.)

This understanding becomes part of the process, especially when placed in the context of competition, even when all else is forgotten. I end almost every talk I give by reciting either one or the other of these two pieces of enduring wisdom because they both represent what I want to get across and so well illustrate my basic philosophy.

Day-to-day improvement is hard to recognize because it involves so many seemingly small parts, so my focus was on a broader scale. My intent annually became to (1) be sure my players had developed confidence in each other, (2) were as fresh as possible physically and mentally at the end of the season, and (3) were confident enough in how they were playing to be able to actually look forward to the challenge of putting it all on the line, independent of worries about possible results!

"Coach loved to win and was always trying to get better, but he seemed to relish the competition and the process even more," adds Jim Grabb, '86. *"Coach's perspective was something that played a key role in my ultimate understanding and valuing of the process. Process really matters!"*

FOCUS

*Dick Gould understood how to perform
well in pressure situations. To be well prepared and look at the challenge as an opportunity. We focused on all the things that
we can control, with the emphasis on execution, and tried to let go of the rest and
not be distracted. We stayed in the moment
and dealt with adversity straight on.*

—*Nick Saviano, '77*

My views on "focus," as articulated by Nick—one of the very best of American teaching pros—came from my own on-court experiences (and failures!) trying to perform under pressure, which is when proper focus is required the most.

Personally, I lacked competitive experience before college. Once there, I thrived in everyday practice against good players, but I still did not know how to focus under pressure. In my senior year, I had beaten some good players in dual matches, including a Davis Cup player or two from foreign countries, and was feeling good going into the Pac-8 conference championship at the end of the year in Ojai, California, near my hometown. I was pumped to play well in front of my local friends! In the quarterfinals against USC great, Ed Atkinson, I was serving in the third set with double match point at 5–2, 40–15—a point away from a major upset. But unfortunately, I lost my focus by letting my mind wander—just one winning point too early—toward "how good this win would feel" and that I had finally "made it." I promptly choked and lost the match.

The next year, as a fifth-year redshirt senior, I was again in the quarterfinals and even on the exact same court! I was playing my friend and great UCLA player, Norman Perry, and again leading in the third set 5–3, 40–0—*triple* match point on my serve. Once more, I started thinking ahead of myself, and predictably, choked again. I was soooo close to entering the upper echelon of college tennis, but I probably needed one more year to gain the confidence and learn how to be focused by staying in the moment to reach that level!

For several years after these matches, I had the same recurring nightmare. I dreamed I was climbing a volcanic mountain, slipping and sliding on the loose shale, but getting ever closer to the top. And, when I finally reached the crest and put my hands on the ledge to pull myself over the top, I slipped, and this time went spinning back down to the bottom of the mountain only to have to start all over again!

The point is that it takes a while, and maybe even a few bad losses and nightmares, to process these kinds of lessons. We often hear competitors or their coaches blame a loss on a lack of experience. At the time, the idea that another player had more experience was too intangible to mean anything to me—but it did serve as a great rationalization for a loss!

I learned that in those two matches I had lost my focus on what I was doing on each point because I was thinking not about the next point, but rather about how great it would feel to finally achieve a truly significant win! Often people who start competing a little later than established athletes and who look up to them early on as the standard can relate to this experience. With this realization, the concept of "experience" finally became more tangible to me.

I also learned that first and foremost I needed to stay in the moment, focusing on the now, the right now, as Nick Saviano suggested! That's what the "experienced" player has learned how to do, and there's nothing intangible about it. It also means not waiting for an opponent to lose, but to stay aggressive. In addition, one must also know their own limitations and play within them—not only against a particular opponent, but during the upcoming point and even with each ball hit.

It is easy to get ahead of oneself by thinking about what might happen. This is a main cause for getting tight and choking. From this point, things usually go downhill quickly.

In a nutshell, the lesson is that we must complete "today" before we start worrying about "tomorrow." Concentrate on this game before we think about the next; think about this shot before the next one. This is important for a team or individual in most any situation. Had I known how to do that, I might have won those two matches. I didn't, of course, but the lesson on focus, on staying in the present moment, was something I could pass on to my players to help prevent them from suffering such excruciating losses.

Focus is also improved by having a game plan going into matches, which gives players something to concentrate on and hence helps them get off to a good start. Team captain Scott Moody, '87, explains:

"Rather than say stuff like 'concentrate, focus,' etc., Coach provided actionable strategies to deal with different mental challenges. For opening match jitters, for example, I remember Coach offering up what he had learned from Bill Walsh, who scripted the first 20-odd plays of each football game, no matter what. This was both to take away the nerves of making decisions, and for information gathering on an unfamiliar opponent to see how they reacted to different shot combinations. The general rule to have a plan that helps get off to a good start is useful in many athletic and business scenarios."

Robert Devens, '94, also found these pre-match strategy sessions helped him focus. He adds:

"I remember on multiple occasions Coach detailing prior to a match exactly how I should play, and steps needed to win and

'if you do it, you will win this match.' [Coach] always said it with such conviction and he had such credibility that I always believed him. It helped me because it focused me not on winning or losing but on the steps I needed to take, one by one, to win. The focus should be on the process not the result. It gave me tremendous confidence and allowed me to stay in the moment during important matches."

The start of the match represents a second chance to reinforce, and perhaps readjust, the focus. I would watch closely as each game I began to see how both my player and his opponent played the first couple of points. Getting the first point of a game is critical, especially when your opponent is serving. Was my player ready? Did my player play a solid, well-constructed point? If so, and he lost the point, no problem. A simple, "That's what I mean" (or "want") reaffirms that; although the point was lost, it was played correctly in terms of what I wished. If my player won the point, the next comment would be something like, "Great—now let's get another."

Matt Mitchell: NCAA Singles Champion; World Singles #53

I might offer a specific strategy to follow, especially when up 0–15, winning the first point on the opponent's serve. This is when I wanted doubt or fear or pressure to be put into the opponent's thinking—as the receiver of his serve, I wanted my player to move around the court to show a new look, move up an obvious step or two before returning the second serve, and so on.

"My favorite was the 'first two points strategy' where Coach schooled me on the value of 'applying insurmountable pressure'

on my opponent," explains NCAA singles champ and world singles #53, Matt Mitchell, '79. *"If I could take the first two points in each game, the pressure for a player to constantly have to come back would eventually take its toll on their shot making and execution. It's a more precise and defined objective than the often quoted 'Be. Here. Now.' It takes your execution to another level of focus."*

After pre-match discussions and early match encouragement, I felt one of the great advantages of college tennis was that on-court and essentially continuous coaching was allowed. This was an incredible opportunity for me to teach my players about strategy—about how to play points the way I wanted them played in certain situations! As such, it also presented continual opportunities to help them stay focused.

To succeed in coaching on court, a coach must know his players and team, teach them to address each and every situation in practice, and then encourage execution. I know my players often hated my on-court coaching the first time any of them were exposed to it. It was something most had not experienced before, and what "Coach was going to say or might say" was only one more thing with which they had to deal. Often what I asked a player to execute was out of their comfort zone and at a critical time in the match. But they absolutely learned from it and were better because of it. It lessened their personal burden because it became "Coach's call" for better or worse.

One of my first examples of trying to get a player to focus through on-court coaching occurred in 1970 during the NCAA doubles semifinal at the University of Utah, when freshman Roscoe Tanner, '73, was paired with senior Rob Rippner, '70. This was the first time one of our doubles teams had reached the NCAA semifinals. Rob and Roscoe seemed like an unlikely doubles combination, but their games and playing styles actually complemented each other very well. Late in the third set, they were up a couple of break points against a great USC team, and if they could convert one of them, Roscoe, with his world-class serve, would be serving for the match.

It was obvious to me that Rob was very nervous, so just before his serve return, I gave him a tip that didn't turn out well at all! Rob picks up the story:

"I had managed to hold serve to 5–5 in the fifth set. As Erik van Dillen, then number one at USC and a Davis Cup star, was set to serve, I walked over to Coach sitting by the fence. Sensing how nervous I was, he whispered, 'Just get the return in play no matter what. Don't overhit!' First point, my return hit the back fence." So much for good coaching and getting my player to focus!

My next bit of advice turned out better, as Rob also generously recounts. *"When I looked over, Coach shot me a reassuring smile, as if to say, 'No problem. All is good.' My nervousness vanished. Roscoe and I went on to win the match."* This was a major upset that put us in the NCAA finals. Rarely have I been prouder of a team!

A coach must realize the competitor also often can get ahead of themself and start thinking about the end result instead of focusing on the *now*! Alan Margot, '73, remembers an excellent example of this. *"I believe the year was 1970, and we played a great UCLA team at home. Haroon Rahim was playing #1 for UCLA on a team that included two future NCAA champions, Jeff Borowiak and Jimmy Connors. He was playing Roscoe Tanner, who was a freshman. There was a time in the match where it was tight, and Rahim's play and attitude were dominant. On a changeover Coach went out to talk to Roscoe and there was a quick moment of silence where he looked at Coach and Coach looked at him . . . Coach then asked, 'What'd you have for lunch?' Roscoe took a breath and attempted to remember what he had eaten for lunch. Coach waited a few seconds and before Roscoe answered, he said, 'Go get 'em, buddy!' and walked off.*

"Roscoe took a couple deep breaths then broke Rahim and served out the match. In the words that were exchanged, which had nothing to do with tennis, Coach created a break in the battle, and a clearing of the mind of what was going on in the moment. His ability to recognize that in that moment, no tactics or strategies needed to be changed . . . what was needed was a clearing of the mind and 'game space' to allow the player to perform. Coach has the gift to create belief and allow the player to compete with the driven passion that he has."

I simply had to get Roscoe Tanner to stop thinking about the pressure from worrying about the results and help get him back into the present. I laugh about it to this day.

Obviously, not everything a coach says to a player on court is well received or guaranteed to work. If things were difficult, a player would often react in a negative way. This gave me a great opportunity to emphasize a critical life lesson as well as to help bring their focus back to the present. *"Coach showed me the importance of not showing negative energy when losing,"* remembers All-American NCAA doubles champ K. J. Hippensteel, '02. *"He didn't focus on the losses/setbacks unless it was a learning moment (i.e., poor effort, lack of focus, etc.), and so we easily moved on to the next goal/task. Any distractions from prior successes he easily cut out by always reminding to 'show me.'"*

Yet another unique opportunity for a coach to take special note is near the end of a close and hard-fought game, the end of a set or tiebreak, or end of the match, and particularly on the verge of an unexpected win. It's very important, as my personal experiences in Ojai had proven long ago, to maintain focus at these crucial points of closure. If I would see a player tightening up, I would sometimes just give a reassuring smile and a positive nod of my head or quick clap, or even a comment, such as, "Here we go," or "That's it!"

If someone seemed to be losing focus at any point in a match, I could usually find a way to bring them back to the point at hand.

For example, I would bring their mind back by giving specific shot or strategic advice: "Serve a kick to his backhand and get in," or "Serve it out wide," or "Shrink the court," to have my player give himself more margin on the sideline. Ricky Becker, '96, calls it *"relaxed focus."*

But as K. J. Hippensteel, '02, says, we also had to focus on the season to be sure we were best prepared for the biggest moment(s), and particularly the NCAAs. *"Coach had all of us focused on May whether it was the opening speech to us or our efforts/focus in practice/matches. A lot of teams were grinding in the fall but fatigued at the end, but he had us fresh and ready to conquer in May.*

"Despite the focus on May, Coach still had me focused on things I could control like coming to the net, showing positive energy, etc., rather than on things I couldn't control such as wins/losses/ weather. These lessons can easily be used in business or my profession of medicine, etc."

Focus is not just an on-court issue. Focus is required off court as well. When a player's college life is falling apart and challenges mount, a coach has to help him keep perspective and focus. We all face challenges outside of the workplace. At least in the workplace or on the team, we have someone available to help. How I as the team leader chose to react to such circumstances depended solely on the personality of the player I was coaching. NCAA singles and doubles champion and world doubles #1 and singles #30 Alex O'Brien, '92, relates just such a circumstance. *"When I was a senior, I was dumped by a girl I really liked. I had not lost a match that year and we were playing Cal. Bent Ove Peterson had me down 6–0, 3–0 and Coach was trying to get me on track. Finally, after trying everything, he simply walked by me at the back on the court and said, 'The net is only three f***ing feet high, hit the damn ball over it.' It shook me out of my funk, and I came back and won the second and lost in a tiebreaker in the third. Coach was great at the unexpected and dealt with it magnificently."*

Or as Geordie McKee, '86, encapsulates the concept, *"Coach completely embodied focus. Long-term focus throughout the year was always on Athens, Georgia in May, with shorter term goals right in front of us to get us there. As Athens approached the focus intensified, to the point that every year, starting three weeks before the NCAAs, the 'Georgia mix' busted out songs on the loudspeakers every day at practice (Georgia on My Mind, Midnight Train to Georgia, etc.)."*

MOTIVATION

Go after what you want—nothing is given in this life. Coach emphasized the perils of complacency. When you are at the top, everyone is coming after what you have. The trick that Coach excelled at was keeping us believing as though we had something to prove every day, something to prove each year. Maintaining motivation for a group of all-star athletes is not easy. He was a master motivator. He didn't always put his foot on the accelerator, but his brilliance lay in knowing 'when' to take it to the next gear in the weeks and days leading up to a big match or tournament. To this day, I struggle to answer what his formula was, but I suspect it was more of a gut feeling. It is one of many intangibles that made Coach a legend during his time at Stanford.

—Scotty (Hugh) Scott, '01

Perspective, process, and focus are critical, but to get the most out of one's team day in and day out, motivation is key, and the leader or manager of any group—coach, athletic director, president, sales director—must figure out a way to provide it in each situation as needed. The more a team has at stake, the easier it is to motivate it. For us, this was when there was a big match or tournament for which we were preparing. But what about day in and day out? Remember, the tennis season runs throughout the entire school year.

"Coach taught me to always compete, work hard, and be disciplined," describes Ali Ansari, '01. *"He never was complacent and always challenged us to give our best. One example I always use with my business teams are analogies to my sports career: You have to operate like a 'well-oiled machine,' which is a quote from Coach from when we were heading to NCAAs. He always kept us hungry, even though we were NCAA champions!"*

As with focus, pre-match discussions and on-court coaching provided excellent opportunities to motivate. Sometimes I was encouraging. James Wan, '07, writes:

"I remember one specific example right before NCAAs where he pulled the whole team into the trophy room. There was a brief moment of silence before Coach told us to look around the room and take in the legacy that was Stanford tennis. That when we went out there, we not only represented ourselves and our team, but Stanford tennis. We not only heard but felt that because we were part of Stanford, we were winners, and everyone (including us) knew that. I think I played one of the best matches of my life following that speech."

Other times, I had to be tougher. Here's Ali again. *"Once, in regionals Dave Martin and I were playing without too much interest against a team from Sac State that we should beat ninety-nine times out of one hundred, and we were losing early. Coach walked up to us and said, 'You are not losing to f***ing Sac State!' Dave and I looked at each other and we said, 'He's right,' and then we went on to win the match pretty handily from there."*

Goals are meant to be a way to motivate. But the team must be able to relate to the goals its leader sets. When I started my coaching career, I was frustrated early on because the teams could not align with my goals; that experience would prove to be a valuable lesson for me. In fairness, in my first few years my teams were good, but certainly not great. What I was trying to accomplish—winning a national championship—was beyond their mental comprehension. They heard it, but in reality, it was so far out there that they could not identify with it. In addition, at the time there was essentially no future in pro tennis, which in itself would have been a very positive motivator. Despite all this, I mistakenly assumed that my players would think that every practice and every match was important and that they would automatically rise to every occasion. I quickly realized I was wrong. It's always difficult to get excited about taking every single match seriously, and these players in particular had other things going on in their lives that made tennis less important for them.

Yet I also believed that every one of those players had untapped potential, and my job was to keep them motivated enough to bring it out. I had to show that I believed in them and believed that they could do more.

Another critical factor in regard to motivation: it has to be grounded in reality, which means that the goal of the team must be one that is realistic. There must be some reasonable chance it can be attained. Otherwise, interest and maximum production, even for the short-term, are hard to sustain. The early teams were a good example of that—winning a national championship was beyond their reach. Getting suntans and winning a few matches were acceptable goals to them. For me, as previously suggested, stepping-stone, attainable goals, worked best. This makes it much easier for team members to enjoy the process and the journey! Otherwise, goals set too high tend to put too much pressure on them. In the best of all worlds, motivation comes from not wanting to let teammates or the program down—it is not something that is asked for or demanded. And their motivation is reinforced with small successes along the way.

Vimal Patel, '94, 1994 NCAA doubles finalist, reveals that he *"wanted to play my best for Coach because I didn't want to let down the man who had led the team to so many successful championship years. Fear of letting Coach down was a tremendous motivator."* I certainly didn't want Vimal to be fearful, but I appreciated his commitment to his teammates.

In the end, there are many ways to motivate. One is by instilling fear, which, Vimal's response notwithstanding, was not my personal style. Another is by yelling or screaming—also not my style as I learned when I was a young football coach. I feel and hope I am best described as a big believer in positive motivation.

"I think one of Coach's biggest strengths was his ability to motivate the team in the right way to get there," says team captain Barry Richards, '90. *"When I say, 'motivate in the right way,' it was rarely if ever through negative motivational tactics, but through using his personal experience or the experiences of other players/teams or situations to deliver his message."*

When talking about motivation, I do not consider "pep talks" the right term. In fact, the overuse of that approach can minimize its effect. Rather, I tried to think in terms of what a team or individual might need the most. I tried to think of a different way to convey the point I was trying to make each time and found that I was able to do so in key situations. Scott Lipsky, '03, an All-American and NCAA doubles finalist in 2003 and future Grand Slam mixed doubles champion, apparently agrees. *"I think Coach's biggest area of strength was his ability to get us motivated to play matches and get through each practice with the goal of performing our best day in and day out."*

In the end, I learned that I had to recognize when to step on the gas and when to ease up. I actually felt that by the end I was pretty good at this. There are times to push harder and other times to recognize that a softer approach might be better. The season is long and provides many ups and downs. Not everything is of paramount importance in a particular moment. Scott Matheson, '75, and now a federal judge, appreciates this. *"Coach is a supremely effective motivator. He knew when to push, when to back off, and how to adapt to different players and situations. That is a gift the best coaches have."*

COMMUNICATION

The main thing is that Coach was simple, direct, communicated easily, and showed he cared. I would come into the courts for practice every day early, and I would come into Dick's office and he'd be eating his lunch. He'd ask me, 'How are you doing? How are things going?' And he'd show an interest in me besides just tennis. I was appreciative that he took an interest in my welfare and it rubbed off on me that I was wanted. I was there to play tennis, but I was also there as a student and as a person.

—Jimmy Gurfein, '81

Communication is central because without it you cannot convey leadership to your team. Communication can be through actions or positive conversations to an individual or group, but either way the coach or leader's most important responsibility is to listen!

Conversations might start as questions. "Is this a problem? How do you propose we address it?" "How can we do this better?" "Is this as good as we can become?" "If you were in my shoes, what would you do?" Never get defensive in this type of conversation!

Jeff Arons, '83, remembers a lot of these team confabs:

"Coach's sanguinity would turn serious, listening to and sometimes calling a team meeting to assuage grievances. Even the most recalcitrant players were given the opportunity to offer their

opinions. Coach Gould allowed his players to voice their frustrations. I cannot recall Coach ever losing his cool during even the most heated and contentious team meetings. I suspect the fact that he allowed you to speak your mind, even criticize him and/or his coaching decisions, empowered his team. Ultimately he would get everyone back to pulling on the same side of the rope."

Mostly, effective communication is related to one's ability to read the atmosphere within the team, to take a calculated risk to go with one's gut. *"I think the biggest thing was being able to set the right tone at the right time depending on the situation,"* adds Jon Wong, '06. *"When we needed our butts kicked, Coach had a sense of knowing when this was needed. Same would be true of when to have more fun. He was usually direct and didn't mince words but gave a sense that he always had our individual best interests in mind."*

Alex O'Brien, '92, calls me a psychologist, which, technically, is a real stretch, but in actuality not far from the truth. *"Coach was a great motivator and gave some ridiculously good speeches,"* he wrote of our team meetings. *"His emotional intelligence was off the chart, and he could step back and see the big picture much better than the competition."*

I also tried to communicate in a way that would give guys confidence in themselves. Alex adds, *"He always told me that everything looked great and that my strokes were great, and my form was great because he knew I worked hard and was very hard on myself. He knew I needed some love and encouragement and rarely did he get on me."*

Team meetings are certainly important, but I always looked in particular for informal chances and environments to communicate with my players. This approach shows genuine interest and often provides the best opportunity for a great, uninhibited conversation. Never hesitate to simply ask, "How are you? How are you doing?"

"Coach was a great listener, and willing to be flexible in reaching his ultimate decisions," says Bill Maze, '78, an NCAA singles and doubles semifinalist and world singles #153, who went on to become an outstanding longtime women's coach at UC Davis. *"He was patient with my moods, and he didn't take my reactions to his decisions personally, or any of my teammates' reactions personally."*

As important as listening and inquiring about the player is, it is just as important to be able to communicate your own feelings— to openly share what you are thinking. It's about being willing to share yourself—even if it leaves you a little vulnerable—and to have enough self-confidence to admit a mistake. Your team performs better if it knows where you stand—what you are pleased with and what the team is doing well; as well as what is driving you crazy and what needs to improve. Unfortunately, some people have a hard time sharing their feelings, and this often adversely affects team relationships and even personal relationships. On a team, just as in a marriage, being vulnerable enough to share your own and true feelings can make a huge difference.

One of the responsibilities of a coach is to help build self-belief in those who may lack it, and this too depends on communication of the positive reinforcement variety. But any praise must be meaningful. Meaningless compliments do not help, but praise where it is earned, even upon completion of a simple task, can go a long way. Those words can often be for what the team has accomplished, but they are particularly meaningful in response to small achievements by a less-accomplished team member. This is especially effective when offered in front of the entire team and can be a strong incentive for others in the same position. It will always be good for building morale and should be based on more than just winning a match. In my sport, it might be as simple as a compliment directed toward improvement of a part of the backswing on the forehand. In essence, this helps to make a team member feel better about themselves.

This is all art, not science, and all these were things I had to learn, even if I was naturally inclined to be empathetic and personal. It's really about what John Letts, '86, calls "EQ" or emotional quotient. One must develop a "feel" for what to say when and how to most effectively say it. This applies to conversations with individuals as well as with the team. John elaborates that *"Coach's unique combination of high intelligence quotient and high emotional intelligence allowed him to finesse the inevitable conflicts that arose between the team and individual players, and to establish unique and different relationships with all his players.*

"Coach was incredibly adept at making each individual team member feel special and feel a unique bond with him. Coach Gould's relationship with each player allowed him to be the best possible coach he could be for that individual."

All of this together—team and individual two-way communications, being vulnerable, developing a high EQ—builds relationships, which is critical because it is on the strength of those individual relationships that one can expect things from players. To get the most out of a player, I needed to be able to show enough confidence in him to ask him to do something he did not have much confidence in doing. The success of this ask relates to the trust and confidence he had in me.

Chapter Five

CHALLENGES OF RECRUITING YOUR TEAM!

Honestly, I didn't have many expectations about the tennis program, there was nothing special. I based my decision solely on the high level of personal interest that Coach took and showed toward me as a person. Not only did he come twice to St. Marks School to visit (recruit) me, daily I received mail from either him, a team member, the university, an alumnus and/ or a tennis booster. Most importantly we became friends.

—Stanley Pasarell, '71

The first rule for success for any enterprise is to recruit the best people!

Charlie Pasarell, Stanley's older brother, was one of the world's top players and a key member of one of the best college teams of all time while at UCLA. One day at a professional tournament very early in my career I asked him if he had any advice for me about what it takes for a coach to win in college tennis. His answer cemented my supposition. He said, *"Dick, the best coach gets the best players!"* How ironic it was that a couple of years later his brother, Stanley, became my first full-scholarship player.

Charlie's advice is just as important when applied to any endeavor, not just sports! Below are examples of how this process developed in particular with our tennis program. It's not easy when starting from scratch, when one's vision must be enthusiastically conveyed without the benefit of proof of accomplishment, tradition, or reputation. Everyone wants to join a winner, but as the following examples indicate, many challenges arise along the recruiting trail. How you deal with those that arise in a particular recruiting situation in athletics or in another field will largely determine your success in landing top people. In any case, after defining and identifying who is important to your success and developing a plan of attack, persistence is key.

Charlie's answer was unquestionably a good one, but the question at that time was, "How was I, with no proven track record at this level and no 'name' outside of Northern California, going to be able to do this?" I didn't really know the top national junior players other than those from Northern California. However, I had a high regard for Southern California junior tennis, so I started by paying special attention there.

The athletic department had promised to help me with scholarships, which were few and far between at the time. They first stepped up by green-lighting the monies for me to take a recruiting trip to the USTA Junior National Championships in Kalamazoo, Michigan where all of the nation's top players in that age group compete annually. This gave me a good "lay of the land," and I met many of the players. Unfortunately, it seemed to me to be an absolute "meat market" of coaches trying to recruit candidates and play up to them. This totally turned me off, and I never again returned.

I thought there must be another way, and I set out to secure the mailing addresses of all participants at Kalamazoo. The first priority then became to find out who among this group of good players might be "admissible" by Stanford's standards. Once I received and reviewed transcripts or talked on the phone to the players to determine whether their academic backgrounds might give them a realistic chance for admission, it would be an understatement to say my list was pared down substantially. With the final candidates identified, my primary strategy was to handwrite a short note on an almost weekly basis to any of these realistically admissible players who were ranked in the top twenty in the nation, or who had reached the final sixteen in both the boys 16s and 18s age group national championships. In some cases, this letter writing started when a potential recruit was fourteen years old.

I have often wondered if anyone was able to read those notes on the five-by-eight-inch letterheads with a specially designed Stanford tennis logo with the words "Home of Champions" at the top because my handwriting was so bad, but apparently they made an impression on David Wheaton, '91. He recalls:

David Wheaton: All-American; World Singles #12, World Doubles #24

"The handwritten notes from Coach Gould began to arrive in our mailbox when I was about 16. I recall first meeting him at a USTA national training camp held at Stanford a year prior. I was one of the top junior players in the country and would be recruited by other leading tennis programs, but Coach beat all of them to it and at it, with congratulations on a win here or an update on Stanford there. The notes were short, punctuated with exclamation marks and key words in ALL CAPS. And there was always at least one smiley face. Coach had perfected the use of the emoji long before the term had been invented. But most impactful for me was the stationery on which the notes were scrawled. Here was the head tennis coach of Stanford

University, the top tennis and academic institution in the country, the 'Home of Champions,' as the plaque on the campus tennis stadium proclaimed, with its litany of pro tour alumni—McEnroe, Mayotte, the Mayer brothers—showing interest in a skinny teenager from Minnesota."

Stanford University itself provided a great product to sell. I could simply let the academic, social reputation, and athletic potential of our great university speak for itself. *"I wanted to go to a school in the 'big leagues' from a sports perspective and one with excellent academics,"* agrees Brian Leck, '67, my first number one player. *"That fit Stanford, perfectly."*

Andy Sands, '87, similarly states, *"Coach had one of the best platforms in Stanford University, which he was able to fully leverage . . . He recruited the best talent in the country his #1 skill) and developed a 'winning' mentality and track record that gained unprecedented momentum."*

That made it easier to enjoy the challenge of recruiting primarily for tennis, especially as successes began to mount. But this could not have been accomplished or sustained without incredible young athletes continuing to enroll—and at Stanford, they had to be great students as well. As Sandy Lawrence, '72, says, *"Almost any serious player would have to consider Stanford as a 'destination university' for such an athlete."*

Our first national team championships in 1973 and 1974 did not diminish the importance of recruiting, as one might guess, but instead reinforced it. Despite my growing national focus, I placed great value on attracting the best local players. Our geographic area was a hotbed for junior tennis in those days. I knew all these players and most of their families from events I had been running or from lessons I had been giving to them as a club pro before starting to coach at Stanford. Besides, if the ones nearby—those who by proximity knew me and our program best—enrolled elsewhere, what would this imply about our program? I needed to get these local guys to Stanford to help establish our/my credibility!

Recruiting siblings was as important as recruiting locals because if a sibling chose to go elsewhere, future recruits would wonder whether that player's older brother had had a good experience. We succeeded in this, and I am very proud that every sibling admitted to Stanford elected to attend, provided adequate financial aid was offered.

Matt Mitchell, '79, was both local *and* a sibling, with older brother Mark Mitchell, '77, in the starting lineup on the varsity. He recalls:

"I was from Palo Alto. I had known Coach Gould since I was eight years old. I played interclub, then NorCal junior tournaments and then national tournaments. It was always the thrill of Burlingame, the nationals in our backyard, which brought out some of the greatest juniors in the country. . . . The tennis program at Stanford was just starting to take off, and I felt I might be able to play a small role in its future success. There would be little or no 'assimilation' issues. I was a local. I was familiar with the team. And Coach was a positive influence on me."

Finding an Edge

These tournaments in our backyard to which Matt refers were almost as important vehicles for recruiting as the university itself because they provided the opportunities I needed to meet top players and make them aware of Stanford University on my home turf without incurring a hefty travel expense on my budget. The summer of national junior competition was kicked off by two of the most important national events: the highly respected California state championship at the San Jose Swim & Racket Club, and, as Matt noted, the national junior hardcourt championships held the next week at the Peninsula Tennis Club in Burlingame. San Jose is an easy twenty miles south of Stanford, and Burlingame is only twenty miles north. Stanford is smack-dab in the middle. Almost all the top junior players from throughout the United States congregated for two weeks to start their summer of competition by playing in these two great and respected tournaments. I naturally made sure to be at each event.

Given the presence of these tournaments, I had an idea that ultimately helped to initiate and sustain a successful recruiting program for Stanford tennis. At the same time, it solved my problem of "not knowing" the players. If I could stage a well-run, first-class activity in the short void at the start of summer and just *before* the Cal state championships and the national hardcourt championships, I could bring the top players directly onto campus at little expense to "experience" Stanford University, to get to know me, and vice versa.

Consequently, I contacted the USTA to begin discussions to permit me to stage the 1969 national Junior Davis Cup (JDC) training camp at Stanford, and hence bring the top junior players in the country to our campus for ten days of intense training together just prior to the start of the two tournaments. There would be regular practices, but the core of the camp would consist of matches between the players, which gave the USTA enough data to select their six- to eight-man national team based on the results.

I needed help putting this together, so I reached out to a friend of mine from my Fremont Hills Country Club teaching days, Ed Scarff, who happened to be the CEO of Transamerica Corporation. Ed got Transamerica to sponsor the camp, providing the top thirty sixteen- and eighteen-years-olds and underage group players in the country with special experiences, some of which are listed below, that were not available to them in previous training camps. The USTA covered the transportation costs to and from Stanford and the room and board for all the players. Those who were selected for the national team based on play at the camp would have all their tournament expenses covered for the rest of the summer. The top players could not afford to miss this opportunity of trying out for the national team.

With the camp set, my next job was to make it one of the best experiences these young players had ever had. Jack Darrah, the coach of neighboring Burlingame High School, was the team traveling coach, and my good friend Barry MacKay, the number one ranked player in the United States in 1960, signed on to be the camp coach. I assumed responsibilities as camp director and host, basically serving as the chief gladhander. In this role, I made certain that campers were fully exposed to the area and Stanford, and were having a great time.

Chris Bradley, '72, whom I had coached as a youngster at Fremont Hills and later became a great local teaching pro, offers a funny story about helping out in the early years of the camp that demonstrates the effort we put into it:

"The biggest behind-the-scenes story of course was how Coach dealt with me when I was the boy-Friday for the United States Junior Davis Cup training camp, hosted at Stanford. I woke up late when I was supposed to pick up Jimmy Connors, Sandy Mayer, Brian Gottfried, Harold Solomon, Steve Krulevitz, and Bob Kreiss from the dorm and get them to San Jose for the Cal state junior championship.

"I said, 'What do I do coach?' Coach said, 'Get your ass down there pronto,' so I got the team in the car drove close to 100 miles per hour in the old station wagon with the right track stereo blasting Country Joe's 'Give a f***, give a f*** . . .'

"We walked into the tournament with all the just-named national team wearing their JDC jackets way after normal default time, but the rest is history. I could have changed the course of American tennis if they had been defaulted and dropped off the team."

Rarely did a top player ever turn down the opportunity to practice together with the other top players in the country to sharpen up for the summer tournaments and play for a spot on this team. I believe we succeeded in making the camp a most special and unforgettable experience. When the players came to the courts for their two-a-day workouts/matches, there were small American flags at the top of each fence post spaced ten feet apart and surrounding the stadium. They were greeted by taped John Philip Sousa marches playing over the loudspeaker, large draw boards posting all the camp matches, and of course sliced oranges (which fast became my trademark), ice water, towels, and personalized scoreboards on each court. To help make the camp fan-friendly, a beautiful glossy program was printed introducing pictures and résumés of all the players.

They lived in the Stanford dorms, but regularly went out to different tennis clubs in the area (and there were twenty-five within seven miles of campus) for evening barbecues and dances. They sat in special box seats at a San Francisco Giants baseball game and were served a delicious dinner in the clubhouse usually reserved for box seat holders. In addition, there was a second special sightseeing trip to San Francisco and dinner. And since Transamerica owned United Artists, we showed a James Bond movie in camp even before it was released to theaters.

The final day of matches was a benefit for the local hospital auxiliary, which sold tickets to the public to help fill the stands. The list of special touches goes on and on—special camp T-shirts, a formal camp-ending banquet at the beautiful Los Altos Golf and Country Club, where the final national team was announced and presented, and so on. Everything was first class. They had a great experience, and Stanford was on everyone's mind!

Between matches, I took them on tours of the campus in informal "get to know you" sessions. After the camp, I was able to watch them all play for the next two weeks at San Jose and Burlingame respectively. The camp was such a success and so well received by the players that we hosted again in 1970 and 1971.

"At the time I did not appreciate the fact that Dick personally engineered hosting the US Jr. Davis Cup camp at Stanford in order to showcase the Stanford campus and program among the prospective national recruit pool," remembers Chip Fisher, '75, a Palo Alto player, JDC participant, and younger brother of Rick Fisher, '73. *"Then he pulled it off! That is a crazy ambitious ini-*

tiative he took (when the program was a juggernaut only in young Coach's imagination) and a crazy amount of work to bring upon himself and others."

The Foundation for Success: Recruiting

You absolutely must win the battle of individual recruiting, but it is extremely competitive and certainly not easy to attract the top people in sports, business, or any field! Much of what I did was not standard procedure for a sport like tennis in those days. So in a sense, I created a unique advantage. You must *never* give up because your success and tenure are largely predicated on getting the best people, and in this case tennis players, on your team! As Geordie McKee, '86, says, *"Simply stated, besides all his great attributes, Coach recruited better than anyone. It was astounding to see year in, year out the finest juniors in the nation commit to Stanford. Most often, he had the best players, then molded them to be great teammates and to carry themselves with pride and integrity."*

The underlying assumption behind my aggressive recruitment of the best players was my belief that we could be successful at the highest level if I could get every potentially admissible player to apply, and if admitted, to enroll. I therefore put a lot of energy into recruiting all the very best potentially admittable players— who were essentially drawn from the ones at the Junior Davis Cup camp.

From my brief experience with our admissions office, I firmly believed that one of the top five nationally ranked high school senior players in the country would be academically admittable to Stanford each year, and that the same would hold true for one of the second five. Occasionally, even a third player in the top ten would be admittable. If I could get them all to apply, get admitted, and then enrolled, I was convinced we had a chance to win consistently at the highest level. This proved to be true.

Once we established ourselves as a top program, I think only one player from the midseventies through the late-nineties who might have been admissible and offered a full scholarship declined to attend. John Ross, whose personal coach was Dennis Ralston—just off the pro tour, where he had established himself as one of the world's top players, elected to join Dennis at SMU. Al Parker, the great University of Georgia player, may have been another, but I can't recall if I had scholarship money available to offer him.

As mentioned before, when I began coaching there were very few full scholarships for Stanford athletes, let alone tennis. Most athletes in all sports to this point worked as servers and waiters in the dining halls in order to receive "free" meals. They also had the opportunity to pay off their housing fees by working in our athletic department's corporation yards mowing lawns, lining fields, and so on. This certainly made recruiting a tougher proposition as other schools were already offering their athletes full scholarships, which essentially covered all their on-campus expenses.

As time went on, though, more money became available, and as long as I had financial aid available to offer, I usually won the recruiting battle. The athletic department knew we were building something big, and they really supported my efforts. At one time, we had eight players on full scholarships. (This was just before Title IX was enacted, and hence before the NCAA reduced the number of scholarships in men's tennis to the equivalent of five, and the next year to four and a half. The effect was to greatly level the playing field at the national level.)

Beyond the handwritten letters on simple but special stationary, the JDC camp, and visiting players at the two local tournaments, my individual visits, often to a player's home, were key for me. I made several home visits after my first year at Stanford in my efforts to build a team for 1967–68. I actually enjoyed these, but at that time, home visits were the exception rather than the norm in tennis. These visits gave me the opportunity see the player in the environment in which he grew up and to get to meet his parents as well. The parents also got to know me a little, which I felt was very important. Would I, as a parent, entrust my eighteen-year-old son to someone I did not know—especially if this person would be serving as basically my son's "dad" while he was away from home for an extended period of time?

My very first trip was among the most memorable of my career, and it went a long way toward making me a good recruiter. It entailed several stops—St. Louis to meet with Bobby McKinley, a straight-A student and the brother of Wimbledon champ, Chuck; then to Lookout Mountain, Tennessee to meet with Zan Guerry, a clay court specialist, a national champion in every age group, and also a straight-A student, and his parents; a stop in Coral Gables, Florida to meet with Mac Claflin and Bill Colson, both outstanding juniors; and finally to St. Mark's School in Dallas to meet with Stanley Pasarell and Mike Estep, also top juniors.

The Bob McKinley visit was particularly interesting. I quickly realized to "really like" anything the mother offered to serve. Mrs. McKinley was most gracious as she asked if I wanted some coffee, which I hated at the time. "Oh, of course, Mrs. McKinley," I replied.

I was sitting in the small living room in Mr. McKinley's recliner when she returned with a hot pot of coffee on a silver tray with a couple of cups. As she started to pour coffee into my cup while holding the tray over my lap, I pulled the release lever to straighten up my chair, promptly knocking the scalding contents all over my lap and onto the only pair of pants I had brought for the trip. Mrs. McKinley was kind and apologetic. She suggested I change into Mr. McKinley's robe, which barely came down to my knees, while she tried to wash my pants in the washing machine. She did a great job! I did not uncross my legs, though, while wearing this extremely short robe! Despite my sacrifice, Bobby ended up at his brother's alma mater, Trinity University in San Antonio, to play for the great coach Clarence Mabry.

From St. Louis, I flew to Chattanooga to visit with Zan Guerry in Lookout Mountain. This meeting taught me more about the importance of being thoroughly prepared than almost any experience I'd ever had, thanks to Zan's father Alex, a pharmaceutical CEO who was a force in junior tennis. I would have been very excited at the time had you told me I would build the entire program on a player from Lookout Mountain and would have assumed you meant Zan, not realizing that it would be his neighbor, Roscoe Tanner, who was a couple of years younger and lived only a few blocks away, who would be the one to do this. But during my visit with the Guerrys, I was not even aware of Roscoe.

Mr. Guerry did most of the talking. Zan was pretty well set on Rice, so I knew going in this was a long shot. Mr. Guerry asked me what the average rainfall in Palo Alto was, and I gave a nebulous answer. I later learned it was 15.75 inches, about a half inch more than in central Los Angeles. This was very surprising to me—even I seemed to think it rained substantially more in Northern California than in Southern California, but this was *not* the case in the microclimate of Palo Alto itself. Mr. Guerry also wanted to know the wind velocity at certain times of year, and a variety of other statistics. For the most part, these questions were easy to research, and I immediately got back to him with the answers. But I did not have them at my fingertips during our visit.

Zan was undefeated as a junior player on clay—a very different surface from the hard cement courts of Stanford. His dad rightfully did not want to see this part of his game neglected, so Alex's biggest question was, "Does Stanford have any clay courts on campus or in the immediate vicinity?" I was stumped—there were none! Upon returning home, I immediately went to our competitive cinder running track and gathered and sent him some samples of the crushed brick that comprised the track's surface as a sample of what could be used for our "clay court" surface. I also went to my athletic director to see if I could put in a clay court for Zan's additional practice. It was to be built adjacent to our existing courts, basically where our swimming complex is now located. Mr. Guerry sounded interested, and if I understood him correctly, he inferred that "if" Zan decided to enroll at Stanford, he would help finance the construction of this court.

Zan subsequently made a visit to Stanford. I later heard that a friend of mine, whom Zan had met at a luncheon, had taken him in his private plane and flown him over the beautiful and forested San Francisco Peninsula area, up the coast and over San Francisco and the Golden Gate Bridge. I was aghast to learn about this—it was clearly a violation of rules. Zan had a great overall visit that created a lot of interest in his mind. He was concerned, however, about being the only top player to enroll at Stanford that next year. He didn't want to enroll by himself.

From Chattanooga, I flew to Coral Gables. It was also an interesting visit. I felt I had a chance to attract two great players and students, both high school juniors at the time: Bill Colson and his friend Mac Claflin. I spent considerable time at Bill's house and thought I had a chance to get him, but as a calculated gamble, I only eventually offered him a half scholarship. He ended up at Princeton, which, as an Ivy League school, did not even offer athletic scholarships. Mac needed the money to attend Stanford, so I offered him a full scholarship, which he accepted.

Finally, I moved on to Dallas. My meeting with Mike Estep and Stanley Pasarell was on the front lawn of St. Mark's School. Mike had an outside chance of admission and ended up at Rice. Stanley was a better student, but I didn't think I could get him away from his brother Charlie's alma mater, UCLA. Thanks to my existing team members, a number of whom were friends with Stanley from their junior tennis days, he subsequently had a great visit in Palo Alto, about which I still have only learned a little. I offered him a full scholarship, but like Zan, he did not want to be the only top player at Stanford.

So I thought if Stanley and Zan came together, both their concerns would be solved. They went back and forth on the phone for a couple of days, each trying to get the other guy to commit to

Stanford. My understanding is the interchanges went something like this: Zan called Stanley and said, "I'll go to Stanford if you do." Stanley replied, "I'm pretty well set on UCLA." This went back and forth for a day or two.

Finally, Stanley called Zan and told him, "I've decided to go Stanford. We can be there together!" Unfortunately, Zan responded, "I just officially committed to Rice."

Fortunately, Stanley stayed with it and became my first full-scholarship player. Among other things, he went on to develop with his brother Charlie a beautiful golf destination resort, the Royal Isabella in Puerto Rico. He has always had a special place in the program and in my heart, and we have indeed been good friends for decades.

But I continued to work hard to ensure Stanley would not be the sole top player on campus. For instance, an additional target was Paul Marienthal, '71, the number one ranked fifteen-and-under player in Southern California. Apparently, the home visit was critical. *"Dick was the most enthusiastic, direct, magnetic person I'd ever encountered in the tennis world,"* writes Marienthal. *"Who wouldn't want to play for him? He was interested in every aspect of who I was. I'm surprised anyone has ever turned down an offer from him to play at Stanford. Coach was so intent and so focused on creating a winner. And so beautifully organized. I feel so fortunate to have been in that first group, getting to experience him as a young coach developing his recruiting chops."*

I was able to arrange some financial aid for Paul. *"I think it was called BAC,"* he recalls. BAC stands for Board of Athletic Control, and this was the group that at that time controlled Stanford athletic department expenditures. *"We worked in the dining room in our off seasons. I always worked the dish rooms because we were the last ones out and could raid the refrigerators. At Roble Hall they put locks on the refrigerators after we (me and a couple of swimmers and football players) polished off about forty hamburgers and three gallons of blueberry ice cream one night."*

Future team captain Bill Atkins, a very good NorCal junior, rounded out the class of '71. Despite some near misses, it was a solid start for building for the future! But what a great learning experience that very first recruiting trip was for a young guy still in his twenties with no reputation outside of NorCal, and with little experience speaking with the top junior players in the country! Not knowing meteorological data wasn't a deal-breaker with Zan Guerry, but the process of recruiting Zan taught me the importance of being prepared. A subsequent recruit—and later my longtime assistant and the future head coach of the program, John Whitlinger, '76, says, *"Coach recruited the best players that could get admitted and didn't let them go anywhere else. He left no stone unturned when he was recruiting. He was always prepared for a home visit or campus visit. As long as he met the recruits' financial needs, it was very difficult for them to go anywhere else."*

John ended up as NCAA singles and doubles champ on a championship team and later became world singles #75.

After the first couple of years, things were starting to pick up, and word was getting out that Stanford was building something special on the West Coast. It was then when I received a call from the Stockton family in New York. They were extremely interested in getting their son Dick, a great student and also one of the top junior phenoms anyone had ever seen, to attend Stanford. They asked if he could transfer for his senior year from his high school in New York to Palo Alto High School, fortuitously located across the street from Stanford University. This would allow him to practice his last year in high school with the Stanford team. In those days, there was no rule against this.

I immediately put them in contact with the high school, which accepted him as a transfer senior. In the meantime, I arranged a room for him at the home of a friend, who lived two or three blocks from Palo Alto High School, and who had played in the Wimbledon championships some years earlier. The idea was that Dickie could walk to high school, and then at the end of the school day, cross the street and walk another block to the Stanford courts to practice.

Dickie had moved to Palo Alto for the start of the high school year, which was around Labor Day. However, Stanford did not begin classes or tennis practice until about one month later. So in the meantime, I arranged several practice sessions with Dickie and top local adult players, and all seemed well. What a team we were quickly building! I had also built a court at my home where I gave lessons in off-hours away from my school teaching responsibilities. Just days before the Stanford guys finally returned to school from the summer break, Dickie came over to my home for some tennis with a friend of mine who was a very good adult player. This was followed by a wonderful and relaxing barbecue with my family. All was good!

But before the sun had come up the next day, I received a call from the family hosting Dickie saying, "Dickie and all his belongings are gone, and we thought we heard a car door close." I quickly dressed and drove straight to the San Francisco airport, which was much smaller then and had only one domestic terminal. I went up and down the concourse trying to find him to see what had happened, but he was nowhere to be found.

When I finally reached him personally via phone a day or two later, he said he had decided he was going to join his good friends Bob McKinley and Brian Gottfried at Trinity University the next year. I assumed that his desire to be with close friends affected his decision. As well as the fact that he was in a high school new to him, and before the Stanford players had come back, which would have afforded him the extra practice opportunities he desired. Whether there was more to the story, I will never know. I was devastated! Dickie later defeated Roscoe Tanner in five sets in the 1972 NCAA singles semifinals and won the singles championship the next day.

Chapter Six

RECRUITING SUCCESS ACHIEVED

As we were shaded by redwood trees, Coach told us to take a deep breath of the fresh air. He knew we were small-town boys, and he wanted us to compare the smog free air around Stanford to the smoggy air around the campus of USC. Coach Gould called us the night before signing day and said that if there was any hesitation in our decision that he would jump in his car and make the five-hour drive down to Camarillo. He didn't get in the car that night. We were already sold.

—Bob Bryan, '00

On the Verge

Though I lost Dickie Stockton in the recruiting wars, the next year for the 1968–69 season I landed an outstanding freshman from Connecticut, Paul Gerken, '72, one of the top five players in the country and a young man clearly destined for the pros. Paul was joined that year by highly ranked Mac Claflin, '72, and a slew of other top players who were among the best in their section. It was truly a great recruiting class. Unfortunately, our conference had not yet fully embraced the new NCAA concept of freshman eligibility, so Paul spent his freshman year playing on our freshman team and not in varsity matches. He was clearly my best player, freshman or otherwise.

That spring of 1969, my top recruit, Roscoe Tanner, '73—the kid who lived around the corner from Zan Guerry in Lookout Mountain, Tennessee—had signed a conference letter of intent to attend the University of Tennessee. Our two *signed* recruits, Rick Fisher, '73—a top local player and future NCAA singles semifinalist, and Gery Groslimond, '73, out of Daytona Beach—were largely unknown to Paul. The future of Stanford tennis, in Paul's mind, looked pretty bleak. In addition, Paul was best friends with Stockton, McKinley, and Gottfried, all of whom were at or on their way to Trinity.

Although the Pac-8 conference did not permit freshmen to compete in varsity events, the NCAA championships were controlled by the NCAA, and freshmen were allowed to compete. Our best freshman were better players than those on my varsity that year. My decision on who to enter in the NCAA tournament was easy. At the conclusion of the NCAA championships in which he led our all-freshman team to an eighth-place finish, Paul came into my office in the old green tennis shack by the courts and told me he felt he had to take advantage of the competition offered at Trinity to get better, and so he asked permission to transfer. Of course I said yes, but the truth is I was shattered! Was I ever going to achieve what I felt could be accomplished and what I had brashly told so many others I intended to do?

Three years later, in 1972, Paul Gerken, Dickie Stockton, and Bobby McKinley led Trinity to the NCAA championship, barely edging us out at the end of the tournament. In down moments I sort of felt they had won with guys who should have been playing for us. The good news was that we were closer than we had ever been, and I had top recruits enrolling like Rick Fisher and Gery Groslimond, and as luck would have it, Roscoe Tanner.

When I was recruiting Roscoe, I said to him he'd "be the one who would lead us to our first championship." Though that appealed to him, he initially elected to stay closer to home, and thus signed a Southeast Conference letter of intent to the University of Tennessee, informing our admissions office and me of his decision. I was crestfallen by yet another "near-miss." However, the SEC letter of intent that committed an athlete to that particular school was only binding to schools within that conference. Roscoe had *not* signed the national letter of intent, to which he would be forever bound.

Halfway through the summer, I received a call from Roscoe saying he was having second thoughts. He asked if Stanford, which had admitted him with all other prospective freshmen on April 1—an offer he had declined to accept by the May 1 deadline—would permit him to undo his no to his acceptance decision. I immediately and metaphorically crawled on my hands and knees directly to our admissions office to beg them to reconsider Roscoe's application on the premise he had been previously admitted. They agreed to do this to "help out the young coach." I relayed this information to Roscoe, who himself was elated, but not as much as I.

Roscoe quickly became the cornerstone of our team, and our team attitude changed primarily because of him and teammate Rick Fisher, from one of "Let's try to make this match close" to one of "Let's go win this thing!" Even though we hadn't yet won a title, all the hard work and disappointing recruiting near misses and transfers were forgotten. The cards were now in play, and I was finally poised to prove to myself and to others that we *could* bring the NCAA team championship to the Farm. The unrelenting recruiting efforts, from that first trip to St. Louis, Lookout Mountain, Coral Gables, and Dallas had been the key. Persistence, despite challenges and disappointments, does pay off.

The next year, recruiting success continued with the addition of Alex (Sandy) Mayer, '74, and Paul Sidone, '74. This led to yet another great recruiting class for the 1971–72 season headed by

Jim Delaney '75 and Rick Fisher's brother, Chip, '75. Roscoe had reached the NCAA singles final both in 1970 (losing to Jeff Boro-wiak of UCLA) and in 1971 (losing to UCLA's Jimmy Connors). Roscoe Tanner and Sandy Mayer combined to win the NCAA doubles title in 1972, exactly thirty years since Stanford's last individual championships in 1942 (Ted Schroeder in singles and Ted Schroeder and Larry Dee in doubles). In Roscoe's third year, we finished a close second for the team championship as well, as Roscoe and Sandy both reached the singles semifinals, losing to Dickie Stockton and Brian Gottfried of Trinity respectively. With every starter on the team slated to return the next year, we finally were in a position to win the championship.

Jim Delaney, '75, team captain, two-time NCAA doubles champion, and world singles #59 underscores the effectiveness of our recruiting, which placed us in this position:

"Dick was the biggest factor for me and not just by a slight margin, but exponentially. He started writing me earlier than anyone (which was flattering) but the quality and the quantity of information he sent was very helpful in telling me about the variety of things Stanford had to offer. I concluded that he was the coach I wanted to play for more than anything else. I believed that far more than any other coach, he would help me grow as a person, student and tennis player. Coach stood out in every way compared to other coaches from the recruiting process in the ability to manage personalities and develop as good a team chemistry as can be developed in an individual sport."

I'm not a pessimist by any means, but I recognize that sometimes Murphy's Law roughly translates as, "When all is going just right, something unaccounted for usually happens!" In this case, Murphy's Law required me to *re-recruit* Roscoe, the most important player on my team, even after he had been on campus for three years!

The bombshell hit when we were preparing to return to Palo Alto from the championships in Athens, Georgia in 1972 after our close second-place finish to Trinity. Roscoe's father, Leonard, a prominent Chattanooga attorney, called the motel and asked if I could meet them at a restaurant called Ireland's. After losing Dickie Stockton and Paul Gerken—two players I had thought were safely in the fold—this turned out to be one of the most devastating meal conversations I had ever had! In the new era of open tennis, there was tremendous pressure from agents to sign the next great "American Hope"—and surely Roscoe was one of them. Mr. Tanner basically said, that after much deliberation, Roscoe was going to turn pro.

To put this into perspective, Roscoe was far more than just my best player and the one on whom our hopes for our first title hung. Roscoe, along with his good friends and fellow freshmen Rick Fisher and Gery Groslimond, had really changed the culture of Stanford tennis from "We think we can win" to "We *will* win." Yes, Roscoe had an air about him—he was cocky and full of self-belief, but in a good way. People loved to watch him play, and our stands would overflow with spectators when he was on the court. And when established world-great Stan Smith, who was serving in the army and stationed at nearby Fort Ord in Monterey, was able to get away for an exhibition at Stanford to play against Roscoe, it attracted a large crowd. This was at a time when Stanford athletics in general had really been struggling. A NCAA men's golf championship in 1953, and finally, a men's swimming championship in 1967 were all Stanford had to show for its athletic team achievements since the early 1940s.

The point is it wasn't just about the tennis! Roscoe was well known among Stanford boosters as well as nationally, and he epitomized hope for the championship-starved-in-all-sports "Stanford fan." That lunch turned out to be the only time in my career I tried to talk a player out of turning pro. The NCAA championship I had promised athletic director Chuck Taylor, who hired me six years earlier, was finally within grasp. But now Roscoe was about to leave before he had the chance to finish what I recruited him for, and for one of the main reasons he came to Stanford—to lead the program to a championship.

In the end, my pleas fell on deaf ears. Roscoe's decision had been made. Surely Roscoe and Sandy and the rest of this great group could have led us to the championship the next year. We would be clear favorites for the first time to win the national tennis collegiate championship! But once again we were so close to doing what I had envisioned achieving only to have it shot down in the end. I was devastated! Roscoe left well prepared for his future and went on to a stellar career that saw him win the Australian Open, reach the finals of Wimbledon, and rise to as high as #5 in the world.

Campus Visits

After those early years, a lot of the rules changed. For instance, a high school senior was barred from practicing with a college team as Dickie and some of our early local recruits were poised to do, so "official" campus visits became increasingly important. In these situations, you must emphasize how you are different, what you intend to accomplish, and show off your best. Emphasize your strengths, and *never* say a bad word about any other school or coach!

My strategy regarding these visits was to wait until the last minute to invite potential recruits to campus. My recruiting budget was small, and I could not afford to waste money on inadmissible athletes, so I wanted to know they were admitted before I incurred the cost of airfare and so on. The added challenge was that, unlike most other schools, I did not hear from our admissions office whether or not a player was admitted until April 1! I had the job of keeping the prospect interested in Stanford in hope that he might be admitted. Essentially all other schools admitted their top recruits earlier in the year and offered their scholarships accordingly. If this offer was not accepted by a certain date, it could be withdrawn. I had to hope my recruit candidate would accept this risk and hold out until he was officially admitted to Stanford.

Jeff Tarango, '90, team captain, All-American and world singles #42 and world doubles #10, offers this very entertaining story about his recruiting visit and a perspective on the larger picture:

"Coach Gould wanted me to come on a recruiting visit when I was only sixteen years old to entertain the idea of coming to Stanford. Coach Gould picked me up at the airport in a baby blue Mercedes Benz that barely fit him into the front seat; the subtle humor in this image was so evident that Gould could not possibly keep a straight face. I knew right then that everything he did and said was actually a test to see if he really wanted me around him for four years. Whether I was smart enough to hang and tough enough to be tested all the time. If I could handle pressure, if I had balance, if I had excellence and greatness in my heart, like he did.

"Coach gave me an hour-and-a-half tour of campus—'the Disneyland of college campuses'—and had me sit and talk with the athletic director privately. And, no, he didn't want to listen or be in on our conversation. Then I met with the assistant athletic director, who oversaw tennis, and, no, Coach didn't have time for that either. It turned out it was because Gould still wanted Al Parker (who subsequently enrolled at Georgia), and it was very clear that Al is who he was going to go call while I met with the others."

Although it was risky because another coach could spark an earlier interest in his own school by getting a potential recruit "on campus" for a visit sooner, my stance was that I wanted the last chance to speak with each of them after they had taken their other visits. This gave me the advantage of talking to them about what they felt had been the pros and cons of each place they had visited. This allowed me to zero in on the applicable strengths of Stanford. I also felt by then I knew them and their families pretty well because I almost always had already made a home visit. I really believed I had a good feel for what to say and what would resonate best with individual players, and each was different.

Perseverance!

The bottom line is that recruiting is an exhausting, sometimes heart-wrenching process, but success in any endeavor—sports or business—is impossible without it. Charlie Pasarell was right all those years ago: *"The best coach gets the best players."*

But the question is *how?* It is particularly relevant to ask before a track record of success has been established. The answer first involves making use of existing assets—in our case a great university with a great campus. Second, a coach must keep finding an edge by being innovative, as we did with the Junior Davis Cup camp and the National Junior Training camp. Later this included building the impressive Heritage Room full of national championship trophies and the Historical Kiosk, which contained a collection of countless videos of our current and former players competing on the world scene. Third, there's no substitute for going the extra mile with early relentless communication with hopeful recruits.

I spent my time recruiting both on the road and on campus trying to convince players that they could become the best tennis players possible by enrolling at Stanford, and by demonstrating that I cared not just about them as tennis players but also about them as people and their success not just on court, but at Stanford and beyond

Recruiting, like everything else, must be genuine and spring from the basic core values you have established for the entire program, including in your own business. And one thing is certain: it will usually provide quite a ride!

In summary, it is critical to never lose your belief in yourself nor your vision. In my case, I felt once I had successfully recruited a player to attend Stanford, it was only the start. To continue to sustain success in recruiting, three things were imperative, the first of which Dan Gerken, '80, adeptly sums up. *"Clearly the tradition would not have been sustained if players did not enjoy the expe-rience and were not willing to convey that to future prospects."*

But in addition to enjoying their experience and conveying such to others, it was critical they also got better, not only while at Stanford, but to make an impact beyond Stanford—meaning on the pro tour. *"A poor trainer or rider can easily blow the race. Coach knew how to train and ride the team,"* says David Wheaton, '91.

It also made a big statement when the admissible local players as well as the siblings of those on the team elected to join us, which all basically did unless I could not meet their financial needs. These points were among the prime reasons that every four-year player at Stanford for thirty-four years earned at least one championship ring.

The preceding examples were mostly related to recruiting the very best players in the country. But especially with the equivalent of only four and a half scholarships, recruitment of top talent from other than the pool of the absolute best players was critical. So many of our championships were decided by other than our "star" players. Robert Devens, '94, surmises:

"I think a secret talent of Coach's was to recruit and retain guys who were lower in the lineup at Stanford, but who could have been number one players at other schools. It was part of the Stanford/Dick Gould mystique, and he was able to effectively communicate it in recruiting and running the team—'every starter over 34 years earned at least one championship ring!' And I would say, Coach's focus on detail, hard work, leaving no stone unturned in the recruiting process paid off, because these number five and six players probably were more important in winning championships than guys in almost any other position on the team."

Championing Stanford Tennis Heritage

The Junior Davis Cup camp was hosted by Stanford in 1969, 1970, and 1971. It was a key to enabling us to land some of the most important early men's players. But I knew we could not rest on that which we had worked so hard to establish—arguably the nation's premiere collegiate tennis program. I enjoyed doing new and different things, so I elected to keep innovating and adding new aspects to our program to keep us fresh and vibrant in the eyes of those considering Stanford. We also needed to tastefully portray the history and tradition of Stanford tennis. In other words, our success did not eliminate the need to continue to find a recruiting edge.

By the mid-1970s, Title IX had brought women onto equal footing with men. We decided to again ask the USTA to "sanction" another national training camp, this time for both men and women players at one site. The intent was once again to get all the best players to experience the unique environment Stanford offered. We hosted the USTA Junior Wightman Cup camp for girls in 1980 and the National Junior Training camp for ranking all the top young men and women for three consecutive years, 1986–1988.

Further, I believe the manner in which our men's tennis program embraced and instigated Title IX in our sport provided a nationwide model for all collegiate sports and enhanced our reputation overall. Initially when I was asked by our athletic department who I thought would be the best choice for our first full-time women's coach, I strongly endorsed a young woman who had been a standout on what was called the women's team prior to Title IX, and who had been working with me doing a great job teaching. And so Anne Connelly Hill was hired for the 1975–76 season as Stanford adopted Title IX. In her four years of coaching, Anne never finished lower than second nationally, including leading her team in 1978 to Stanford's first national women's team championship in any sport since the advent of Title IX. (Our men's team, led by John McEnroe, also won the championship that year.)

I felt we did an exemplary job of merging our two teams into a singular program—joint spring break practices, mixed team matches (World TeamTennis style), social activities, community service, fundraising events, Thanksgiving "fun" trips, shared media guides, team banquets, season tickets combined for *both* teams, and on and on. In addition, we worked so well together that I was soon blessed to have Anne become my wife. I was a double winner due to Title IX! My wife was followed by the great women's coach Frank Brennan, a close and dear friend, and one with whom I also worked very well.

Visibility and successes brought many improvements to the Stanford's Taube Tennis Center, such as the Ralph Rodriguez Clubhouse, the Craig Johnson Player's Lounge, the Phil and Penny Knight Scoreboard, and so on, but we still found many additional ways to be creative. Our success at winning national titles naturally brought trophies, pictures, and various other memorabilia, and we needed somewhere to suitably display them. Humility is always of utmost importance, but so is tastefully displaying pride in what has been accomplished. As a result, we built the Mike Orsak Family Heritage Room on the ground level of the tennis clubhouse to feature one of the most impressive displays of men's and women's collegiate success stories in any sport in the nation and to serve as a profound influence on impressionable potential recruits making official visits, as well as reminding current players of the responsibility they have to uphold the tradition of success.

In the spring of 1996, even before I took them out to see the beautiful hills behind Stanford, the Orsak Heritage Room did the trick with the Bryan brothers. *"We flew up north and Coach Gould first showed us the majestic trophy room,"* begins

Mike Bryan: NCAA Doubles Champion; All-Time World Doubles #1

Bob Bryan: NCAA Singles and Doubles Champion; World Doubles #1

NCAA singles and doubles champion and longtime doubles pro #1 Bob Bryan, '00. *He explained to us that never had a four-year player ever left the program without a ring. We saw the murals, the numbers, the banners, framed magazine covers, and the impressive Stanford tennis memorabilia that Coach had preserved and displayed. Mike and I were historians of the game, and this tennis shrine blew us away."*

I wanted not only my current team, but my recruits to see what former stars, from Tanner and Mayer to McEnroe and Mayotte to the Bryans and the many in between had accomplished. The material was certainly there as tennis matches and events had been appearing on television since the sport had gone "open" in 1968. I had a seven-foot satellite dish at home, and every time I knew one of my players was playing in a final or was playing in a televised match, I tried to record the competition. In 2014, I engaged one of my grandsons to convert those videotapes to DVDs for the sake of better preservation.

Even though we had a slew of national titles, seventeen-year-old tennis players are rarely historians. Thus, in 2010 we made Stanford tennis history more accessible by designing an outdoor all-weather kiosk to house video archives. The use of a touch screen calls up three general topics for videos: (a) Stanford Players in the Pros, (b) Collegiate Events (team indoors, dual matches, NCAAs, etc.), and (c) Special Events (Bank of the West matches, instructional videos by our coaches, etc.). These videos can also be projected, when desired, onto the large screen above the stadium entrance or even onto the stadium video/scoreboard. They are also stored in the cloud for immediate access.

Title IX Revisited

I must add that I have *never* agreed with the manner in which Title IX was implemented. In order to create equal opportunity for women, the decision was made to include football in the equation. Since football awards about eighty-five scholarships, an equal number of scholarships for women had to be made up by either adding more women's sports than men's or by reducing the number of scholarships for men competing in the same sport. As an example, men's tennis had no limits on the number of scholarships when I started coaching, and the number was soon capped at the equivalent of eight. With the advent of Title IX for the 1976 season, women athletes rightfully started to receive scholarships. *But* because of the added cost of providing them, as well as the imbalance of scholarships created by the large number of football scholarships, legislation reduced scholarships for men's sports— in tennis to five, and the next year to the equivalent of four and a half. Women's sports scholarship offerings increased across the board and more women's sports were added. By NCAA edict, women's tennis was gradually increased to permit up to eight full scholarships. I ask, is this equal opportunity? It certainly is not when two teams in the same sport are compared! If football were out of the equation (the Power 5 conferences and their TV contracts show us how much money football can actually bring in), tennis would have six scholarships for each team. True equity would be sport-by-sport equalization in like-sport scholarships. Title IX now reverse discriminates! I felt bad for my guys whom I now thought were being short-changed.

Other negative results of Title IX include the dropping of a disproportionate number of men's tennis programs. True, many programs, both for men and women, have been dropped for budgetary reasons, but men's programs are dropped at a rate over twice that of women! Other sports such as wrestling have suffered the same fate.

Our facility was not large enough to accommodate both a men's junior varsity team and a women's varsity team. The men's junior varsity team was discontinued as of the 1975 season. The net result is that opportunities for men's participation has decreased substantially. And finally, men's teams were being told to cap or reduce the number of participants, while women's teams were told to increase squad size to demonstrate more women were getting high-level sports opportunities.

In summary, Title IX has had both good and bad repercussions. In addition, I also *do* think if one truly believes in equal opportunity and in Title IX, there should be a commitment for administrators to hire women's coaches for women's sports. How can the field of coaching for women be advanced and opened up without this opportunity? Billie Jean King's Women's Sports Foundation (of which I am a proud supporter) is doing its best to encourage more female coaches, but this is hard to do if so many men are taking those positions.

Chapter Seven

BEHIND THE SCENES SCHEDULING

Coach didn't overdo our schedule so that we were worn out or injured later in the season, and we didn't put so much emphasis on any one match/tournament during the season so that it would have a negative effect on our mindset going into the NCAAs. And we believed in the way Coach approached our preparation because it had been so successful before.

—Barry Richards, '90

Momentum and feeling good at the right time are so important! I wanted to be sure my guys felt good about themselves at the right time—which was the end of the season—so scheduling was an important factor. David Wheaton, '91, explains, *"It's the Holy Grail of sports to play your best when it matters most."*

This is true in most organizations.

One of the important strategies in this regard is managing the home and away schedule. First of all, there is huge home court advantage in tennis, so I really did not go out of my way to schedule a lot of away matches. Teams liked coming to California in general and Stanford in particular to play, so I took advantage of this. With the matches we were obligated to play, I was always searching for an advantage that would leave us feeling good about ourselves at season's end when I wanted our team to be fresh, physically *and* mentally. Not exhausting ourselves on the road and skewing home matches at the end of the season was part of this.

"The one thing Coach did was that he was so good with timing," says Jimmy Gurfein, '81. *"We got there in the fall and started a little bit with practicing. As we'd continue through the year, we wouldn't have as many matches, unlike other teams that had tons of matches. I think he was trying to prevent burnout. We peaked in May—that's when he wanted us to peak."*

Our matches with our major conference opponents, USC and UCLA, with whom we had home and away matches, were great examples. When I was a player, we always played them away in Los Angeles the first weekend in April and hosted them at Stanford the third weekend in April. This had been the case since shortly after World War II. During my coaching career and once we had finally established ourselves, we often got "mashed" in SoCal, but two weeks later in front of a raucous home crowd urging us on, we would rebound with two wins. This made my players feel good about themselves at a critical time of year. "Guys, here comes the 'The Big Red Machine'" and "We're getting better and better and better" were phrases I could employ effectively as the climax of the season approached.

By the time I was a coach, each spring at our conference championship all the conference coaches would meet to set the upcoming year's schedule. This was not as easy when our conference grew from eight to ten and then twelve teams, and then when women's teams were added to the scheduling mix. I liked ending the season at home because this schedule gave us every opportunity to avoid the added challenge of traveling during a heavy academic study time and playing matches in front of the raucous opponents' crowds. And it helped us to build tremendous momentum heading into the NCAAs. It was a part of the "Feel good! Here we come!" mentality we had entering the championships. To me, this was a major factor in our success! Of course I never said this publicly. In our annual conference coach scheduling meeting, I would always say something to the other coaches like, "Well, we have been doing this for so long and it has served the conference well, so why change it now?" It worked, and the coaches, maybe with some reluctance, accepted it.

Today, the conference itself does the scheduling, and it's hard to believe that regularly two of our main rivals for the national championship—USC and UCLA—are played at home either in January when it is cold outside and before people even realize it is tennis season, or during spring break, when no students are on campus to support the team. This kind of scheduling does nothing to take advantage of a great opportunity to promote our sport!

Of course there were a lot of nonconference matches as well. My good friend, Coach Allen Fox of Pepperdine, rightfully wanted to play in SoCal one year and at Stanford the next. Because of the Pac-12 dual meet schedule, the only feasible time we really both had on our schedules was the near the end of the year. I always managed to find an excuse as to why we could not travel to play at Pepperdine that late in the year—schoolwork, guys hurt, budget, and so on. As a result, Allen and his great teams would always have to make the trip to Stanford if he wanted to play us. Again, the home team advantage was so great, this only helped us in terms of confidence building heading into the NCAAs. My responsibility was to watch out for my guys. *"Coach had an uncanny ability to get the team to peak at NCAA,"* says Greg Hing, '81. *"I'm not sure how he did this. I always thought part of it was how he scheduled matches and the number of matches (fewer)."*

Stanford's "quarter system"—four academic quarters (including summer) during the year—represented another scheduling opportunity. The first quarter ended with all final exams prior to the Christmas break, and the second ended at the end of winter quarter and prior to the start of spring break.

We took advantage of this by capping off our heavy fall practice season with an annual fun trip with boosters, usually to Hawaii. (More about this trip later.) Our winter match schedule ended just before final exams with a trip to La Jolla in Southern California to play in the USTA Pacific Coast Men's Doubles Championship at the beautiful La Jolla Beach and Tennis Club. This event presented a nice change of pace from dual matches and a chance to focus on doubles (and a little touch football in the sand) in an incredible atmosphere.

These provided great team experiences heading into each of our final exam sessions and our academic breaks. I could not have dreamed for more!

USING THE "OFF-SEASON"

In my day, fall was for technical changes and tactical application. . . . Unfortunately, in this day and age, it's much more difficult because of all the events that the Intercollegiate Tennis Association has put on the fall schedule. Guys have trouble changing some things when they have a tournament coming up.

—John Whitlinger, '76

Using the fall "off-season" correctly was one of the most important parts of scheduling because it was the one time, after a full summer of competition for most of the players, when they could return to a safe haven and have two to three months to make changes in their techniques and tactics/styles of play without having to worry about a match the next day. I have deep regrets that the college "season" of competition has morphed into a full year of competition. There now remains essentially no time to "take one's game apart" or make major changes without the risk of losing confidence in oneself.

One of the first early-in-the-year interruptions began in 1979 when the Intercollegiate Tennis Association (ITA) established an All-American event in the fall and invited all the nation's best players. UCLA hosted the event in 1980. Stanford's Scott Davis, '84, later to become world singles #11 and world doubles #2, was from Los Angeles, and he ended up winning the title that year. But since this was an era before we could hire assistant coaches, I did not feel I could justify traveling with just him when I had eleven other players left at home with no practice direction. Thus, it was not unusual for one of my players to travel on his own to play this event.

On the other hand, the ITA began to give out individual "ranking points" based on how well an individual performed and thus this event established the first individual ranking list of the season. If one of my invited players chose not to play and therefore passed on the opportunity to get some good early season wins, he could be penalized later with a lower ranking and thus lower seeding in the NCAA tournament. This put tremendous pressure on college players to compete in the tournaments rather than stay at home and work on developing parts of their game.

Jim Grabb: Team Captain; NCAA Singles Semifinals; World Singles #24, World Doubles #1

"There was a lot of focus on improving various aspects of one's game," explains Jim Grabb, '86. *"Coach was aggressive about getting players to embrace change, to move into uncomfortable areas, etc. in order to get better. Change doesn't often come easy and often results in a step back. As a result, very rarely did any of us perform well in the fall. Certainly most of us bought into the idea of breaking things apart and taking some lumps in October in order to be more effective in May."*

PRACTICES

Although training sessions were well-de-signed and intense, they were also fun and relatively short. Players did not overtrain, and Coach did a great job changing up our training routines, which kept the team engaged and fresh. Under Coach Gould, Stanford was universally respected in the college tennis world for playing its best tennis at the NCAA tournament. Coach Gould's approach to training and competition made this possible.

—Jeff Arons, '83

The day-to-day practice schedule was just as important as the month-to-month match schedule. Our practices never began before 2:30 (but at 2:30 *sharp*) and ended by 5:00, Monday–Friday only. Since I completed the next day's practice schedule including the assignment of practice partners before I left for home each night, I was a stickler for my guys letting me know as far ahead as possible if anyone was going to be late or miss practice. They were great about this.

I allotted thirty minutes to our strength and conditioning coach, once we had the privilege of having one. I attended every post-practice workout, and if it took more time than thirty minutes, the strength and conditioning coach and I would sit down together to find a way to be more efficient and release my players sooner! With the exception of spring break or the weekend prior to the NCAAs, we never had a team practice on a weekend.

Mostly, I was still just trying to keep my guys fresh enough, both mentally and physically, to be able to play their best at the NCAA championships. This objective permeated everything I did.

"I just know Coach was focused on peaking," remembers Jeff Salzenstein, '96. *"His eye was on Athens. He didn't need to push us early. He didn't need to overwork us. He didn't need to overtrain us. He just wanted us to be fresh at year-end. Coach knew how to balance practice and rest. He did a very good job of that. I never felt overtrained. I never felt tired. I felt fresh, except for those darn fartleks just preceding the NCAA championships that I was not very good at."*

"Fartlek" is a name for a conditioning drill based on different intervals of running and kinds of continuous movement. It provided an intense workout at a time when I really wanted to be certain I had the full attention of my guys in the final weeks leading up to the NCAAs.

It is so very important for the leader to do all that is possible to make everyone feel valued and included. Thus, as I mentioned earlier, we made every effort to mix practice partners. Much of our team time was spent on practicing themes or actual situations with regular practice partner rotations every ten minutes or so. (Themes included serving and volleying combinations, attacking serve returns, playing only the backcourt, etc.). After five minutes, winners would move up a court; losers would move down. We played points rather than sets, always trying to create and maximize pressure situations.

"Coach knew how to create pressure when it really did not matter, either through intersquad matches or individual tournaments, so that when the pressure mounted as we were reaching our goals, I would be prepared," says Ryan Wolters, '99, team captain, NCAA doubles champ and singles semifinalist. While Joe Kao, '04, finds a double rationale to our approach. *"There were two lessons in my mind—one tactical and one philosophical. The tactical lesson is that Coach had us practice the pressure situations. All our prac-*

tices replicating game time situations like consolidating breaks and tie-breaks were tactical. From a philosophical view, it's to manage the panic factor that inhibits performance."

When I finally was able to hire an assistant coach, the great Coach John Whitlinger, most of the time I would run the general practice and that would free up John to do one-on-one work with individuals in our full-team workouts.

Sometimes though there were also outside resources, such as when an individual asked if he could go outside of practice time to work with a local pro on a particular thing, I had no objection. Often the local pro was a former Stanford player who was teaching in the area, like Jeff Arons. Another example would be Sandor Mayer, Sandy and Gene's father. He was a great coach to whom they would often turn during his annual spring vacation visit. I had no problem with this—it only made us better. In addition, I learned a ton from Dr. Mayer and incorporated much of his coaching philosophy into my routine.

LINEUPS

I think a lot of ladder sport coaches rely heavily on challenge matches. Coach did as well, but he always made it clear that he had the final decision. Sometimes the results of a challenge match didn't make sense for the team. Because of that, I think he tried to avoid challenges unless truly necessary. What was more important was how each individual was performing at their spot on the team. If there was an issue, then Coach would work on a way to solve it.

It happened my sophomore year. No one knew if I'd ever play singles on the team, but I earned the sixth spot and started well. And then I kept winning, surprising myself as much as anyone. Doctor (Ricky) Becker was playing number five and having mixed results. I'm sure Coach knew in a challenge match I probably wouldn't beat Ricky, but he wanted to give me a chance and see if Ricky would pick it up at number six. He sat both of us down together, and we talked it out and came to an agreement. I kept winning and Ricky did as well. Somehow, because of his honest and direct approach, we were able to make the change, make everyone happy (at least content), and no challenge match was played.

—Grant Elliott, '97

Setting the lineup to decide who starts or who plays at what position (in an orchestra it's called a chair, in a choir it might be a soloist, in dance it might be the lead, in school, it might be who is selected as graduation speaker, and in business, it might be who's awarded the promotion or named partner).

It's a challenge to demonstrate caring and a feeling of relevancy when it comes to setting a lineup or filling like positions. This is one of the most agonizing parts of the job of any coach or team leader! You look a person in the eye and tell them that they're getting better and improving. You would never say this to them if you did not truly feel such. But then in what seems like a contradiction, you immediately turn around and play that person in the lineup in a position that might not seem to validate your comment. As a player myself who was only in the starting lineup for the last two of my five years, I knew the importance of working to make all players feel engaged—to help them feel relevant, even though they might never be a starter.

In tennis, a coach has the opportunity to have players "play-off" for a spot on the team. These are called ladder or challenge matches. It is not always the best way to determine a lineup or team positions. The process of selecting a lineup can produce wear not only on the team leader, but even more on the players. How one deals with that stress can make or break a team. It can create adversity as well as adversarial conditions, which can destroy a team. In my forty-four years of coaching (the last thirty-eight at Stanford), I used a different method of selecting my lineup almost every year.

An early decision in my career, and one of my first with a great team, involved my top two players, arguably the two best players in the country. Roscoe Tanner had come to Stanford as my biggest recruit, in his words, "to establish the program and to lead Stanford to its first championship"—a feat we *both* felt was possible! By his sophomore year, Sandy Mayer was playing at Roscoe's level. Both soon became top ten in the world pro singles rankings. I felt a loyalty to Roscoe for being the first to accept the challenge of leading Stanford to the top, and I did not want to rock the boat. One method of determining a position in a lineup is to have a challenge ladder match. It is another to decide when such should be played.

Paul Larson, '71, who was there at the time, describes the process. *"Coach knew when to play a challenge match. I remember the Tanner / Mayer rivalry. Both great players but only one could be number one. Sandy was hot to play Roscoe for that position. I don't know for certain, but Sandy was a better gamer and could have beaten Roscoe on any given day. Roscoe had just won a major fall tournament in San Francisco, the Transamerica Open. The very next day Coach had Roscoe play Sandy in that challenge match. Roscoe was full of confidence and Coach knew it. Roscoe won, kept his spot and confidence. Who knows what would have happened to Roscoe if he had lost? As for Sandy, confidence was never an issue, and Coach also understood that."*

Promoter Barry MacKay was great about giving a Stanford player a wild card each year into his major Northern California fall pro event, then named the Transamerica Open. By the end of the next year, 1972, both Roscoe and Sandy reached the NCAA semifinals in singles. It was a fair question as to who was the better player at that time! I *did* elect to keep Roscoe at number one, but Sandy could have just as effectively and easily played at that position. The next year after Roscoe had turned pro, Sandy won the NCAA singles (and once again, the NCAA doubles, this time not with Roscoe, but with Jim Delaney).

Much of my decision-making on how to do handle these things was based on the personalities of those comprising my team. There is no secret formula for this—whether or not to play intrasquad matches, and in turn, determine who plays whom in such (ranging from everyone playing everyone else to only matches between small clusters of nearly equal-in-ability players) or simply for the coach select the lineup arbitrarily.

Jimmy Gurfein, '81, recounts just such a situation that occurred with Tim Mayotte. At the time, they were two of my most improved players. *"I remember before my sophomore year, I was already playing and winning matches on the international circuit. I came into Stanford thinking, 'Here I am, I'll be one of the top players.' When we got to the team meeting, at the time Tim Mayotte was part of that team and had just defeated Jimmy Connors right before the Stanford season started in the Transamerica championships in San Francisco in September. And though I had a really good summer, so did Tim. We had a team meeting to discuss lineups. The meeting ended up going against me, I guess you'd say, because Coach wanted me to play some challenge matches despite the success I'd had over the summer. I was complaining and acting out, and Coach said a couple words and got my thinking to click on to a positive state. He was firm, not wishy-washy, to the point. He said, 'Jim, just play.'"*

Later that year, Jim and Tim would meet in the singles final of the NCAA championships, which Tim would win in three close sets. Not everyone will be happy, and some will carry a grudge forever because they will feel they have received the short end of the stick—that they never got a fair chance! Or feel that the matches were rigged (scheduled at a time when they were not at their best physically, or after beating someone, had to play that person yet again, and on and on).

Jim Healy, '73, remembers the angst this can cause on a team. *"It was spring break 1971, and that entire week the top players were playing an intense series of challenge matches to determine the lineup for upcoming matches against USC and/or UCLA. Paul Sidone beat Jim Delaney in a very close challenge match and seemingly won the right to play number five in the upcoming matches. The dilemma Coach had was that, in his gut, he was convinced that Delaney had a better chance of winning against USC/UCLA than Sidone. That match could make the difference between the team winning or losing. I remember Coach walked all the way across campus to Paul's fraternity to tell him that he wanted to start Delaney despite the outcome of the challenge match. Paul ended up watching and cheering the match in the stands and Delaney won his match. My respect for him as a coach and for Paul as a teammate spiked even higher."*

Although my players might not have thought I felt this, I really did empathize with them in these lower lineup positions because I had been there myself! This was especially difficult for me to manage these positions on the team—number seven was really an "extra" player in the event any "starter" got hurt. I know because I played number seven one entire year. The next year, I played number six, but my position was always in jeopardy, and I felt the pressure of always having to justify that I was the rightful selection to play that spot. Balancing what was fair and what was best for the team was always a very difficult challenge. At least I understood it from a player's standpoint because I'd been there myself.

Scott Moody, '87, describes the relationship this way. *"The culture was as pure a meritocracy as I've been involved in. Coach never played favorites, and always fielded the team that had the best chance of success in a particular match. That didn't mean if you had a few bad days you were out of the lineup. He understood the ups and downs of our uniquely individual and pressure-filled sport. But over time he put the best team on the field. I can't think of one player who truly disagreed with where they were in the lineup, whether starting or not. Although he cared truly about each player, nothing was personal when it came to game day; it was all about putting the best team on the court."*

As a team leader, how these positions are handled is of key importance. These are difficult decisions, but normal ones for a coach to have to make. There really is no right or wrong answer—often it is not clear cut, and one must go with their gut feeling, including how this might affect other members of the team. This is *very* hard to convey effectively to those negatively affected, especially when you care greatly about the individuals who are concerned.

But you *must* accept that you *cannot* please everyone all the time. The responsibility of the coach is to put his best players at that time on the court in the correct playing position. Fairness cannot always be a factor!

Jim Hodges, '80, adds, *"I think this was the real key to Coach's, and Stanford's, success. First, he had an uncanny ability to do what was best for the team, even if it was not strictly fair. As a college kid, I (and some others) resented the fact that some players essentially never played challenge matches, while others always played them. In hindsight though, his method (almost his instinct) was correct. In my last two years, Peter Rennert was the best player, but even his confidence/ego was a little suspect. He might well have lost a challenge match to Tim Mayotte. But keeping Peter at number one brought the best out in Peter; and Tim would always play his best no matter where he was in the lineup. It had to have been really hard for Coach in John McEnroe's year. I think he felt that he had to have challenge matches, but I think he would have been just as happy (and correct) to have Mac automatically at one, with either Bill Maze or Matt Mitchell at two. It all worked out, but I'm sure it was not easy."*

Sensitivities caused by ladder matches were magnified if siblings ever had to play against each other to determine their positions on the team—a mistake I regrettably made once or twice. Team captain and All-American Mark Mitchell, '77, recalls, *"Playing my younger brother in a challenge match should have never happened. Coach should have stepped in and stopped it from happening."* When it comes to setting lineups, a coach must have thick skin.

In dealing with situations case by case, a coach may decide to sit down and ask the team how they would handle a particular case. Sometimes it is good for the team to air it all out in front of everyone. The coach may or may not decide to explain why and how a decision was made. A coach must remember that the only one who will ultimately be happy is the person who is playing number one. It can be especially challenging if it involves the final starting spot on a team. Jeff Arons, '83, describes better than I could how this can often work for the best. *"During my sophomore year, I was replaced in the starting singles lineup right before NCAAs by freshman Jimmy Gurfein. Jimmy was hyper-competitive, and he was one of my main on-court rivals. I was very disappointed and angry with the decision. I recall Coach Gould emphasizing how important it would be for me to support 'Gurf' during the tournament. I ended up rooting for Jimmy the entire tournament. I remember feeling inspired by his clutch play and his tenacity. I also took a lot of pride in encouraging Jimmy and doing what was best for the team. I had teammates like Greg Hing, John Corse and Andy Chase who had backed me after I'd replaced them in the starting lineup. Greg, John and Andy were great friends and role models, and it felt good to follow their example. The addition of Jimmy to the starting lineup made us a much stronger team, and his play propelled us to the 1980 NCAA team title!"*

Often the "challenge match chips" don't fall the way a coach thinks they should. Consequently, after seeing my players in matches against other schools, I always reserved the right (and responsibility) to make arbitrary changes. I would usually have some matches earlier in the year so that the loser(s) would have time to recover. Some players play very well against teammates they know, but not so well against others who may be unknown to them.

"The attribute of being tough, yet fair, which gave each player an honest and consistent understanding as to what their current standing on the team was, as well the hope and vision that it could improve, in my view was one of the essential qualities of a winning program," is how Craig Johnson, '76, answers the question. *"No doubt at times it may have not felt fair to each of us as players not getting a spot in a particular match or road trip, but we each, to my eye, knew an opportunity was just around the corner if we earned it."*

By the time of the NCAA championships, I had had the entire year to see how my guys were progressing, who could best rise to the occasion, and so on. At that point, I had to assume sole responsibility for the lineup and accept that I would never be able to please everyone all the time! Dana Treister, '87, sums up the best approach a player can take, because the matches or my decisions won't always work out to their liking—but hopefully the season will. *"Compete every day. Nothing is given to you, you have to work hard and earn your position, and if that means competing within your own team, then that's the reality of being part of a winning program. Status is earned, it is not given to you and does not come with seniority. If you aren't improving, new talent will come along behind you and take your spot. That's just the nature of big-time athletic programs and successful business enterprises."*

Well said, Dana. There is a price to pay plus a lot of pressure from those who are chasing you when you are sitting on top of the pyramid!

EXPECTATIONS—A SLOW BUILD
"Georgia on My Mind"

Playing for the end of the year was always the goal. We peaked at the right time, and all knew the early matches were not the time to stress. Win the NCAA tournament. Fear no one and respect everyone.

This feeling was conveyed through "Georgia music" and spirit and a drive to win. There was a slow build every year and we all knew when the Georgia tape played that it was game time!

—Alex O'Brien, '92

Alex O'Brien: Team Captain; NCAA Singles and Doubles Champion; World Singles #30, World Doubles #1

Alex was right, and he did it very well, winning a rare "Triple Crown"—the NCAA singles, doubles, and team championships in the same year. (Actually, Alex, who entered Stanford without scholarship aid, was a key component of three team championships. Seldom have I had as much respect for a player as I did for him.)

The NCAA team championships were held in Athens, Georgia with the University of Georgia serving as an incredible host beginning with the first team championship in 1977 for twenty-two of the next twenty-five years. This represented a *tremendous* home court advantage, especially as a vastly improved Georgia team became an annual challenger for the title and as their enthusiastic fans gathered to support them.

As a result, and to help make my own team feel more at home, I methodically collected every song I could find that had the word Georgia in it ("Georgia on my Mind," "Midnight Train to Georgia," "A Rainy Day in Georgia," "Georgia," etc.) and compiled them in a tape. It became a staple. This is an example of comfort and excitement with which my teams really seemed to identify. *"During the year,"* remembers Ryan Wolters, '99, *"the team could play music that we chose before matches. But before Georgia, Coach would play this music at practice that only had songs that contained the word Georgia in them. When you heard that music it triggered something inside. You knew it was time to get serious and that our goal was near."*

I would usually play this tape on our first day of practice to begin the year, as well as always at practice daily in the final ten days/two weeks leading up to the championships. I even made a separate copy so we could play the tapes in each of our two rental cars as we drove to practice each day in Athens.

May was NCAA time—"our" time. The stage was set, and the important part of the season was now beginning. As hard as it might be to believe, we won more NCAA championships (seventeen) than we did conference championships (fourteen). Henry "Jeff" Brandon, '78, confirms this. *"I can't for the life of me remember if we were Pac-12 champions. We certainly didn't celebrate it, and it was never a goal. We only had one goal—to win the NCAA championship. It was all about winning the big one!"*

We were the undefeated Pac-12 champions in 1978, which Jeff was a part of. In the end, we won thirteen of our seventeen championships played at the University of Georgia in a twenty-four-year period. Our overall NCAA win/loss ratio in Athens (62 wins,

4 losses) was incredible and even better than our win/loss ratio at home during that time. I have to believe this was at least in some part due to learning how to make my team feel "at home" in Athens by appreciating the fantastic atmosphere. This is in fact an important aspect of any away match, but particularly the national championships! I wanted to make certain they relished playing before the rabid Bulldog fans and looked forward to this great challenge—to accept it rather than fear it!

"We all knew from the first practice in Palo Alto that the objective was to win the final match in Athens," remembers David Wheaton, '91. *"And that permeated everything Coach did and said throughout the entire year. His intensity naturally heightened at the NCAA tournament, but I never felt that failing to lift the team trophy would be a train wreck for him personally or professionally. We felt enough pressure on our own; he didn't add to it."*

The focus after my first few years of coaching was always on getting better—a constant build toward the last competition of the year. The key was to be able to show my players tangibly how this was happening. It was realized partly by the results of scheduling and approach to practice, as well as by my personal buildup. This meant creating an atmosphere in which expectations could best be realized. I did all I could to increase the expectation and excitement of the challenge of traveling to Athens for the NCAAs. This was their time to shine. And, more often than not, they did!

John Letts, '86, writes, *"Our team goal, indeed, expectation, was to win the NCAA title, nothing more, nothing less. All practices and matches leading up to the NCAAs were merely a means to improve, learn, and get ready to perform when it counted. When we arrived at Athens, it was 'now' time. As the ultimate leader, Coach Gould was able to convince his teams that no matter what had transpired before we arrived at Athens, we were ready. He calmly and confidently would relay our team's record at Athens each year, usually 30–4, or something of the sort, and nearly always better than our overall team record, even at home. Athens was even better than a home court advantage. We were young and wide-eyed, and when Coach told us it was time, we knew we were there to deliver and keep the tradition going."*

Team captain Grant Elliott, '97, puts it another way. *"Coach had created a chemistry and expectation for winning. That expectation was felt by the teams we played. There was a feeling, across the country, that when the big moment came, regardless of our seeding, we were the team to beat in the tournament. That couldn't have been truer than in 1996 when we beat UCLA. They handled us twice in the regular season, and I believe they were undefeated. But we felt something going into the tournament. The cream rises to the top. Give us a chance on the big stage in May and the odds were on our side. The result of that match was stunning. Not that we won (maybe a little), but that we were in every match. We won the bottom four but were still in it and fighting on one and two. We could have swept (in singles) the best team in the country on the biggest stage. The focus was very clear, and the expectation was to be great when the time came. And, generally, our teams were."*

Despite this accepted goal of winning a national championship each year, there were always different challenges along the way. Most of the time we overcame them, but a couple of times we could not. In Athens, Georgia in 2001, we played Pepperdine in the round of sixteen match. Our leader, Alex Kim, the defending NCAA singles champion, went into full-body cramps due to dehydration caused by the extreme heat and humidity. The pain must have been unbearable. How helpless I felt as he lay writhing on the court! He was taken to the University Med Center to receive intravenous fluid but did not respond. He was then taken to the hospital for added treatment, where he received more fluid. But he entered a coma-like state and was unresponsive—he'd received too much fluid and his brain was starting to swell.

Fortunately, this was diagnosed in time, and he turned out fine. *But*, it was a very scary situation in which we could have lost him!

Obviously, he could not compete the next day in the quarterfinals against Tennessee, and we lost a close 4–2 decision without him in the lineup. Still, we played great as a team. Rarely had I felt as good about a team entering a championship as I did that particular year. I would never have bet against us. But the loss of our number one singles and doubles player was just too much to overcome. As it turned out, we would never win another team championship.

Scott Lipsky, '03, concludes, *"Our team goal every year was to win the NCAA title, and I loved it and appreciated the lofty goal. We were number one for all or part of all four years I was in school, and we wanted to win it all. Since I graduated and have spoken to many guys who played college tennis, they all talk about winning a conference title or winning the indoor title like it's something great. I appreciate more and more that we did not really celebrate winning the Pac-10 (12) titles or winning the indoor titles because they were just a means to an end for us. I truly believe that we would have won at least one more title if Alex Kim did not have to be in the hospital in 2001, if our number one singles and doubles player, K. J. Hippensteel, had not been lost for the season in our last competition of the year leading into the NCAAs in 2002, and if one of our key players did not leave the team in 2003."*

Chapter Eight

COMPETING AT THE HIGHEST LEVEL

One of my most vivid memories was one of the first team meetings of my junior season, the fall of 1994. The meeting was in the trophy room. The NCAA team runner-up trophy from 1994 was in the front of the room, with an 8 X 11 hand-printed sign saying "Silver Sucks" taped to its base.

My recollection is Coach had us sit in this room, with the sign as the focal point, for some time . . . definitely past the beginning time for the meeting.

—Jim Thomas, '96

Clearly this made an impression on a bunch of competitive guys who did not like losing any more than I did because we proceeded to win the championship each of the next four years—the first time this had ever been accomplished!

Playing a team sport at the college level requires a manager to organize practices, matches, and games. *Competing* at a championship level in any activity—sports or otherwise—requires a coach or leader who can consistently get the best out of each and every player, and out of the team as a whole, but particularly at the right times. As a coach, it is imperative to encourage people to try their best, and this often means helping them prove to themselves that their best is usually far greater than they thought it could be! For the team leader, this is both an art and a science. For me it was a joy, but it was also a massive challenge because it almost never involved taking the path of least resistance for the coach or the players.

There are many elements involved in a team's success, such as preparation, setting expectations, managing egos, and creating a culture of winning, but whether sports or business, eventually it all comes down to performance on the court, on the field, or during the sales call. To perform well, one must be able to produce at a very high level *at a specific time*, and often in collaboration with the coach. When it all comes together, win or lose, it is satisfying to know that one has put forth their absolute best effort. But there are far more moving parts to this process of competing at the highest level than just expending great effort. Here are five more important elements to keep in mind:

- Relish the challenge
- Adapt
- Be proactive
- Lead effectively
- Foster competitiveness

RELISH THE CHALLENGE

There are several attributes that made Coach succeed. One was his burning desire to win. His physical presence was intimidating. You saw it in his eyes. He always had a look of success. During matches, he would roam the courts projecting confidence. There was never a look of doubt or outward fear.

—Greg Tusher, '93

One of my freshmen was not excited about the challenge he faced on his first day of practice. Jeff Tarango, '90, recalls, *"My first day of practice at Stanford University, I was nervous, not knowing what to expect. I walked into the tennis stadium and Coach Gould greeted me and handed me two new tennis balls and said go to court 1 and hit with Patrick McEnroe. I asked where the third ball was. Coach said: 'When you get good you only need one ball. I have a limited budget so two balls is plenty for you and Patrick.'*

"Seven years later Patrick and I stayed at my house at Manhattan Beach, and we were now both Top 100 on the ATP Tour. We had a can of balls and we decided we were having an extreme Gould practice this week and the rest fitness. We decided to take one ball a day to Live Oak Park and hit that one ball only. Our first rally was over two hundred balls. We had four more rallies over fifty. Then we went for our beach fitness workout at John's Malibu Colony House. In 'Gould and John Mac Spirit,' we played ONLY volleys in deep sand with one ball until we could not bend anymore."

Speaking of Johnny Mac, here's a more poignant example of facing a challenge. This one involves the best shot under pressure I have ever seen, one that only a true champion could produce by one who relished such challenges. In 1978, we were playing at UCLA against one of their best teams ever. Stanford was trailing after five singles matches 2–3. John McEnroe was still on the court playing his nemesis, Eliot Teltscher. All members of both teams were standing courtside and the packed stands were going crazy. Mac was down a set and 5–3 in the second set. We were using no-ad sudden-death scoring, meaning the first player to win four points wins the game. It was match point for Eliot, who was serving to win the deciding point at three points all. After a long backcourt rally in itself full of suspense, Eliot took advantage of a short ball and charged the net with a great approach shot wide to John's backhand. Mac ran at full speed all the way across the court and hit a backhand pass shot winner barely out of Eliot's reach to break serve, stay alive, and now serve at 4–5. Mac held serve to even the set, and Eliot—a future top ten world player—began to fold. Mac won a fairly routine third set to tie the match score at 3–3. UCLA had great doubles, but gathering inspiration from Mac's great and almost unbelievable comeback, Stanford won two of three doubles to win the match. Stanford escaped with a victory on its way to an undefeated season and an NCAA championship! I doubt the thought of losing ever occurred to John McEnroe.

True champions in any field relish competition and become better because of it. *"It's about creating an environment where players expect to win but are not fearful of losing,"* says Jim Miller, '82. *"And whether in a given match, in a season, or over a career, it's about adapting to keep finding a way to make it work. And in a very high-pressure sport, it's about making it fun."*

One cannot be afraid to fail in any endeavor, be it in sports or business! This is first and foremost. It's such an important concept. For many great competitors, the thought of failure never enters their minds. Roscoe Tanner, '73, was one of these people.

"I was brought in to help create a winning culture. Baylor School, where I played in high school, didn't lose, so I never considered not winning in the long run. We didn't fear anyone. We might lose, but we intended to win."

Of course the fact is that we all fail often because life is full of challenges. In many ways, there is no such thing as failure. It can help to think of challenging situations not as potential chances for failure, but as opportunities to succeed or as experiences. I have yet to see a baby successfully stand up and immediately start walking. Before that first step is successfully taken, there are many failures—too many to count! Or to guide the first spoonful of food to one's mouth. Or to immediately start talking. But, usually with some encouragement, we keep trying; we embrace the challenge. At that early stage, we really don't know or care whether another baby starts to walk earlier or later than ourselves. We measure our success only in terms of ourselves.

Later, we begin to become aware of the expectations others have for us, as well as those we have for ourselves. Later still, as we grow older and begin school, and especially by our teenage years, we become more aware of the successes of others. Too often that leads us to measuring our accomplishments by whether we were able to keep up with our friends. Worse, we might look down on those who cannot keep up with us. This is often applied to the physical appearance of others, to their athletic abilities, to their academic accomplishments, and to things as superfluous as the number of friends they have or how much those friends are respected by others. Unfortunately, this can create a false sense of value or lack of such within us.

The first thing we must accept is that each of us is different. Think first of your own family and how different your siblings may be from you. One might be more athletic, another more outgoing, and another more intelligent. And you all probably have different interests. But each difference brings something of value to the family. Just think how much positive impact we can make by recognizing and encouraging achievement or success by others, no matter how small it might seem. This helps to show we truly care!

The second thing is to realize that imperfection is part of our individual uniqueness, and more important, *always* a necessary part of any success, not only in sports, but in relationships, business, and any field of endeavor. When we are facing a challenge, we are often under the impression that we must perform perfectly in order to succeed. We grow up thinking that to be successful, we must be perfect. At an early age, we hear that word so often that it becomes synonymous with success. These are false assumptions because human beings are simply not perfect.

Unfortunately, although we know this is problematic, we unconsciously reinforce the idea of perfection. A parent says, "Great job—just perfect." A teacher puts a smiley face and a gold star on a simple first-grade spelling test where we spelled all ten words— DOG, CAT, and so on—correctly and writes "PERFECT!" across the top of the page. We begin to equate success with being perfect, and conversely, anything less than that as failure. We quickly forget that even in sports, examples of the greatest successes also include failure: the top batter in all of baseball "fails" to get a hit two-thirds of the time; the top quarterback in football "fails" to complete a third of his passes. Rarely does anyone record a perfect bagel by winning twenty-four straight points in a tennis set. And no one has ever shot an eighteen on a golf course!

Many of my players arrived at Stanford with these types of self-expectations of perfection and success, and I always worked hard to defuse this mindset. *"I think the best thing Coach did for me was get me to understand that I didn't have to be perfect to win,"* explains Jared Palmer, '93. *"That I could contribute to the overall team effort by being a good teammate, even if I personally didn't win."*

These two things—the expectations of others and the misinterpretation of perfection as a measure of success—not only tend to undermine one's sense of well-being, but also erode the beauty of facing a challenge and overcoming it. Our own or others' expectations of perfection tend to make us afraid to fail, and in turn, afraid to sometimes even try! The antidote is often to lighten the mood and focus on the enjoyment of the sport. Scott Moody, '87, remembers when *"we huddled before each match, Coach would say, 'Hey, have fun out there, enjoy this.' That was a wonderful way to put it in perspective, and I draw on it to this day. If you can look at something difficult and fraught with doubt not as an opportunity to fail, but a chance to embrace a great challenge and see what you can do, it frees you up to do your best."*

This idea extends far beyond sport, as Walt Disney understood in telling his "imagineers" that if they could dream it, they could do it. Along the way, along *any* way, there are many failures in each of many iterations, but gradually progress is made and very often a breakthrough finally occurs. Thomas Edison famously counted each of the hundreds of failures in his attempt to invent the lightbulb not as a failure but as a step closer to success. The important thing is to keep at it.

"Coach didn't let me quit," recounts Joe Kao, '04. *"I talked previously about his helping me with my mental game, but that period during my junior year eventually brought out some of my best tennis. I also learned life lessons that I cherish to this day on how to deal with failure and a general approach to life that recognizes that tomorrow is another day to compete, and to be grateful that there is that opportunity."*

Of course, reaching a breakthrough involves far more than just not quitting. We must build a supportive and respectful culture within our team where failure is allowed in order to maximize achievement. And this culture is a team thing. Fortunately, most of us in our occupations are on teams where it is not a life-and-death matter. When adversity happens and one falls down, we must all work hard to pick that person up! If it happens to our team or group, as leaders we must find a way to get everyone back on track. We must create an environment where members of our team are not afraid to try for fear of failure! We must not put pressure on them to be perfect.

Another example is more subtle. An athlete is often told that they have great potential or have great talent. The result all too often is that without even realizing it, the athlete subconsciously avoids making a true effort to achieve because of a fear they cannot live up to expectations. I learned to avoid saying, "He has great potential" or "He's very talented."

I believe that continuously emphasizing the journey rather than the end result, looking forward, emphasizing preparation and effort, setting realistic goals that can be reached and then resetting them, and creating an upbeat and positive attitude, all go a long way in helping an individual or team maximize performance as challenges arise. There is no magic to this or specific steps to follow, as every situation and team is different. As a leader, a coach must create by example an atmosphere of enthusiasm about accepting and meeting challenges. The leader earns credibility by constantly showing that they are prepared for every eventuality.

Alex O'Brien, '92, tells a great story about one way we did this during a very important time, the NCAA championships in Athens, Georgia. *"In Georgia the blue laws did not allow alcohol sales on Sunday. We played the finals on Sunday and asked Coach what the plan was. He quickly dismissed our question and said everything was organized. That summed up how we operated and enjoyed life as a team. Hurdles were always there but we enjoyed the challenge of overcoming them on all fronts."*

I still laugh about this—the thought that I might not be prepared with a bottle of cold champagne to help us celebrate if we won. Fortunately, we did win, and we all were able to enjoy a celebratory sip or two. The challenge of preparation had been met, and the result was relished by all! *Always* be prepared for any occasion!

FIND A WAY/ADAPT

One of Coach's favorite phrases was "Find a way to win." That meant to us that the player ultimately is accountable for his performance on the court. The core principle to me in "finding a way" is being able to diagnose problems and make creative adjustments in real time during a match.

I remember a teammate who was frustrated during a practice set yelling, "Oh my God!" after missing a shot. From a few courts away, Coach responded, "He's not going to help you out here; you'd better figure it out."

—Scott Moody, '87

I consider myself a realist; I think most successful leaders are. In my occupation, I must expect the worst: the physical environment such as weather, a physical injury or mental health issue, and of course, a game plan that can be adjusted in real time. One must always be prepared to adapt. It's my duty to be certain that my players are taught the ability to adapt as well. For example, a certain style of play might not be working against a particular opponent. What my player does best, and thus probably likes to do the most, may simply not be working. I must be able to convince that player to practice for every conceivable eventuality. They must all be prepared, and able, to adapt their games to what I see may be necessary or at least worth a try.

Alex O'Brien, '92, understands this. *"If things are not working, change them,"* he writes, echoing one of our fundamental team philosophies. *"Coach was great at looking at a situation and disrupting it by radical thinking. If the momentum of a match moved against a player, he would force the player to take a radically different approach to try and find a way to win."*

Jim Miller, '82, adds, *"Adapt to the situation. In tennis, when you're a bit off, or when your strengths feed the strengths of your opponent, you need to adjust. Whether it's taking off some pace, or shifting to the Aussie formation in dubs, or something else, keep trying new ways to succeed. The same is true of leading business teams—the need to keep adapting."*

Adaptability is important in every situation. Examples in my sport of tennis pertain of course to both singles and doubles and might include general categories such as where to serve or what kind of serve to hit, where to stand on return, whether to play more aggressively and apply more pressure, play more conservatively and slow down the overall pace of the match, change of speed and spin of the ball, direct shots to a certain part of the court, and on and on. But I cannot expect my players to do what I ask in a match, especially if it involves getting out of their basic comfort zone, unless we have spent enough time in practice ensuring that they are able to execute, even if it's not their strength. Therefore, much of our practice time was spent on adapting to different situations.

"We practiced the drive/lob combination in doubles a lot, for situations where we had trouble breaking serve in doubles," Scott Moody, '87, recalls. *"Not many other teams that I know of used this consciously, and it worked."*

Another regular practice I espoused, which was often not overly popular with more conservative players but to which I reverted if a match was going against one of my guys, was to become what I called "aggressive with margin." John Letts, '86, describes the concept in greater detail. *"Be aggressive with margin meant that in critical moments we should play aggressively but hit our shots well clear of lines and the net. In other words, rather than getting tight and playing nervously ('pushing') or going the other way and trying to play too aggressively and out of our comfort zones, Coach Gould gave us the confidence to know that if we just played our game rather than getting tight, if we just 'hit out' on our shots with great margin for error, we would inevitably come out on top."*

Here is yet another example of having to adjust under trying circumstances to "find a way," as Scotty (Hugh) Scott, '01, describes it. This one falls into the category of perseverance. *"My freshman year I was playing a challenge match for the last traveling spot on the team. It was down to one final match between me and Ali Ansari. The winner would travel and play in roughly half the matches, the other would likely stay home for the year and practice with the other nontraveling team members. I was sick as a dog. It was pouring rain and it was a Sunday. Coach called, and when I told him how sick I was, I recall him reminding me that, 'This is the situation you are in, and this will happen again in your life. You either play the match and get through it or you don't, and I'll give the spot to Ali. Life won't be perfect so do your best with what you have.'*

"I won the match (somehow), went outside and threw up in the parking lot. I was in bed with a 102-degree temperature the rest of the day and while deathly sick, it was a huge turning point in my life. I knew what I could get done in even the hardest circumstances. I was pushed past what I thought was my breaking point and I not only survived but I succeeded. For this lesson from Coach, I will forever be grateful."

Changing the pace or coming to net or being aggressive with margin are some examples of "finding a way." Or sometimes, as Scotty suggests, it's just pushing through. Scott Moody, '87, agrees. *"The personal accountability required to succeed at Stanford tennis and the ability to 'find a way' to compete I believe are core life skills. I have tried to draw upon them as much as possible in business and in all areas of life."*

THE STANFORD WAY
Be Proactive: Strike First

Coach knew that by being aggressive his players were less nervous about attacking. Coach knew that this style of play led to a sense of commitment and more purpose-driven tennis. As a player, I loved having Coach on my court because he would push me to attack and play aggressive "Stanford tennis." This style of play involved always putting constant pressure on your opponent by coming to net and not waiting for your opponent to miss. Coach instilled this attacking mentality in my game, which definitely helped my talent blossom. He would remind me to take the initiative and be bold. He'd be on the side of the court and gesture with his hand to hit the return and come in or serve and volley. That is where I learned to take it to my opponents and win the match rather than try not to lose.

—Mike Bryan, '00

All too often, competitions in sports as well as business are lost by those who choose to wait to win, rather than to go after the win! The alternative aggressive philosophy is to be proactive rather than reactive. This was absolutely a key to our success. In my sport, this is known as "first-strike tennis." First-strike tennis is essentially an attacking style of play symbolized by beating your opponent to the net. This forces them to hit the ball to a smaller target area. Playing closer to the net also opens up more angles and allows you to return the ball back to your opponent quicker, which gives him/her less time to prepare and get to the ball. Although this involved some risk because despite what you did, the ball could be hit by you, it characterized the playing style of our teams: "the Stanford Way!"

My responsibility was to teach my players the skills (an improved serve, and a strong volley—both from midcourt and finishing—with strong overheads and a shorter-stroke return of serve) so they could feel comfortable attacking when I asked them to. For the vast majority, it became incorporated into their basic game.

I am convinced that this philosophy of staying aggressive by finding a way to be the first to the net—to be proactive rather than reactive—was a major key to our success, especially at crunch time. It takes a while to develop the skills and the confidence to lay it all out there, but we spent a lot of time practicing this style of play. In college tennis, this meant that *all* my players became reasonable serve and volley players, even though only a small handful entered Stanford with this skill high on their list of abilities. *"Coach made me a serve and volley player and I made it to number one in the world in doubles,"* reports Alex O'Brien, '92. *"In juniors the only time I ventured to the net was to pick up a ball or shake hands after the match."*

All-American and NCAA doubles finalist Vimal Patel, '94, adds, *"I had no net game or attack from the transition, which was my weakness. Coach changed that. He didn't let me stop coming to the net even when I lost several matches doing it, and only encouraged me even more. Coach took a kid who had no clue what a volley or coming to the net was, and in one year brought him to the finals of the NCAA doubles tourney at the end of the year. Knowing players like Roscoe Tanner and John McEnroe before me had been shown these same tactics allowed me to have the confidence and belief I could do the same things, even though my game was the polar opposite of what was being taught to me now."*

I taught this because I have always believed that the first-to-attack style puts incredible pressure on one's opponent to react time and again. *But* a fact not many understood was that it also kept my players in an offensive frame of mind instead of waiting for their opponent to lose. My challenge was to get my players to embrace this concept when all was on the line.

K. J. Hippensteel, '02, recalls, *"It amazed me how Coach was willing to progress my game by forcing me to come to net in huge matches that had implications for the season even though he knew I wasn't comfortable or skilled at it yet. I can remember it being 4–4 in the third and 30–40 break point, and Coach wanted me to serve and volley or come in off the second serve to put pressure on my opponent. It gave me the confidence to try that, and I gradually became more comfortable at it. I found success at playing a more aggressive game, which was where my future was at."*

Over time, my players recognized this and took great pride in the Stanford Way of first-strike tennis! It was our trademark! One might think a trademark unnecessary for a tennis program, or a business, but I believe that establishing a brand is important to any endeavor, both for internal morale, as well as for outward appearance, as long as it is core to your principles. First-strike tennis was definitely our brand!

David Wheaton, '91, sums this up very well. *"I came to Stanford tall and lean with the kind of body well-suited for a net-rushing player. And yet, even with good hands and reach for playing at the net, most of my time was spent stroking from the baseline with only occasional ventures forward. Coach Gould decided early for me that 'occasionally' would change to 'constantly.'*

"Broadly categorizing, there are two styles of tennis players: those who rally from the baseline, and those who look to move forward to the net. Net rushing is a higher risk style of play—sometimes you get passed, sometimes you force an error, but according to Coach, the result of constantly pressuring an opponent tips the percentages in your favor. Rolling the dice was not the

comfort zone for my personality, but Coach's strong belief and constant urging that getting to the net was the right style for me eventually engendered a belief in me that he was right. So convincing was he that serve-and-volleying became the style I would take on the pro tour."

David rolled the dice and reached world singles #12.

COACHING DURING COMPETITION

From Coach's vast experience of coaching college tennis and seeing the best players, his strategic instruction was invaluable. He also had a very good sense of when to leave a player alone and when they needed to hear from him during a match (and what to say). This is a skill I have seen missing in some coaches, despite them having been at it for a long time.

—Greg Hing, '81

When a leader says something and *how* it needs to be said to each individual or group is key. It could be within one's family, within a group of friends, or a department within a business. In any case, this trait is developed as one's confidence grows.

As an example in tennis, early on in my career I feared on-court coaching because I lacked confidence in what I believed. That was not without good reason because very often a player I was approaching during a match would essentially tell me to "get lost," even in front of a crowd. He simply did not want to hear from me! And if I sensed that the time was not right, I usually would respond by giving him a little space—at least for a few moments.

It's also true that other players welcome and thrive with more help. My advice in these cases was usually simple, such as, "take your time" or "toss the ball a little more to your right on your serve." Occasionally it was more complex and involved strategies such as "play his forehand more when attacking" or "slow the match down." The bottom line is that a coach/team leader must know his players/team and what they can handle. Then they must gain/ have the confidence to convey their beliefs in an effective manner.

Eventually I grew to love on-court coaching as I saw my style of play working and being embraced by my players—even the ones originally resistant to it. Like my players, I gained more confidence in myself, even though I might make a mistake. This confidence is important because so often a match can turn based on an adjustment in technique or on the strategy used. The original plan does not always work successfully.

This is where a coach can really help a player and one reason why a young person has such an opportunity when playing college tennis: it's the one place where unlimited coaching in tennis is essentially nonrestricted. Fortunately, coaching on the job also has few restraints, as well as many similarities. It starts with the leader's trust in the mission, and then of the confidence himself/ herself has to believe he/she can aid in making the process more successful. Enter variables such as style of coaching, determination of what value can be added, and good judgment on how it can most effectively be applied.

As an example, in tennis there are several stages in on-court coaching. We all face similar decision points in other phases of our lives. Think outside of opportunities at the start of a new process where your team may be a little overwhelmed and need extra encouragement. As the process continues, there often is a loss of focus for any number of reasons—boredom, sloppiness, looking ahead, ability to work together, and on and on. How can you effectively get everyone back on track? And at crunch time when deadlines are looming, what might you do to better bring it all home and complete the project well and on time? Or in other terms, "complete the deal"?

Applicable similarities may be creatively found in how I approached coaching during the multiple stages of a match.

- Pre-match. I knew most of our opponents from pre-vious matches, and I always had a small notecard in my pocket with their tendencies and weaknesses, as well as strengths. I would review this with my player pre-match.

- Warm-ups. Much of this time was dedicated to my player. First, I checked to be sure he was moving his feet because nerves almost always play a part, and when nervous, one's feet stop moving. A simple com-ment such as, "That's the way to move your feet" or a "Now you're moving better," accompanied by a quick hand clap usually worked fine. (Note: this is different from simply saying "Move your feet" or "Your feet ar-en't moving.") I also checked to be certain my player was developing a good hitting rhythm.

- Also during warm-ups, I would look for any of the opponent's stroke weaknesses I might have missed—backhand volley, forehand out wide, and so on. When taking practice serves, I would ask my player to serve one out wide to the forehand, one tight into the body, and a kick up high to the backhand and note how well his opponent responded!

- Once a match started, I looked first at my player to be sure he was doing what I wanted. Then, once again, I continued to watch the opponent to see how he would handle certain shots—how he would return a wide serve to the forehand, a high kick serve to the back-hand, a serve and volley point where the serve was in tight to his forehand, and so on. (I might even ask my player to try any of these to see how his opponent responded.) If he was very fast from the backcourt and good out wide, we might attack more down the middle to nullify his speed and cut down his angle of return. If he attacked and volleyed well to the angles, we might direct more passing shots at his body.

- I was always aware of the tempo of the match. Should my player slow it down and take more time, or should he attempt to speed things up to break the tempo?

- I watched to see if our original game plan was working. If not, I would tell my player what to try/do next.

- As the match neared conclusion, I watched carefully to see if my player unconsciously was changing his style of play, which usually manifests itself by waiting for his opponent to lose.

- I also watched to see if my player would start to lose focus, which meant he probably was thinking ahead of himself—how good it would feel to win, and so forth. Usually this was a simple fix. Instead of saying "concentrate," I might tell him where to serve the next point or tell him what to do on the return—play down the middle, attack, and so on.

How beautiful it was to see a player—usually in college, about midway through his second year—start to do what you were about to tell him to do *before* you could tell him yourself! This meant he finally understood what you had been preaching, especially about being aggressive *and* feeling confident enough to do it.

"By far the most helpful thing I learned was staying aggressive, taking it to the opponent," says Alex Kim, '01, who went from playing number five or six as basically a backcourt player to becoming the NCAA singles

**Alex Kim: Team Captain;
NCAA Singles Champion;
World Singles #106**

champion as a serve and volley player two years later. *"Coach's famous phrase, 'Show me!' was the cue to being aggressive, especially on a second serve return. I remember one time I didn't serve and volley during a doubles match. During the point, I could see in my peripheral vision his flabbergasted reaction from the bench. That was the last time I served and stayed back in a doubles match!"*

I didn't always stay on the sidelines. I would regularly go onto the court to tell a player what to do or to try. It was not unusual for me on a changeover to take a seat courtside with my player and ask him what *he* thought. Remember, I'm watching at least three matches (six matches before I had an assistant coach) at once. This was important because maybe I had missed a service break while watching another court. In this case I might ask, "How were you broken?" to get a point-by-point account. I learned quickly where I should be directing most of my attention at any one time, but I would still miss things, especially when two players reached a critical point in their respective matches simultaneously.

Although trying different things is often necessary in a match, one never knows for sure whether it will work until it's tried. This being said, simple strategies seemed to work best for most. This is in fact the term John Letts, '86, uses to describe my approach: *"Simple strategies! Coach instilled confidence in each and every one of his players their ability to bring out their best when it counted. His coaching advice would be simple."*

Because of the nature of the player he was, I had a particular simple strategy for David Wheaton, '91. In his words, *"One of my enduring memories of Coach is the advice, actually the command, he would give during a match as he sat in the changeover chair on the side of the court. At some tense moment I would look over at him for counsel. With one hand cupped around his mouth and the other pointing to the net, he would invariably mouth: 'Get in!' Mind you, the direction did not waver—it was 'get to net' after my first serve, 'get to net' after my second serve, 'get to net' after returning serve . . . just 'Get in NOW!'"*

The worst thing is never to try something different if what one is doing as a player or coach or leader is not working. Again, you can't be afraid to fail. A suggestion doesn't always work, and a leader (and player) must be willing to accept this. If you are not thick-skinned, you should not be a coach. It is as impossible to be right all the time as it is to please everyone all the time! But a coach must also know when to back off.

In on-court coaching, I was basically playing the match with my player. Robert Devens, '94, gives an example of the type of coach–player collaboration I loved. *"Coach was incredible about picking up on (and cataloging) weaknesses of our opponents. My freshman year I played a match against a freshman at another Pac-10 school. In juniors, I had played the guy ten times and so felt I knew his game. After the warm-up, I went to my chair and Coach said, 'Okay, watch the backhand pass down the line, he doesn't like the slice, weak backhand volley, and make him beat you down the line on forehand side.' Coach had dissected the guy after a five-minute warm-up and gave me insights I did not have after ten matches in the juniors. Coach could spot a weakness a mile away."*

Unfortunately, today watching a tennis match and not being able to participate rarely gives me much pleasure. I've been spoiled by the opportunity to play the match with my players!

COACHING AND COMPETITIVENESS

Coach is the warmest person you will ever meet and also the most competitive person you will ever get to know. He can be one scary son of a bitch when he wants to be. I know that for a fact. Behind his unique ability to connect with someone, remember their name, remember their kid's names, and go out of his way to look them in the eye and welcome them, there was a fire burning that simply never went out. Coach wanted to win, not just today but every day and every year. It was uncanny. Some people have some of that. Coach had a different motor than anyone I've ever known. In the years since I left school, I've often joked that Coach would have been an incredible CEO as his ability to lead and sincerely connect was unlike anyone I've ever met!

—*Scotty (Hugh) Scott, '01*

Scotty's right, but today I've used up my jollies by coaching my players for forty-four years. Coaching tennis completely replaced my overall competitive desire. Everything I do from playing other sports to playing card games is now purely for recreation. I can appreciate a sport or activity for the intrinsic artistry of it. For instance, I would rather walk the golf course and take in the natural beauty around me than win the hole. People who have seen me coach or been my players probably would not believe me, but I honestly do not care who wins; I may now be the least competitive person there is.

Though as the coach on the court, it was a very different matter for me. I invested so much in my players that I *really* wanted them to succeed, and even more important, to feel good about themselves! This feeling made a very big impact on me! Their success was my responsibility! When you care about someone, you want to see their hard work pay off. You want to see them satisfied and happy with their performance. And this is, once again, the collaborative approach to competition that I love.

At the same time, your competitiveness cannot be allowed to overwhelm your care and concern for the player himself. I hope I never did that. *"I think Coach is one of the most competitive people I have ever met,"* adds NCAA doubles finalist and world doubles #1 and singles #36 Jonathan Stark, '93. *"But he had an amazing ability to separate the competitive with the coaching and mentoring aspects. I think my biggest takeaway is that I never felt tons of pressure to win for him. Coach wanted us to have fun while becoming better tennis players. This made it easier to play our best for him."*

In short, a coach's job is to be certain the players are prepared and able to execute anything he asks them to do. I trusted that I had earned enough respect that they would give what I asked an honest try.

All this being said, I had to teach my guys to never be satisfied; that individually and collectively, they can always do more. They must realize that there are always more mountains to climb. The bar can always be raised higher. *"After beating Georgia in Los Angeles in the finals in 1997, all I wanted to do was to hug the trophy,"* remembers Bob Bryan, '00. *"At that moment, it was the greatest day of my life. I couldn't believe we were national champions. I was relieved, tired, elated, so many emotions were flying through me. Coach Gould told me to take the trophy back to my hotel room, sleep with it, but then when I woke up in the morning, we would start our quest for next year's championship. Champions don't rest on their laurels. They find the next mountain to climb."*

That was our plan, our protocol, for continuing to win after a victory. Enjoy the feeling for a bit, then immediately focus on the future, on the next success, on the next championship. But if there was a protocol to winning, there was a similar protocol for losing: sit with it (just like with winning), feel it deeply, and then look ahead.

SUMMARY ON COMPETING

We all have a tendency to play safe, to become content with habits that make us feel good and that are easy. Coach Gould forced me out of my comfort zone.

—Bob Bryan, '00

Relishing a challenge often means overcoming our fear of trying. Finding a way means not knuckling under to sometimes overwhelming circumstances. First-strike tennis means being aggressive, even when being tentative feels safer. Accepting coaching means being open to input when your impulse is to do it by yourself. And being a competitor means overcoming the habit of resting on your laurels or wallowing in defeat and instead looking ahead to the next challenge.

All these elements of competing have one thing in common: not only are they often difficult, but they are very often counterintuitive, and as such, they all, at some level, involve a degree of discomfort. My job is not to make it easy, but to push players into these areas. Often only by being in a situation with some regularity do we begin to feel more comfortable with it. Bob Bryan clearly learned to push himself all the way into becoming a world champion with more doubles titles than anyone ever, except for his brother, Mike. (Bob was injured for part of a year, and Mike won a couple of majors with a different partner while Bob was recovering.)

If a coach's job description can be put into several salient nutshells, that's certainly one of them. Consistently forcing yourself, your players, and your team out of everyone's comfort zone is not just important for playing tennis, or any sport, or any endeavor, it's also critical for both the coach and the players if they are to win championships, and for anyone who wants to reach their potential and succeed beyond what they thought possible.

Chapter Nine

BALANCE

There needs to be a balance in everyone's life . . . a balance that gives you enough personal time away from the pressure and monotony of your job or sport (Coach encouraging us to be a part of the fraternity gave us this), and a balance in your job or sport that is intertwined with laughter, hard work, passion, and competition.

—Scotty (Hugh) Scott, '01

Balance in one's life is so very important. While most of us have many interests, we often find it hard to prioritize them. Work, such as coaching, is one example. If we give all our time to any job, let alone a sport, it's hard to be a great parent or spouse. If we give parenting our complete attention, we might not keep our job. The same applies if we are the best spouse we can be. Careers are important, but other things are important as well. There must be a balance in life!

This chapter deals with how we tried to accomplish it with Stanford tennis. It may require out-of-the box thinking to apply to your own situation and look a lot different, but it is also scalable. I am convinced it is worthy of your full consideration. I let the examples speak for themselves while recognizing that every situation is different and that some would not be appropriate in today's world or with certain groups. I always tried to convey this by word and example to my players.

Steve Winterbauer, '83, recalls the message clearly. *"Coach showed me that one's career is very important, but it is not one's life. My sense was that he was very driven and ambitious about his career, but far from consumed by it. It did not define him. I always felt there was Dick Gould the tennis coach and Dick Gould the person. They were remarkably similar to be sure. But they were distinct. This is important in any profession, including mine—law. Much is out of my control. I can construct a sound defense, make strong opening and closing arguments, present material evidence, basically make all the right moves—and still lose. There is a certain foundational security one needs as a person, lest he find himself constantly experiencing alternately crushing lows and exhilarating highs as a lawyer. Being comfortable and distinct as a person allows me to be steadier and more effective as a lawyer."*

We always hear the phrase, "Be the best you can be!" While noble, this is totally unrealistic. It must be modified to: "Be the best you can be, commensurate with how much you are able and willing to put into doing so!" As a coach, all I had to do was keep reminding myself of my own struggles as a college student to balance tennis, studies, and my social life; naturally, I carried this personal struggle over into my coaching career. I could not forget, therefore, that my guys were college students, like I had been, who were experiencing more freedom than ever before and facing a variety of competing priorities at the same time. I truly felt they had to have the freedom to make decisions for themselves and to experience the consequences. Of course, one priority was to not let their teammates down.

"The best teams," advises David Hauser, '00, who also applies ideas about balance to his career as an engineering executive, *"are the ones who always put in the time and effort and can turn up the dial around deadlines and milestones, but at the same*

time make sure to balance family, sleep, etc., along with dedicated times for strategic thinking where we take a break from the day-to-day grind."

One of the most important things to recognize and remember is that at Stanford, one is there to be a student first. Because of the academic demands, this is especially relevant with pre-med students, of whom I have had many on my teams. Geoff Abrams, '00, currently the director of sports medicine at Stanford, calls it *"a culture of athletic success, but not at the expense of academics,"* and relates a story by way of example. *"I was upset about a poor performance on a chemistry test and came to practice one day upset. Coach Gould and Coach Whit had the perspective that I would not be productive that day (or would distract the team); that if I missed a practice, it would not affect my athletic performance. Coach sent me back to the dorm to recover. He also allowed me to modify some of my afternoon practice schedule to allow for an occasional conflicting class."*

The number one ranked player in college tennis during most of his sophomore year and an NCAA doubles champion, K. J. Hippensteel, '02, was also a pre-med student. *"No matter my successes, Coach always pushed me and never let me rest on my laurels,"* he describes. *"After becoming number one in the nation my sophomore year, I had to take pre-med labs my junior year and miss two days of practice a week, and he never gave me difficulty for this. My game suffered that year accordingly, but I appreciated that he understood I was at Stanford not just for tennis but also for academics."*

FRESH AND FUN

December 6, 1973

Dear Mr. Hefner,

I am bringing my national championship tennis team to Los Angeles to play USC and UCLA the 1st weekend in April. I have seen pictures of your beautiful court at the Playboy Mansion. I ask if you would care to have us play an exhibition and intermingle with your guests on the Sunday following our Friday–Saturday intercollegiate matches. I look forward to hearing from you.

Sincerely,
Dick Gould
Men's Tennis Coach
Stanford University

***

February 20, 1974

Dear Mr. Gould:

Thank you for your letter of December 6 to Mr. Hefner. I have discussed with Mr. Hefner the possibility of yourself and the Stanford tennis team taking a tour of the Mansion West and he said that he would be pleased to have you, although he could not personally attend. If it is convenient for you, we would like you and the team to come to the Mansion on Sunday, April 6 during the day for a small luncheon and a tour of the grounds. Mr. Hefner also thought it might be fun if your team could put on a short doubles demonstration with some of our guests at the Mansion who are tennis players. Please let me know your thoughts on this and if it would at all be possible.

I would appreciate it if you could contact me either by letter or telephone to let me know your exact plans so that we can make arrangements with our staff. I am looking forward to hearing from you in the near future and to meeting you and your team.

Sincerely,
Les Marshall
Assistant to Mr. Hefner

Having fun was really important to me. Basically, it was meant to lessen the pressure and to teach that winning a match was not the most important thing in the world. But as one reads this, one must understand that I coached in a different era—some of the things we did to lighten the mood could not be done in today's world! I truly felt my players were in college to study and enjoy the total college experience, but when one adds in the requirements and additional stress of competing on an athletic team, it becomes critical to offer some outside fun experiences. I had written Hugh Hefner because a monthly tennis magazine I read always featured a private home tennis "Court of the Month." One of these was the especially beautiful court at the Playboy Mansion near UCLA. When I received the response, my reaction was, "If it is convenient?" Are you kidding me? I couldn't write the acceptance letter fast enough!

We set our visit date for Sunday after playing UCLA and USC on Friday and Saturday respectively. However, we got a late start playing UCLA on Friday due to wet courts. Since UCLA had no lights, our dual match was stopped because of darkness with Stanford leading 3–1 in singles. We would normally finish the match on Sunday, but with the Playboy Mansion visit on tap, there was no way this was going to happen. I offered my athletic director a very feeble excuse for not being able to complete the match on Sunday, and the experience proved to be a day not to be forgotten, which Tim Noonan, '75, world #187, captures well. *"Jim Delaney and I played an exhibition with Bill Cosby and Jimmy Boyd, who is the guy who sang, 'I Saw Mommy Kissing Santa Claus' at the Playboy Mansion. This turned out to be the day of the 'Bunny of the Year' contest. We spent time in the game room shooting pool and playing pinball and hanging out by the pool with all the visiting bunnies. We even took a hot tub in the famous grotto before we left. At one point, through a doorway, I saw Hef's outstretched legs, in pajamas and slippers, extending out from a chair he was sitting in, but he never made an appearance. It was, to say the least, not an experience I had anticipated when thinking about my college career!"*

The grotto to which Tim refers was a cave constructed under a hill with swim-in access from the pool, featuring three different-sized hot tubs, pillows, mood lighting, and music. It was almost my undoing. After a great lunch and our exhibition and tour, I returned to the grotto for a soak. No one was present, so I promptly stripped down to nothing and hopped into one of the tubs. As fate would have it, in walked a couple of young ladies who removed their robes to reveal bikinis. They entered an adjacent tub and began discussing their day. I was stuck! Then Tim and a couple other of my guys finally entered the spa. When they realized my predicament of being in my "birthday suit," they cracked up. Now they had me. They were relentless in encouraging me to get out of the tub. Finally, I asked the gals to look the other way, and I quickly dressed and barely escaped.

There were many, many other memorable side trips, albeit less high profile than the Playboy Mansion, that we took over the years.

"I still vividly remember the team's trek to Pebble Beach to play the Pebble Beach All Stars in 1969," writes Alex McGilvray, '71, *"and us being honored at the dinner/dance/fashion show after the matches. Paul Marienthal in his Roman toga played the flute at the fashion show and followed the models into their dressing room (and stayed in there for an extraordinary amount of time)."*

Tim Noonan, '75, remembers the Pebble Beach exhibition this way: *"Rick Fisher and I were scheduled to play an exhibition with some celebrities and were changing in the Pebble Beach locker room. The latest Dirty Harry movie had just come out, and we got to talking with some guy on the other side of the lockers about it. We were saying how great Eastwood was in it, and this guy kept saying Eastwood couldn't act, had the same squint all the time, etc. etc. Fortunately, we kept defending Eastwood's performance and telling this guy to go see the movie, because when he came around the locker it was . . . Clint Eastwood, grinning. Or squinting. 'Oh,' said Fish. 'I guess you've seen it.' We then proceeded to play the exhibition with Dirty Harry and a couple of others."*

Most of the extracurricular and fun team trips we took were close to home or tacked onto existing schedules and involved some degree of ingenuity as we had a very meager travel budget. Many of these were one-offs or only occurred for a couple of years. At one of our NCAA championships in Georgia, for example, our host family was joined by the great country singer, Kenny Rogers, who was serving as a visiting team cohost, which happened to be Stanford. Kenny invited us to visit his ranch spread just outside Athens. But the only time it would work for all was on the day before the start of the tournament. How could I turn down the opportunity for my players to play on his home personal golf course, to ride his four-wheelers around his lake stocked with bass and alongside his incredible Arabian horses, as well as spend some time in his home with his beautiful wife, Marianne, as our hostess?

After a full season of hard work, I did not feel missing two hours of practice time would have any negative effect on our performance.

We all loved this experience, and it perfectly set a relaxed tone for entering the serious competition. To that point, Glenn Solomon, '91, recalls, *"Coach did a great job of not overworking us and getting too intense before it really mattered. He had us prepared but loose before the NCAAs each year. That one time when we skipped practice the day before the NCAAs started to go to Kenny Rogers's house is a good example. No other coach would've done that, but it kept us loose and fresh."*

We were invited on several occasions by Notre Dame's great coach, Bobby Bayliss, to play them in their indoor tennis complex on the Friday night before the Stanford–Notre Dame football game the next day. Not *all* of us saw Stanford football come back to win on one of these trips: in the fall of 1990, Jared Palmer and Jonathan Stark had partied heavily following the match with their friends on the Notre Dame team the night before the football game! Our football team was way behind at halftime, and as a result, Jared and Jonathan left the game early. I actually tripped over them sleeping on the lawn just outside the stadium at game's end. When I woke them, they sheepishly asked, "Who won?" I was determined not to tell them that Stanford had come back to score an incredible victory!

"The social part of the team was so important," adds Charles Hoeveler, '98. *"We had way more fun than any other team, and prospective recruits could see that."*

My general philosophy centered around the feeling that if I were with my guys as much as possible, I would have a great feel for what was going on and could exercise more control of the situation. I am sure we pushed the envelope at times with off-court activities. And in fairness, it was a different era. But what we did was all in good fun, and we emerged relatively unscathed.

Relaxing off court, as Eric Wente, '73, notes, didn't always have to involve special trips to unusual locales with celebrities; sometimes they were just weekend outings around Stanford. *"Having fun together helped relax the team, so Friday afternoon golf on occasion, as well as the odd pitcher on Friday afternoon, were important. Tennis is generally an individual performance sport, but Coach was able to instill a sense of team. A couple of players played to a much higher level each year as part of the team than their summer performance would have led one to believe."*

Michael Flanagan, '94, has his own stories. *"Some of the ones I remember the best and enjoyed the most were the trips to the Dutch Goose after a round of golf during spring break for beers and deviled eggs. These were low-key events where we got to know each other better as well as our boosters. I really enjoyed all our team outings."*

Having fun like this also helped me project a certain looseness into our daily routine and convey that playing tennis was more than grind, grind, grind! This also made all that we did both on and off the court more enjoyable to me personally. There was plenty of time to be serious. *"I absolutely loved how loose and fun Coach Gould was,"* Paul Galichia, '96, says. *"He was never wound tight, and he didn't want his players tight either. The guy was having a blast, and it was infectious."*

In general, I felt it was a much better approach to give my players a lot of freedom rather than to have strict team rules I might not be able to enforce. How could I enforce a no drinking rule when as soon as these guys left practice and went back to the dorm or frat house they could pretty much have a beer, party, and do as they wanted? Basically, all they were told was to not embarrass themselves, their family, their team, or their university. In retrospect, at least with the general concept, I think we were right on, and I feel this philosophy was an important ingredient to our success.

As previously noted, the implementation of Title IX in Stanford athletics in the fall of 1975 had the effect of putting women's sports on equal footing with men in terms of scholarships, money, equipment, and so on. In the wake of that ruling, my wife-to-be Anne was named the Stanford women's coach. We immediately merged the men's and women's team activities and functions. This included fun trips, kids' community clinics, spring break practices, mixed matches, team banquets, and even combined media guides and composite team schedule posters and schedule cards. A season ticket for tennis was issued for *all* tennis matches. Coach Frank Brennan and I continued this practice when he took over the reins of the women's program from Anne. In fact, it changed the social aspect and dynamics of team functions for the better.

My guys relished this joint participation/responsibility, which really served to create one large team, with the sharing of fundraising efforts and other benefits. As Michael Flanagan, '94, points out, *"One component that I thought was great was that most of the off-court outings involved the women's team as well. It was great to get to form such a close bond with them, and this helped motivate us all toward achieving greatness as well since the women's teams were also winning national championships each year. Of course, probably the best outing of the year was after NCAAs to measure our championships ring size at Zott's. (Zott's—Rossotti's Alpine Inn—a historic family pub in Portola Valley behind the campus, with a great outdoor picnic area immediately adjacent to a creek)."*

I also felt that it was important for these guys to see more of the immediate area around Stanford during their time here than simply the campus itself, or what the local beer and burger joints had to offer! The adjacent foothill nature preserves all had great hiking trails. Thus, the "nature walk"! During spring break and often after two-a-day practices, we would meet in the foothills immediately behind campus for a late-afternoon hike on local park land through the beautiful redwood forests and streams on great trails. Most guys hated this. David Martin, '03, even refers to them as *"infamous."* Afterward, we would meet at a family pub for burgers and refreshments. Fortunately, no one broke a leg chasing after a deer, stepped on a rattlesnake, or received a bad case of poison oak.

Underlying all this activity is one central philosophy: never fail to think outside the box to make something possible—in this case, fun and unique experiences! Perhaps one of the best examples of this occurred when we were invited several years in a row to play in a tournament in Reno, Nevada—about a six-hour drive over the Sierra Mountain range from Stanford, and a trip that no one wanted to make in the winter in a car or van. Plane fares were out of the question. Adidas sponsored the tourney, and if we could figure out a way to get there, our rooms were comped, several meals were included, and the guys would receive free admission to great stage shows—*fun*! How could we not participate?

Our challenge was the cost of our transportation. The creative solution was to meet at the Stanford Shopping Center bus stop (on campus) to board the local commuter to the San Francisco transportation hub for fifty cents each. There we transferred to the "Gambler's Special" bus bound for a casino adjacent to our hotel. Not only was this bus trip free, but each player got a coupon for a free breakfast and a coupon worth ten dollars for poker chips. I collected all the poker chip coupons, and upon arrival took them to the casino cashier and turned them in for cash, which provided enough money for dinner for one night for each player. The players did use the second coupon for breakfast. This turned out to be an event we looked forward to each year.

Sometimes I knew to find an excuse to *not* be present and—like Sergeant Schultz on the old *Hogan's Heroes* TV show—*"know nothing"* about an event. The Zete Beer Tennis event was one of them. Most of my guys were in the same fraternity—the same one I was in as a student. The frat was always stretching the boundaries, and this impromptu event became a legend of sorts. *"How can I forget Zete Beer Tennis?"* laughs John Whitlinger, '76. *"It's hard to describe all the fun that was had on the courts. It's still something my frat brothers talk about."*

One time much later, as my successor Whit and I were talking about Zete Beer Tennis, he remarked, "It's good you weren't there!" Evidently, each fraternity member who was on the tennis team (and most of the team were proud members of the Zeta Psi fraternity) was in charge of a court. Every time one of the frat brothers hit a good shot, as determined by the court captain (tennis team member), a cup of refreshment had to be downed. At the end of the afternoon, most kegs were empty. I'm sure Whit also had to consciously not attend a few of these events when he was appointed head coach!

I was also a party to many of the good times, another of which Coach Whit recalls: *"I remember the Frog Pond Lounge at our 'go to' hotel, the Ramada Inn in Athens. I always booked the same rooms every year, 523–530 facing the hill in back. Those rooms worked out well. The Frog Pond Lounge needs no explanation."*

While I made a point of skipping the Zete Beer Tennis, I did put in a few "after practice/competition" hours at the Frog Pond Lounge along with my other pals in coaching. So did Whit when he came in to coach. We both should have owned stock in that lounge!

We all shared so many wonderful and unique experiences together, but I was always struck by how positive my guys were regarding what I would call "duties"—participation in out-of-practice events, many related to fundraising, which for the most part, participation was highly recommended. These provided great "touches" with our community, and the benefits from of our fans actually getting to know the members of our team were tremendous. It absolutely helped to build a great following, which worked both ways.

One of the biggest fund- and fan-raisers was the Silver Bucket Champagne'ships. The genesis of this event occurred when I co-founded the Los Altos Tennis Patrons Association (LATPA) in 1964 while serving as a club teaching professional. We needed to raise extra money to help our top juniors and non-income producing young adults (college students) travel in the summer. I had heard about a popular adult doubles social tourney in Pasadena in Southern California held mostly on private courts—the "Wretched Round Robin" fundraiser. I thought maybe we could do an adaptation of this concept on the mid-Peninsula, as there were many private home tennis courts sprouting up. I presented this to our LATPA board, and they agreed to give it a try. The first year or so it was a mammoth effort to even locate twenty-five or so private home courts in the immediately adjacent communities. And then we had to get the court owners to agree to give up their court for one Saturday for the first day of the two-day event. One good result was that suddenly I had a lot of new court-owner friends and potential supporters of my college tennis programs.

My players were to contact the homeowners to arrange a time to go to their assigned court the week of the tourney and clean/wash it. The day of the event we met at six o'clock in the morning at my office for final instructions. The team then carpooled to their respective courts with a case of champagne and packaged hors d'oeuvres for each of three flights of play. Their primary job was to be certain each of these three flights (comprised of doubles only; four teams; twelve players) finished on time (three hours of play), and that each flight was served an equal amount champagne (not to exceed four bottles) and snacks. I frankly was amazed at how my guys bought into such things in an effort to help the program! Craig Johnson, '76, remembers:

"Fundraisers for the team like the Champagne'ships were just one of many unique and fun ways to get Coach's players involved in 'selling' the idea that Stanford tennis was building national champions. Each of us had a responsibility to be a part of what it took off the court financially to keep that going! All of these events and ideas had the impact of creating teams that truly played together both on the court and off. In a way, that illuminated year in and year out an atmosphere and picture for the next generation of junior players of a place and environment in which they could take their tennis careers to the next level AND have the time of their lives doing it."

From its modest beginning, the Champagne'ships grew quickly, and the last year I ran this event there were 1,200 entries and we used forty-four private home tennis courts. I enjoyed hearing the stories the Stanford team court captains (managers/hosts for the entire day at each court) returned to tell. Paul Marienthal, '71, jokes, *"Those crazy Champagne'ships! Utterly hilarious watching the drunk mixed doubles matches. One of these was held at the court of Dr. Arthur Kornberg, a Nobel Prize-winning biologist, and I was assigned to be the Stanford player host. He was such a nice person. He came out to talk with me, and helped me with my homework, which I was trying to do in between pouring champagne!"*

"Everybody was in charge of an individual private court," says team captain, NCAA singles semifinalist and pro #113, Rick Fisher, '73, and then goes on to spill the beans about something I never knew about. *"I remember we reported back to the courts when we finished at the end of the day. We were supposed to bring back all the unused champagne bottles to Dick in the old shack. Paul Sidone and I sat outside his office and told the team newcomers that 'We'll collect those. They go in these boxes here and you can go in and report to Coach.' We ended up getting a whole case of champagne. Dick never knew."*

These are only a few of the many creative enterprises, none of which we could have participated in if they would cost our budget any money. Bill Maze, '78, reminisces:

"Coach created unity with all the fun road trips and events that he invented, besides the usual team trips to play other schools. The Champagne'ships, exhibitions, Playboy Mansion West, Ojai, the National Team Indoors at Madison, WI . . . the list goes on. So many things happen while traveling together that great bonds are created like the trip Coach and I took to Washington, DC for me to play in a mixed match with Lele Forood (now longtime women's coach). She and I beat Stephanie Tolleson and Bill Scanlon to win it, I believe."

Bill is right. That was a great trip and included a VIP personal tour of the White House, including the Oval Office.

THANKSGIVING WEEK TRIPS

Coach brought us to Hawaii during Thanksgiving, and we had a great time. We would help the coaches teach some of the boosters who came with us. We'd go out on the island of Hawaii, and we'd go all over the island with friends, including one of the top amateur players, Professor Michael Boskin, who is a world-renowned economist. We went on a hike through this mountain, which was the rainiest spot in the world. I remember a few of us went on a helicopter over the mountains. And the experience of being in Hawaii as a team, not competing, but teaching at the beginning part of the day and experiencing the island in the afternoon, was a lot of fun. I remember those times in Hawaii with great fondness.

—Jimmy Gurfein, '81

When I was a member of the team at Stanford, we played in maybe twelve to fifteen matches and two tournaments a year—the Northern California Intercollegiate Championships in February and the Ojai Championships (to which we drove for six hours) the end of April. I enjoyed practice and matches, but that was all the college athletic experience was. By about 1969 or 1970, I had come to feel that there could, and should, be more!

My first thought was to place my men's team on a cruise ship. I would give a lecture or two to the guests, and my team would help me give clinics to those on board on stops along the Mexican Riviera. In return, we would receive our onboard cabins and meals. I felt the guys would enjoy this as a break in their monotonous practice schedule and that it would serve as a good bonding experience.

Princess Cruises made regular stops in San Francisco before heading to the Mexican Riviera. I called Princess and presented my proposal to them. On the phone, they verbally said it was a great idea and that they would like to do it. They asked me to provide dates, which I did in a subsequent letter. I stated we would be available over Christmas vacation or perhaps Thanksgiving week. The reply came back that they were excited, but could not do this over heavy vacation periods, as the ship was always filled then. Same for the summer months. That ended this thought.

My next idea was to arrange a trip to Hawaii—my players were from all over the United States, and few had ever visited the Hawaiian Islands. We certainly had no team budget for that type of trip, so it would have to be self-sustaining. In December of 1972, Pan Am Airways agreed to donate ten seats from San Francisco to Hawaii (Oahu) over our Christmas break for our team. This accounted for free airfare for eight players, my wife, and myself.

Now we had to find a place to stay. I had heard about a brand-new Sheraton hotel right in the center of Waikiki Beach. When I called the hotel, they referred me to their manager. It turned out he happened to have been a recent captain of the Michigan State tennis team. He said he would give my team, my wife, and me free rooms for the week if we could bring some guests to help fill the new hotel. I said I would try. (This is also the reason Pan American agreed to the free air for my wife, myself, and eight players.) I promptly sent a letter to our growing list of "Friends of Stanford Tennis" announcing this trip and inviting them and their families to accompany us. We had a great response, and a sizable travel party, so now our hotel rooms were secured.

We still needed a way to fund our major meals. I talked to a couple of my tennis-playing buddies on the island of Oahu, and a sixteen-person all-island tournament was suggested—eight Hawaiian "all-stars" versus eight Stanford players. As it developed, the four quadrants of the tourney were held in four different locations over a couple of days. In each location—Kailua Racquet Club, Diamond Head Tennis Center, and so on—the players would be treated to lunch and a big evening barbecue. The semifinals and finals were played in the McKinley High School gymnasium, on wood, in Honolulu. The newspaper picked up on this, and it became a big deal. Between this and a couple of travel group dinners, our major meals were now assured.

As a sidelight, I wanted my team to experience another island for a couple of days. My friend and early mentor, John Gardiner, proprietor of John Gardiner's Tennis Ranch in Carmel Valley, came to my rescue. He had just taken over the tennis concession at the new Royal Lahaina Hotel in Maui. He arranged for free room and board at the hotel in exchange for an exhibition and a clinic given by the team for hotel guests, so this is where we spent Christmas Eve and Christmas Day before returning home.

It was a great team bonding experience and a fantastic trip at no cost to our athletic department nor our program. Furthermore, we never had a team practice—I just wanted the guys to have a blast together, and they did. It was so successful that I began planning what to do next.

My best friend, Tom Chivington, had taken over my coaching duties at my former school, Foothill College. Together, we went to another friend who was a travel agent to help us figure how we could get both of our teams to Hawaii, but this time during Thanksgiving week. Our travel agent negotiated for free rooms and court time for our teams at a new development on the island of Kauai—the Kiahuna Plantation. This was based on bringing a certain number of paying guests with us. We decided that if Tom and I staged a daily morning clinic for our guests, which featured hitting with our respective team players, we could charge our guests a fee that would cover our airfare. In addition, we would put on an exhibition for the resort guests. Our travel agent printed a flier announcing the trip, which he, Tom, and I widely distributed. It worked—we got enough people to sign up and were on our way! The teams "worked" for their vacation on the court practicing with our guests from 8:00–12:00 each morning. This was in the fall of 1975 and set the stage for subsequent annual Thanksgiving trips throughout my coaching tenure.

Beginning in 1976, Anne and I took both our men's and women's teams and guests on these Thanksgiving week trips. We never took fewer than our projected starting lineups, and often—depending on how many guests signed up and paid the clinic fee—our participation would include almost every player on our teams. It was not unusual for our travel party to include 125 players, coaches, and guests. The format remained the same—a morning clinic for guests led by the coaches and with team "hitting" participation. Then time off for the team with complete freedom after the clinic ended each day at noon until 8:00 a.m. the next morning. They had a blast!

"The Thanksgiving trips were great," recalls Scott Moody, '87, *"because how many kids from New York get to go to Hawaii on break? This was another example of Coach's out-of-the box think-*

Typical Thanksgiving trip turnout of over 100 friends

ing and 24-7 fundraising and program building!"

My next thought was to expand on this experience. I decided to use the same format but take the team to a different location in each of their four years at Stanford. For several years, we alternated annually between one island in Hawaii, the Mexican Riviera, a different island in Hawaii, and then the Caribbean. Our travel guest pool remained strong, and they really enjoyed getting to know our players so intimately and in an informal situation. These were among the first people I would approach for funding requests. It was standard procedure at this time each year to announce to our travel party some project we were preparing to undertake to better our program or facility. I always invited anyone who might be interested in supporting such to contact me for more information.

"Clearly, the Thanksgiving trips—for me the highlights were the Bahamas, Hawaii, Mexico, and Hawaii again," adds Team captain Mark McKeen, '84. *"I can still remember those trips and the wonderful alums/people on them—great moments in time. And, on the first Hawaii trip (during my sophomore year), we had* Sports Illustrated*'s Walter Iooss photograph me, Scott Davis, Steve Winterbauer and a few others in tennis clothes for the* Italian Vogue *magazine—and I believe that I still have a copy of that* Vogue *somewhere! Love it."*

Unfortunately, NCAA regulations changed: no more "fun in the sun" vacations without playing an actual match! But when this rule change was announced, we had already booked our team and guests for a trip to Manzanillo. There were no college teams in the area, but technically the rules at that time did not specify we had to play a college team. The hotel tennis club assembled a team of locals and hotel guests, and we played the "Manzanillo All-Stars." When my athletic director found out what had happened, I "heard" about it and received an in-the-spirit-of-the-rules lecture in no uncertain words.

Subsequent to this, another even more restrictive rule was enacted. A team could not travel to a destination to play earlier than forty-eight hours ahead of time and had to leave thirty-six hours after the competition—not much time for fun. The exception to the rule, however, was travel either to Alaska or Hawaii, where schools in both states needed help in attracting teams to travel this distance to play. Thereafter, our trips were to an island in Hawaii. Thanks to a good friend and a graduate of the Stanford Graduate School of Education, University of Hawaii Coach John Nelson, the University of Hawaii teams would travel from Honolulu to play us at our island of choice on the final day of our trip. In return, we would host them on our schedule at home every other year. It was a win-win!

"Hawaii Thanksgiving trips were amazing," Alex Kim, '01, remembers. *"The islands themselves are amazing, but being able to not only bond with the team, but also bond with successful investors/entrepreneurs (like VC's Barr Dolan, Tim Draper, etc.) literally shaped my future career goals."*

The Hawaiian analog to the Frog Pond Lounge was the Hano Hano Room in the Sheraton Waikiki. I thought my guys were going to study because they'd say: "Coach, we're going to the Hano Hano Library to study." Roscoe Tanner, '73, remembers calling *"team meetings at the top of the Sheraton in the Hano Hano Room."* It took me almost a full week on our first trip to realize the Hano Hano Room was not a study hall, but the rooftop hotel bar, and the "librarian," the guy behind the bar, knew the whole team very well.

Scott Bondurant, '82, sums it all up very well. *"Playing touch football in Jamaica; hitting golf balls from the deck of our rooms into the ocean at Princeville, Kauai, Hawaii; playing bridge with patrons in Hawaii—little did I know that Andy Chase and I were playing with the lawyer and Stanford faculty member who oversaw the government break-up of AT&T, Professor Bill Baxter. And then getting caught in a riptide on Hanalei Beach and having Jeff Arons swim out to help me—two days later we found out that two people drowned there that day."*

Our trip to Jamaica was extra special to me for a couple of reasons. The club at Montego Bay had been a key stop on the Caribbean circuit before open tennis began, and I was always enthralled to read about all the great players who had competed there. But more important, I invited my eldest child—my tennis-playing daughter, Sue—to fly down from Princeton to join us for the week. This was a big thing for both of us as we really had spent no one-on-one time together since my marriage with her mother had broken up when Sue was sixteen years old. It was great to have her with us, and in addition, she knew many of my players from her junior playing days.

Another of the highlights was always Thanksgiving dinner with all our travel party. In this case, the Montego Bay Club agreed to stage a special dinner on the roof of one of their buildings. We were served a scrawny chicken in place of turkey and had fun staging crab races. All crabs had numbers painted on their backs. We put them in a can and emptied them in the middle of a chalk-drawn circle. Whichever crab made it out of the circle first was deemed the winner. I have conveniently forgotten what consti-tuted first prize!

OVERSEAS TRIPS

The Germany trip is one I will never for-
get. All those guys are my closest friends
to this day.

—Jonathan Stark, '93

Eventually, thanks to a former Stanford financial aid administrator, Ken Kaufman, we found several opportunities to go to
Europe. These international team trips were arranged to benefit
and promote his mentoring work with the John Ernest Foundation. Those journeys were all unique and incredible. Unlike the
Thanksgiving trips, none of these involved any tennis boosters.
Two were to Germany, and a third was to Switzerland. My basic
goal was to incorporate as many fun activities and visits to incredible places as possible, all the while playing as little tennis as
absolutely necessary.

"Germany," writes Alex O'Brien, '92, *"was off the charts. We*
learned about an amazing country and toured the countryside.
Jason Yee had a few too many large beers at Neuschwanstein
Castle. I also miss the art of the slow pour with warm beers back
in the day. The head of the beer had to come down before the bar-
tender could pour more."

The second trip to Germany in 1997 was aided by Nike, our
sportswear supplier, and led by their European rep at the time, one
of my former players, Dave Larson, '78. He reminisces: *"One*
of my best memories is when I helped Coach facilitate a trip to
Germany for his team twenty years after I graduated. We had a
team dinner in Heidelberg, which was truly a night of stories and

merriment. He was forever grateful, but I was the one who felt that I could finally give something back to the great program in which I was allowed to participate."

On this trip, among our visits was the college town of Heidelberg. We ended up in a college bar just off the main town square and had a great time. But this watering hole was special for me because Anne and I had visited it years before on a personal trip following a week of leading a group of Stanford alums to Wimbledon. For some reason, she remembers it far better than I. She was unable to accompany us on this second trip, but I did call home to her from this bar that night because it happened to be our twentieth wedding anniversary. Never forget the anniversary of you and your spouse, no matter where you are! It brought back great memories for both of us.

"The trip to Germany/Prague in '97 was an amazing time," Paul Goldstein, '98, says with a laugh. *"Going to that bar in Heidelberg. Walking around Prague with Misha Palecek's father. He was so proud to be showing Misha and his teammates post-Communist Prague for the first time."*

Neither of these trips were without challenges. Getting passports updated was one of them. I gave repeated warnings to the team about not only having passports but being sure they were in order. On the first trip, two of my most experienced world travelers due to their junior international travels—Jonathan Stark and Jared Palmer—went to show their passports to the airline ticket agent at the San Francisco airport and only then realized they had expired! Fortunately, it was before 9/11 and easier to quietly and quickly pass around passports during the group check-in with a very busy ticket agent, and we all got on board. But as soon as we landed, we made the trip to the American embassy to rectify the situation.

For the second trip, I again gave repeated warnings to the team to be sure their passports were updated, and all had the example of Palmer and Stark from five years earlier with expired passports ringing in their ears. My most traveled players were the Bryan brothers. But naturally, they forgot their passports. At group check in, we simply repeated our drill of five years earlier and kept the brothers in the back of the group. We passed other checked-in player passports back to them. The harried and hurried group check-in attendant just nodded when Mike and Bob held up the passports of one of the other guys, and they got their boarding passes without any problem. Fortunately, once again, on arrival the American embassy was able to help us out.

And then our trip to Switzerland in 2001! We boarded our flight to Zurich on a beautiful San Francisco day. But unbeknownst to us, some major international event occurred while we were in the air. Midflight, there was some confusion and anxiety exhibited by our cabin crew. When we landed and retrieved our bags, we were met by cameramen and newscasters. They all wanted to know what we thought. We had no idea what they were talking about. Then we noticed the airport television monitors. It turned out that we were the first flight to land from America after the 9/11 terrorist attacks had taken place while we were in the air. Our eyes stayed glued to CNN throughout the trip. *"I remember well our trip to Switzerland,"* recalls Scott Lipsky, '03, *"and especially remember getting off the plane just after the attacks on 9/11 and all the TV cameras in our faces when we landed. We had no idea what was going on with the Twin Towers,"*

Of all the things I have ever done as coach, perhaps the extra effort of organizing trips that would not be an expense to our athletic department, but which provided an outlet of fun for our players, were the best. Needless to say, these experiences were unique enough that they were extremely attractive to recruits. But the biggest lesson was about the importance of bonding, both within the actual team itself and between our players and guests. As David Martin, '03, says, *"Coach is a fun-loving person and a high-energy, positive coach. He created a sense of unity through events off the court like hosting barbecues at his house, team trips . . . even the dreaded 'fartleks' prior to NCAAs were an oc-*

casion. Coach drew us together by creating shared experiences off the court."

Whether Thanksgiving or overseas trips or outings in the San Francisco Bay Area, many lifelong friendships were formed through off-court activities. These relationships also resulted in greater attendance at our annual team dinner and matches, and even in significant financial donations to our program. The trips in particular turned out to be among our team's most meaningful experiences at Stanford and set us ever further apart from other programs. Even though the team usually had to be on court to help as hitting partners for a clinic as early 8:00 a.m. each morning and often spend an hour trying to dry wet courts due to rain, these trips proved to be among their most cherished memories. As such, I believe they provided an added dimension of both fun and education that was crucial to our success.

Chapter Ten

FLEXIBILITY AND RESILIENCE

FLEXIBILITY

From Vince Lombardi to Coach K, a lot of great football and basketball coaches have had a system that they used to develop their players and their teams. They recruit people who they think will work in their system, and if the player doesn't fit the system, too bad for the player. During the time when Coach coached tennis, if he wanted the best players and the best performance out of them, he couldn't have a cookie-cutter system approach. Not everyone will serve and volley (or be a baseliner). Not everyone will hit a two-handed backhand (or one-handed). So, in tennis you need to find a way to bring out the best from the players that you have. That's the Dick Gould system. That's the Dick Gould magic.

—Jim Miller, '82

Flexibility is an incredibly important trait for a leader in any field. It might be required in dealing with an individual or even by adjusting a company's own business plan. Nimbleness can be required. Never are things always the same, and while keeping within one's own personal parameters, the ability to adjust can lead to success or failure.

I have always felt that being flexible—being willing and able to adapt when the situation warranted—is a personal strength of mine and very important to our success as a team. I firmly believe that everyone is different, and to get the best out of my teams, players could not always be treated the same. This requires a different variety of management skills and a tolerance for fluidity because challenges, situations, and personnel are consistently changing.

"Dick's ability to work with a wide range of player personalities, often difficult ones, while keeping an ever-present positive outlook was absolutely unique," writes Mark Conroe, '80. *"While he had a firm hand on the team, he allowed players to express themselves in a way that worked best for them. This flexible approach allowed each player to be his best."*

John McEnroe presented me with one of my early challenges in being flexible because, as we all know, John certainly wasn't just another player, and as a result, the circumstances under which he entered his freshman year were unusual and required a very definite departure from the norm.

John had had a great summer on tour before his scheduled arrival for his freshman fall at Stanford. However, I was not completely certain whether or not he was accepting prize money, which would have rendered him ineligible for collegiate competition. When he called me from the airport to say he had arrived for fall quarter and asked if I could pick him up (which the rules allowed in those days), I said, only half-jokingly, "Mac, I thought you turned pro; I've given your scholarship away!" There was a moment of silence until I could not hold it anymore, and I started laughing.

My primary concern, however, stemmed from the fact that in the winter and spring of his senior year of high school and when his academic schedule permitted, he had played a lot of pro events as an amateur, which in collegiate tennis one can do as long as no prize money is claimed. Upon his high school graduation, he traveled directly to Wimbledon to represent the US in the junior event there, which would start the second week of the main tourney. John had done so well in the winter and spring pro tourneys that he had also been accepted into the Wimbledon qualifying event, which almost was as difficult to get into as the main draw.

Playing at Roehampton, the site of Wimbledon's qualifying, he won enough matches to actually make the men's draw, and then he *kept* winning throughout that first week. All of a sudden, it was time for the junior event to begin, but he was still in the men's tournament. Obviously, he dropped out of the juniors, and then famously went on to reach the men's semifinals. That was when I thought I might lose him—that he would never remain an amateur and matriculate at Stanford.

He continued to play throughout the summer with solid results. I'm not sure he ever took a week off, but I did feel he had overplayed, which might have led to him being stale and tired the following spring when I needed him to be at his best. I therefore decided—and this relates to flexibility—to give him the fall off. I told him I did not want to see him at the tennis courts until January. This was only the second time I had ever done this: Stanley Pasarell, my first full-scholarship player, reminded me that I had given him his first fall term off as well.

The fall season of competition was very light in those days, so John would not be missing any competition of great value. When I explained my decision to his teammates, no one complained in any way. To be totally truthful, I knew John was not a good practice player in the normal sense of the word. Rather, he improved by playing matches, so standard practice repetitions would be of limited value for him. He would quickly lose interest in months of practice without matches.

Michael Flanagan, '94, sums up the philosophy behind this approach: *"Coach did a masterful job of motivating players and knowing what each player needed to get the most out of his game. For some players and teams, he would apply pressure like challenge matches or be in their face about their performance. With some players and teams, he was very laid back and let the situation play out. He was always striving to get the very best out of each individual player."*

And that's what I was trying to do with Johnny Mac.

John was joining an outstanding defending NCAA championship team with a lot of returnees, including Matt Mitchell, the then-reigning NCAA singles champ; Bill Maze, a great player and longtime rival of Matt's in NorCal juniors; Perry Wright, a top player from Southern California, and several others. With the addition of John, I believed this would be one of the best teams we had ever had. My hunch was borne out when we completed that 1977–78 season undefeated and with all the four players—McEnroe, Maze, Mitchell, and Wright—ranked in the final top twelve collegiate national rankings. In addition, two other members of that team went on to be ranked in the top one hundred in the world in singles (Peter Rennert at #40 as well as #9 in world doubles, and in 1980 as the #1 college player in the nation, and Lloyd Bourne at world singles #73). It also included two other great players, team captain John Rast and Jim Hodges.

At the beginning of the season, this abundance of riches presented some challenges, starting with setting the lineup for our first real competition of the year—the ITA Division National Men's Team Indoor Championships in Madison, Wisconsin in February. In good faith, I felt I had to have John, Matt, and Bill play each other. I had to give both Matt, as the defending NCAA champ, and Bill a shot at number one. In these matches, Bill defeated Matt in three sets, and Mac defeated Matt and Bill, both also in three-set matches. So the top three spots were set, except that Perry Wright then upset Matt to start the season at number three. Matt, the defending NCAA singles champ, was starting the year as number four on the team!

Challenge matches are always stressful, but these were extreme. I remember it was raining on one of the match days, and I had left myself no wiggle room in which to complete the matches before leaving for the national indoor event. Thus, we played some of them at a nearby indoor facility. I will never forget my ride home at rush hour on the freeway in the rain with darkness falling. Johnny Mac was driving, and he was still so wound up, I thought he was going to run into someone or drive off the road. Fortunately for us both, we survived a harrowing thirty minutes.

When we arrived at the National Team Indoor Championships in Madison, Wisconsin, it was the first time I had seen Mac compete in person as a college player. What a great competitor! In addition, I quickly learned in those four days what a great team player he was. He often finished his match before many of his teammates. Before I could say or do anything, he would be on his teammate's court to congratulate him or console him. This revelation affected how I was to treat him in some trying moments later in the year at the NCAA championships. (Not surprisingly, in subsequent years he always answered the call when asked to represent his country in Davis Cup competition, no matter how exhausted he might have been. What an incredibly loyal person!)

I say, fondly, that I have had a lot of outspoken characters on my teams over the years, but none of them generated as many questions from tennis fans as John McEnroe. I love John. At that time, he was a young eighteen and a ton of fun to be around. For example, one night during the indoor tourney in Wisconsin, I was out a little late having some refreshments with my fellow coaching buddies. At two o'clock in the morning when I headed for my room, common sense dictated that I return inconspicuously via the fire escape stairway. But who did I run into? Here was Mac coming off the elevator at the other end of the hall after his own fun night on the town. And Madison is *fun*! Mac knew he was caught red-handed, and as we passed in the hallway, he wasn't sure what to say or do. I simply said, "It's a little late, Mac. Better hit the rack soon." He writes in one of his books that he thought that was pretty cool, but little did he know I needed in the worst way to hit the rack myself!

Dan Goldie: NCAA Singles Champion; World Singles #27

"I think one of Coach's greatest assets," says Dan Goldie, '86, NCAA singles champ and world pro #27, in summing up my approach to Mac and everyone else, *"was being able to understand each player's unique personality and needs. He was able to adjust his coaching and relationship style to get the most out of everyone and gain their respect. He tailored the art of coaching and development to fit the unique personality of each student. For me, it was positive encouragement, making me less serious, taking the pressure off, helping me enjoy my successes."*

Everyone always asks about Johnny Mac's behavior. I must say he really comported himself well almost all year. It was a foregone conclusion Mac would only complete his freshman year, but because of this, he put an immense amount of pressure on himself to cap off his one year in college as the NCAA singles champion. Wimbledon semifinalist or not, John would have to truly earn the NCAA singles title on the court because there was some great competition in the college ranks, from his lifelong nemesis, Larry Gottfried of Trinity, to future top ten player Eliot Teltscher of UCLA, and, among others—perhaps most of all—his own teammates! John knew this, and as the season wound down, I could literally see the self-imposed pressure building inside him!

The last regular season match was at home against Pepperdine. Their ace was a really nice guy and talented player from South

Africa named Eddie Edwards. Suddenly, it was as if the dam burst somewhere inside Mac, and with no provocation I could sense, he basically lost all composure playing Eddie. Because of the great year he had had, I chose to ignore it, and I don't think I ever mentioned it to him.

By the time we got to Georgia for the NCAAs, John was wound even tighter. Seemingly little things, such as a spectator talking too loudly or moving between points, would set him off. Our linesmen and chair umpires in those days were not trained and certified as professional umpires as they are today; they more often than not consisted of tennis fanatics, many of them University of Georgia professors who played tennis at lunchtime and local club members. With Mac seemingly itching for a fight in order to blow off steam, they were prime targets for his frustrations.

During the championships, he was less than a good citizen to the point where I eventually had a decision to make. Should I sit John or let him continue to play in the individual tournament following the team win. John had done so much for me and his teammates all year that I ultimately decided to stick with him. I also honestly felt that he would not learn any redeeming or lasting lesson if I pulled him from competition. Yet, here was a guy I *really* liked and cared about bringing the wrath of much of the crowd down on himself!

In one of the gutsiest performances I have ever seen—over eight days in ninety-degree heat and humidity, a total of eighteen matches with the last being three of five sets—Mac won the title. I was so proud of him! I have never met a fiercer competitor, and I have had many great ones. Although this book is intended to be about more than tennis, and although this is yet another tennis story, this feat was too amazing to omit here. It vividly describes how flexibility with a coach's personal values, this time relating to standards of behavior, can lead to an extraordinary effort and result.

BEST COMPETITIVE EFFORT EVER (FINAL MATCH OF JOHN MCENROE'S COLLEGE CAREER)

NCAA Championships
The Singles Finals—1978

Monday, May 29, 1978—Memorial Day: a day to remember the incredible efforts, feats, and costs of our worldwide Battle for Freedom! Celebrations with parades, backyard picnics, and barbecues. And also a day historically marked by great sporting events such as the Indianapolis 500 motor car races held since 1911. A newcomer to the crowded activities block was added in 1977 with the first combined NCAA Team and Individual Championships at Coach Dan Magill's great shrine to college tennis at the University of Georgia. The NCAA Men's Team Championship in 1978 was the second year of a true team championship.

I was the chauffeur for Peter Rennert and John McEnroe, who were in the back seat of our rental car in Athens, Georgia. Peter, John's teammate and best friend, was to give him a brief "loosen-up" hit prior to the final match of his collegiate season. We wove through the crowd to find a parking place. As we stepped out of the air-conditioned car, we were met head-on by a midday blast of boiling air. Not only was the temperature in the stifling nineties, but the humidity was almost unbearable.

This was to be John's eighteenth match in eight days—four days of singles and doubles in the Team Championship Monday through Thursday, in which John led us to victory. The team event was followed immediately on Friday by the Individual Championships with two singles matches. On Saturday, play consisted of two singles and a doubles match, then on Sunday one singles and two doubles. Finally on Monday, the final singles match. (John and his partner Bill Maze were defeated in the doubles semifinals the day before.) John didn't even have the chance to celebrate the team championship nor have any time between the two separate events to catch his breath and mentally regroup.

Understandably, John's back was starting to tighten, so in addition to the light hit-around with Peter, he also had a date with the trainer to put some heat on his back and have it stretched out. This was a legitimate concern. John's opponent in the finals was hard-serving John Sadri of North Carolina State. The Wolfpack did not qualify for the team event, so John Sadri was four days and eight matches fresher to start. In addition, he was playing at an extremely high level and had not lost a set on his march to the finals. Mac had been forced to three sets in the quarterfinals against Erik Iskersky of Trinity and again to three in the semifinals against teammate Bill Maze. He was exhausted, and by tradition, the finals were the best of five sets!

The style of play of each player was very different. Although both lived and died at the net, Mac relied on touch, soft hands, and a serve he used especially well—in this match, a wide left-handed slice to Sadri's backhand. The physically much stronger and bigger six-foot, two-inch, 180-pound Sadri bludgeoned the ball and had one of the hardest serves I had ever seen. He was to reach a world high of #14. In addition, the crowd loves the underdog and Mac had not done a lot to endear himself to the 3,500 fans present during the week. It would be like playing a second opponent!

It is now 11:00 a.m. and time for the match to start. Both players walk onto the court to the roar of the crowd in anticipation of a special match. The coaches, J. W. Isenhour of NCS and myself, follow, and we are probably as nervous as the players. All four individuals—the two players and coaches—are already sweating profusely from the oppressive heat and humidity. Hydration would be critical. This is no-ad, sudden-death scoring—the first player to reach four points wins the game. If the score reaches 6–6, a best of nine-point tie break is played to determine the set.

At 2–2 in the first set, Sadri draws first blood and breaks Mac's serve and has break points in a couple of other games to be on the verge of taking a commanding lead. But Mac fights them off and holds on to get to 3–5 and serve. Sadri has another break point, which is also set point. But Mac somehow battles back, finally breaks Sadri's serve to tie the score at 5–5. Both players hold serve to send the first set into overtime, and Mac escapes by winning a close tie break. Despite John McEnroe's fighting spirit, I know if he had lost this first set, he would face an almost insurmountable challenge based on what he had done the last eight days—his tank was almost on empty!

Mac had won that all-important first set 7–6 in over an hour—the first set Sadri had lost in the tournament! All the time I am asking the ball kids for dry towels and soaking them in my ice bucket to have them ready, wet, and cold on the changeovers, along with continually reminding John to drink plenty of water. There are no service breaks in the second set, and Mac again wins a 5–3 tie break for a 7–6, 7–6 lead. The third set goes to 5–5 on serve until Sadri finally earns the service break and serves out the set the next game. Both players leave the court at the ten-minute break for some shade and dry clothes. The score is 7–6, 7–6, 5–7. The heat has only gotten worse!

The fourth set starts almost four hours after the start of the match. Mac's back is starting to tighten up big time after the break. On every changeover, he must lie prone on his back and get stretched to the limit by the trainer. He is surviving on sheer determination and will to win! In my mind, however, there is no way he will be physically able to play a competitive fifth set—so it had better be *now* in the fourth! There had been only three service breaks in the first three sets, and there will be none in set four. The score reaches 6–6, and 3–3 in the tie break, Sadri's serve. He has the final three serves and has served twenty-four aces in the match so far (an average of one ace per serving game). He must only win two of the next three points to win the set and even the match at two sets all. McEnroe takes the next point for a 4–3 lead. Then a forehand passing shot by Mac wins it all, 7–6, 7–6, 5–7, 7–6 in an epic final.

John jumped for joy and hurled his racket into the net while coming forward to congratulate John Sadri on a great match. John McEnroe had won 144 points; John Sadri 143. That is exactly how close this match really was! John became the youngest NCAA singles champion to date. The crowd realized what they had witnessed and went crazy.

I believe I was just as exhausted as John, and I had done nothing. Mac was able to stay standing to accept the championship trophy presented by former Secretary of State Dean Rusk. As I sat on the bench during the awards cere-

John McEnroe: NCAA Singles Champion, NCAA Doubles Finalist; World Singles and Doubles #1

mony for the presentations to both players, I thought back to what a great team player and competitor John McEnroe truly is. He has the heart of a lion—few could have matched what he did over those eight days. Fortunately, the format was changed for the next year so that no one was asked to go through such a scenario again.

I think of how blessed I am to have been associated with John. I have had the pleasure of working with many great competitors, but none who could come through under pressure better than him. I guess that is why he soon became the world's #1 player.

I also had a fleeting moment of disbelief. I realized that was my fourth different NCAA singles champion in six years—this for a guy who did not even want to play tennis in his youth.

In retrospect, I am so glad I was flexible with my treatment of John! I was less mad at him than I was sad he could not quite complete such a great year without maintaining proper behavior on the court. I am certain he was bothered by this as well.

Subsequent players benefited from the lessons I learned—some of them from Mac—about being flexible. For instance, Rod Coull, '86, notes, *"Coach's skill and success, in my opinion, was in identifying potential as well as mental toughness and then gently molding that potential without being rigid about it for a given individual. He nudged them rather than pushed them because he knew when to nudge and when not to."*

"Coach allowed all of us to be individuals, he didn't tell us we all had to do something in a certain way," writes Jonathan Stark, '93. *"I don't think I ever hit a ball on the weekends at school. Some of the guys would hit over the weekends. I never felt the pressure to play from Coach or anyone else. This was what I needed to play my best tennis when it mattered. Because he allowed us this individuality and freedom, I didn't want to let him or the team down."*

Styles of play differ as much as personalities, and this is also a factor. Again, Mac is a prime example of someone whose playing style was as unique as his personality and anything but classic— he often slapped at his forehand and flicked at his backhand and had a long, almost torturous, sidewinder service motion, *but* he became a world champion with that rather unusual game! How poor a coach would I have been if I tried to impose my style of classic stroke production onto him?

Having said that, I built my teaching reputation on developing a first-strike attacking tennis style with all of my players—always trying to apply pressure on the opponent. Every player I coached had to learn how to serve and volley and to attack opponents' second serves. Yet I was somewhat flexible in how I enforced this, depending on a player's strengths as well as the strengths and weaknesses of a particular opponent. In other words, my responsibility was not to change my players' games, but to add to their arsenals so that they could do whatever I asked them to do in a match or even on a particular point. I had to be sure they had enough confidence from what we had practiced to do this. Even in a match, when a strategy was not working, it was my job to find one that would/might work better. This did not mean changing their style of play, but rather making certain it was adaptable to a variety of situations. I also had to consider not only their tennis strengths but their situations and personalities as well.

Eric Peus, '90, discusses this from a player's perspective. *"A great team has to have great players. But what sets a winning team apart from another talented one is its commitment to sacrificing individual goals and success to those of the team. Coach's ability to make the best players trust that he cared about their individual development (and future pro career) encouraged them to reciprocate and emphasize the team goals during the spring season. The fact that he treated and coached players a little differently depending on their personality or their personal circumstances was one of his strengths as a coach and leader of the program."*

A coach has to adapt to changes in the sport itself. Maybe the biggest change in the last twenty to thirty years has been the forehand grip adjustment from an Eastern "shaking hands" grip to a semi-Western or even true-Western grip. This necessitated changing the path of the racket on the swing, and subsequently the footwork as well, as the stroke became more body rotational. And beyond this, rules changes, equipment (racket sizes, types of strings), and court surfaces evolve, all of which in turn further influence how style of play changes. Nimbleness is key as a sport or business evolves and members of a team change! Or as four-year letterman Michael Flanagan, '94, concludes, *"The biggest takeaway I have from the Stanford tennis team is how every single team is different from year to year."*

Michael's comment is why I might treat a team or individual differently from one year to the next. I think my greatest example of flexibility was in how I approached and treated each player—not just stars like John McEnroe. Everyone is different, so a good leader will treat everyone as an individual. But everyone must feel he will be treated fairly. Even siblings, let alone twins, in the same family have different buttons to push that will elicit the response one wants. Some work better with praise; others respond better to harsher, more direct approaches. This can even vary from day to day. I wholeheartedly believe that the best coaches can find these buttons. I feel that I was flexible enough to be able to adapt quickly and decisively for the good of the team (or even individual) and thus rate this as one of my strengths.

"I have great respect for Coach's ability/gift to manage differing personalities and to get everyone working together for a common goal," says Jim Delaney '75. "As a coach or manager, you try and foster a sense of team and camaraderie, but also individual opportunity. This leads to better results and productivity from everyone. I observed Coach with other players on the team and how he communicated with them. For most of us it was different, and as a result he was able to get more out of the individual player."

RESILIENCE

Resilience—yes, I think Stanford tennis had it in spades. First, I think there was innate toughness in Coach and in the players he recruited. There was a belief that we could stumble along the way but, ultimately, we would be there at the end. I remember we lost a match late in the spring one year. Coach gathered us after the match and said, "We are right where we want to be, we are going to improve more than they all will over the next two weeks because we are a young team." I still don't really understand his comment, but I believed with conviction that we were "right where we wanted to be" after Coach finished speaking. He was resilient and so were his teams.

—Robert Devens, '94

We all have goals with our professional lives, our families, our personal lives, even our hobbies. We will always encounter setbacks in health, our relationships with friends and family, and in our work life with these goals, but goals give life more meaning. Each day we have things to strive for or improve upon. But they can consume us and make life more of a struggle, especially if they are unrealistic. However, if we constantly work to reach them, these positive steps can give us fulfillment and satisfaction.

In athletics as in business, these challenges occur almost daily, but we can choose how we deal with them. I have always greatly admired those who realize that failure—often described as the inability to reach a goal, or adversity, such as an illness or defeat—is unavoidable. These people understand we must not be so afraid to fail that we become afraid to try!

Scott Moody, '87, explains how we assimilated failure on our team. *"Coach's great attention to every detail off court left little for the players to worry about. To handle wins and losses, I think the importance of personal accountability and not being afraid to fail really helped. He instilled that in us from day one."*

When failure occurs, as it will, the ability to bounce back is critical. This is resilience, and it's vital to the success of any team and any long-standing business. The coach and leader must know/feel when to pick his/her spots, and this might vary from team to team and individual to individual. It's important to know how much emphasis to put on each setback. Regardless of the situation, the key to resilience is *always* being eager for the next challenge and considering it an opportunity to do better!

Jonathan Stark, '93, notes that example of resilience occurred during the national championship. *"The best example for me of bouncing back after a setback was at the NCAA finals in Palm Desert, California. I was playing after a couple of months off because of a foot injury. I think we were playing Oklahoma State in the first round, and I was horrendous and a complete train wreck on the court. I lost my match, but we beat them and were playing Texas in the second round.*

"In our team meeting before the match, Coach pulled me aside and said he was going to lay into me a bit. He basically called me out in front of the team and said to quit being a pussy and that the team needed me to step up. I trusted him, and because of the camaraderie and team culture that he had created, I didn't want to let him or the team down, and I went out and played good tennis for the rest of the tournament. I believe Coach knew each individual on the team and he had an uncanny ability to know what made them tick to get them to play their best tennis. For me, it was not letting him or the team down."

It was not uncommon for us to start the season slowly in our first team competition, the ITA Division National Team Indoor Men's Championships, *but* we were usually able to keep our focus on improving and bouncing back to win it all. The particular tack I would take if a disappointment occurred would depend on the character of the team or individual.

"Coach knew exactly what route to take after a setback," says Mike Bryan '00. *"He knew when to be positive and uplifting. He also knew when to be stern and come down on his team or an individual. I lost my first six college matches for Stanford. I got swept as a freshman at the ITA indoor team tournament in both singles and doubles in February. My confidence was crushed, and I felt like I had let the team down. This experience could have easily hurt me down the road, but Coach knew exactly what to say to me. He could see that I didn't need a kick in the ass, and he could tell that I was already my toughest critic. He just simply told me that it's early in the season and that I'm going to be unstoppable when I started playing the right way. He told me that he was very excited to get working with me on a few things and that we'd get right to work next week. I didn't see any doubt in his eyes. He didn't treat me any differently. He was simply saying in so many words: 'You'll be fine. I got you.'*

"I then went on to only lose only one more dual match for the next two seasons. He was right. His vision for my style of play worked like a charm."

Sometimes bouncing back is a year-to-year thing, often due to missing our starters who graduate or turn pro. The latter is often unforeseeable because, unlike graduations, which are anticipated and planned for, sometimes a player doesn't decide to turn pro until the seasons ends in the late spring and he reflects on what he has accomplished. Unfortunately, by that time it's too late to recruit any new players due to our unbendable admission application deadlines. This situation occurred twice after we won the national championship (1981 and 1986) and had lost players to injury, graduation, and to the pros. We started each of the following seasons slowly. Despite the setbacks, we regrouped over the academic year and were playing well by the end of the 1982 and 1987 seasons. But unfortunately, we had incurred too many early season losses to have a record that merited selection into the sixteen-team championship field.

"We always had our focus on the ultimate goal, and any setbacks or disappointments were just bumps along the way," says Barry Richards '90. *"One of the most disappointing and yet coolest memories is from my freshman year when we had a series of injuries/setbacks for different players and ended up losing a ton of matches we would have normally won (including to several teams Coach had never lost to before) and were very out of contention to make the NCAA tournament. However, toward the end of the season, we got a few guys back and went into 'NCAA focus mode' and won a string of matches including beating the top three ranked teams (Long Beach State, USC, and UCLA) all in the last week of the season. Unfortunately, we finished as the first team out of the tournament, which I'm positive we would have won had we gotten in. It was a bummer, but it showed the resilience of the team."*

Barry is right! We had the resilience to bounce back after not being invited to the Big Dance, and though we couldn't work our way into the tournament in those two years, 1982 and 1987, we were playing great by the end of the year, and actually won the title back in each of the following years, 1983 and 1988 respectively. The point is that both of those titles came a year after not even making it into the tournament! Little has made me prouder than this obvious resilience.

How a leader publicly handles personal disappointments—like not making the tournament or a player leaving the team—is critical. Coaches, of course, have their own lives to live. I was no more immune than my players from life's adversities, but I strongly feel the measure of a person is regularly determined by how one deals with these setbacks. I always took pride in the fact that my teams rarely suspected if I was dealing with a particular personal challenge. As an example, I don't think they had any idea when my father died in midseason. Glenn Solomon, '91, simply says, *"Coach had a good ability to not let setbacks impact other aspects of his life or his relationships with the players—this was key to our resilience."*

It was really difficult for me to accept that on occasion a player might choose to leave the program, usually to turn professional before his graduation date. As an example, perhaps he wins the NCAA individual championship—the pinnacle of collegiate tennis—and feels he has nothing else to prove. Or maybe he is swamped by agents trying to represent him, all telling him how great he is. On the one hand, I was complimented that the player felt he was ready to turn pro. On the other hand, I tended to take such situations personally, *but* I could certainly not let this be known to the team. I think I did a pretty good job of moving on.

However, one time a player's departure really hurt was in 2003, and it was not related to him turning pro. This was not my strongest team, but we had a chance to win the championship if our team was at full strength. David Martin, '03, was a player on that team. *"My senior year we lost to Cal-Berkeley,"* he says. *"A few weeks later, one of our key starters abruptly quit the team, and we were not very deep that year. It was very emotional for a lot of guys, and we were stunned. Coach went about business as usual, kept our heads up, and refused to let us wallow in self-pity. We later beat Berkeley two times that year without that player. Coach's positivity spread through the team."*

This particular "defection" was initiated because I wanted to adjust the lineup. A really good player and a great guy with an amazing work ethic had finally worked his way to the number one position to start his senior year. This is exactly the kind of effort a coach wants to reward, if at all possible. But after about eight matches, his record was just so-so. I had two other players who I felt were playing at least equally as well. Under the circumstances, I felt they also deserved a chance to see what they could do at this key position. I proposed on the plane returning from the team indoors that these two be given a chance and that they would split the remaining matches at number one equally. This would give my top three players—all very good ones—an equal number of matches at number one. Further, I said I then would have these results to help me decide my final lineup for the NCAAs, which we absolutely had a chance to win.

This did not sit well with my player who felt he was being demoted. He said that if I followed through with this thought, especially since one of these two players did not exhibit as good a work ethic as he, he would leave the team. And this is exactly what happened. Without him, it may have cost us a realistic chance at another championship, but I stuck to my beliefs. Hopefully, I did so in a way that was seamless to the rest of my team.

HANDLING WINS & LOSSES

Movies are often made of coaches who can inspire the players when things are not going well. When running such a successful program, I feel teaching your players how to handle such levels of success is equally important. Coach was an expert in this area.

—Vijay Sekhon, '00

"'Respect everyone, fear no one' was the phrase I remember that we used in the locker room," says Michael Flanagan, '94. *"On the rare occasion that we did lose, Coach would often use those as teaching moments to get us motivated for the bigger picture of the NCAAs when we would likely encounter that opponent again. I remember specifically, after one Rolex fall regional tournament in which none of us performed very well, Coach brought the team together and analyzed every opponent whom each of us lost to and what he thought of our effort. One of the opponents that a teammate lost to Coach described as a nice 'club C-level player,' which brought a laugh from everyone on the team and is still talked about by our teammates to this day. However, the guy on our team felt so bad about being called out in front of his peers as having lost to a nice 'club C player' that he was never going to lose to a player of that caliber again, least of all when it counted most in the NCAAs."*

We all regularly experience highs and lows. Disappointments are a fact of life, *but* they can truly help us grow. This represents the practical side of resilience, for it can make a difference in wins and losses. We learn so much about a person by how they deal with both a win and a loss, and as coaches and leaders, we are afforded a prime opportunity to teach others by example on how to deal with these highs and lows. Above all, we must never let a team see how a disappointing result affects us negatively as long as our team has prepared well and given its best effort. This is perhaps when leadership by example is most important. In addition, we must not discount that the disappointment may have been at least partly attributed to our own efforts and effectiveness as the leader.

These can be temporary, especially if we have learned to be resilient. *"Coach wouldn't get too high or too low,"* remembers Jeff Salzenstein, '96. *"He'd say, 'Let's just keep an even keel. Let's keep rocking. Let's keep moving.' He just stayed calm. He didn't freak out—he let everyone kind of do their thing, but he did have a way of keeping everyone together."*

Jonathan Stark: NCAA Doubles Finalist; World Singles #36, World Doubles #1

It's often difficult to keep that "even keel" because I think it's not unusual for a coach to take a disappointment harder than his team. The losses all hurt! For the most part, I kept this frustration inside myself and tried to not let it show to my players. *"Coach handled both wins and losses the same, which led to his understanding that it was a process,"* says Jonathan Stark, '93. *"And wins and losses weren't the important thing—it was playing your best tennis when it mattered the most."*

Jonathan is right to a point. Playing to one's capability in any given moment is most important *provided* there is a total effort both in preparation for the competition and during the match itself. If effort lagged, I would be livid and react accordingly. But for the most part, even if I were inwardly frustrated, I never lost sight of my vision for Stanford tennis. This vision was furthered mostly by staying positive, as I tried to do with Vimal Patel, '94, who needed not to get down on himself or to try harder, but to learn how to learn from his losses. He writes:

"I had a real problem with letting the team down. Coach told me specifically to take a loss and think about it for ten minutes: what I did well . . . what I could have improved on . . . what my opponent did to expose my weakness . . . and then forget about it as there was nothing I could do to change it once it was over. This was a new way of looking at a loss for me at the time based on what I had been taught. Coach made it OK to lose and [showed] how to cope with that loss in a positive manner."

The way I handled team losses depended on whether I felt the team was playing up to its potential, and on the personalities of the individuals on my team, realizing that all teams are different. Geordie McKee, '86, describes one approach I took to address this problem. *"In the spring of '86, the team was struggling, guys seemed burned out, efforts were lagging, and the results showed. This was, on paper, the best team in the country, and we were expected to win the title—the same group of freshmen who made up a majority of the '83 championship lineup was on this '86 team playing in their final season as seniors.*

"The downward spiral culminated in a blowout loss to UC Irvine, at home no less! Coach had seen enough and felt the need to take immediate action. He called a special team meeting the next day; I think we all went into that meeting expecting to get blasted, however, Coach really wanted to hear from all of us about what was going on. Why were we losing? Why such a mediocre effort? Each of the seniors spoke initially and gave their opinions/feelings on the state of the team. Then the others followed: a true 'airing of the grievances' (to quote Seinfeld). The meeting turned

collaborative and eventually cathartic as we talked through the issues and how we could turn it around in time for the NCAAs only weeks away.

"I think we all left the clubhouse that day feeling a weight had been lifted, a closer bond with each other, and certainly more optimistic about the balance of the season. Fast forward less than six weeks later, this group played its best tennis of the year to capture the championship in a lopsided win over a powerful Pepperdine team."

Six or seven years later, I had an entirely different team in a very different set of circumstances, and so I handled things entirely differently, as Alex O'Brien, '92, relates. *"My freshman year we were the number one seed in Kentucky at the National Team Indoors and lost every match. After our final loss, we sat at the bar and Coach berated every one of us and said what a joke of a team we were. He went down the line and ripped us all as we deserved. I remember thinking this guy is crazy. He was not crazy, but he knew when it was time to press and when it was time to let off the gas. He had a sneaky sense of timing and pressure and applied pressure very efficaciously."*

I found the best way to manage my frustrations and/or disappointments was to focus on where I felt we could be by year-end at the NCAA championships, because this is what we were preparing for! *"Coach emphasized the growth process and progression toward the NCAAs,"* adds Robert Devens, '94. *"There was less of a focus on individual wins or losses, so long as guys were growing and improving in anticipation of playing their best in May."*

In short, I rarely responded to wins and losses on their own terms, but rather what they meant or said about our progress toward getting ready for the NCAAs in May. A loss might even be helpful in learning a critical lesson that could bring a victory at the championships. The point in any endeavor is to keep one's eye on the ultimate prize.

Chapter Eleven

DEALING WITH SPECIAL ISSUES

One particular memory speaks to Coach's responsiveness to others. I think it also demonstrates his willingness to listen respectfully to difference. I think it was an extraordinary moment. We were scheduled to play the University of Washington. It was the day after the discovery of the secret bombing of Cambodia.

We were warming up on the courts for our match, and hundreds of our classmates were filing into the Frost Amphitheater across the street to gather and talk and figure out a response. Many of us were part of the anti-Vietnam War movement. I was on the court right in front of the little shed.

I think John Spiegel and Rob Rippner were next to me. We kept looking at each other as the flow of students came past us, staring through the fence at us in our tennis warm-ups.

At some point, we spontaneously gathered in the center court and said, 'We can't play this match.' I don't remember which of us said that, but we all felt it. Coach came

*down out of the stands and met with us at
the net. We discussed it.*

*He had the final say of course. The deci-
sion Coach made was powerful. He agreed
that we would forfeit the match officially,
but we would play as a sign of respect to
these guys who'd taken a bus all the way
to California.*

*I remember well Coach standing with all
of us on the court, respectfully discussing
it. It was an extraordinary time to be starting a coaching career in the Bay Area, but
his willingness to respect his players was
powerful. It said Coach took us seriously.
It said he was responsive. It said he was
willing to deal with difference. And it was
a powerful gesture of team building. We
could trust that Coach would not devolve
into unpredictable behavior.*

—Paul Marienthal, '71

Any college sports team, like the college itself, exists within a
much larger context of local, national and world events, and social movements that impact the players on the team. The same is
true of any group or organization outside the college sports scene.
These global or personal life issues can easily overshadow day-
to-day life, and certainly matters relating to one's team, and they
can happen at any time. The COVID-19 pandemic is a great example. As a result, no matter how much we feel we are in control
of things or how well we have things planned out, there is *always*
something that arises that poses a special challenge.

How a leader deals with these challenges will naturally have a direct influence on their team (family, athletic, or business). These
can range from international issues, national issues, health issues
(even life or death), to extremely personal issues, and on and on.
The word compassion comes to mind. A strong leader must gen-

uinely care. Here are a few such instances where compassion was needed and helpful during my coaching tenure, beginning with a couple of examples during the student protests in the Vietnam era and including much more personally traumatic ones later.

VIETNAM WAR, CIVIL RIGHTS, AND PERSONAL ISSUES

Coach accepted the multiple demands upon us all: Understanding and contributing to the civil rights movement, trying to end an imperialistic war in Southeast Asia, and trivial academic requirements. He appreciated that a win or loss on the tennis court would not impact the advancement of mankind or solve the significant problems plaguing the country. The equanimity and uniform support that he provided held a disparate group together.

—John Shepherd, '70

Until the midsixties, coaches were generally considered authority figures. One rarely questioned what a coach or team leader said. But the Vietnam War changed that thinking dramatically. Young people were losing confidence in traditional authority figures at the team level. If a coach was hung up on short hair, for example, his players might let theirs grow out as a way to state their identity and independence. Rebellion was the order of the day. On-campus riots protesting the war were often the norm. Students were genuinely concerned about where the leaders of our country were taking us. Against this backdrop, many found "playing games" less relevant.

Increasingly for coaches, teachers, and even parents, respecting the views of others—whether or not we agreed—became essential! This was apparent my first season on the job in the fall of

1966 when three good freshmen, who had been recommended for admission by Coach Bob Renker before I arrived, entered Stanford with me. All three were very concerned with the complex state of the world in general, and the Vietnam War, racial injustice, the Los Angeles Watts riots (near some of their homes), and the assassination of Bobby Kennedy and Martin Luther King, Jr. in particular. Our capitalist system was being questioned, and many students, my players included, were intrigued with socialism as an alternative.

John Spiegel, '70, slated to be my #1 player that year (later to become the father of Snapchat founder, Evan), chose to forego his senior season of competition, graduate early in December, and join a group of revolutionaries. Here's how he describes his story:

John Spiegel: Former Team #1

"My years at Stanford, from 1966 to 1970, were years of campus turmoil, student strikes, building sit-ins, and police interventions. The focal point of student protests was the Vietnam War, which was dramatically escalated by the Johnson Administration, threatened all of us with the draft upon graduation, and caused classmates to refuse induction and face prosecution. Racial injustice was another focus, with the Watts riots in LA, the assassination of Martin Luther King, Jr., the founding of the Black Panther Party in Oakland, and so forth.

"Each spring, in 1967 through 1970, the academic quarter was disrupted by protests, occupation of buildings, and violence on campus. I finished my undergraduate coursework by December of

my senior year and decided not to remain in school and compete on the tennis team my senior year.

"I had heard about a group called the Venceremos Brigade, which was recruiting US 'revolutionaries' to work in the Cuban sugarcane fields. We traveled by bus to Mexico City, flew to Havana, and traveled by bus to a cane harvesting camp about ninety minutes from Havana near a sugar mill formerly owned by The Hershey Company. We returned to the US on a converted cattle boat that traveled up to St. John's in Canada in very rough seas, and then took a bus across the country to Berkeley.

"My experience with the Cuban socialist economy and political system convinced me that our market system, for all its flaws, was much better, so I entered economics graduate school at Stanford that fall, ultimately ending up in law school and law practice for the next forty years.

"Fortunately, Roscoe Tanner had arrived as a freshman that year ('69–'70), so my doubles partner Rob Rippner got a trip to the NCAA finals in doubles, and the Stanford tennis dynasty was under way. I admire the persistence of Coach Gould through those difficult years to calmer times more conducive to athletic excellence."

This was my first experience with a player leaving the team, but he was following his conscience and morals, and I respected his decisions.

A second player in this group, Rob Rippner, '70, to whom John refers as his former doubles partner, also decided tennis no longer held an important place in his life. He chose to study abroad for an academic quarter at the Stanford overseas campus in Italy.

After Rob returned from Italy, he moved back into a starting role but played a very unenthusiastic match against Cal-Berkeley, essentially tanking, or throwing the match. I was so livid at the time that despite it being one of last matches of the year and a player I really liked, I strongly suggested he take the rest of the year off. Here's how he remembers it:

"My junior year in 1969 was fraught with political turmoil on campus. After the assassinations of Martin Luther King, Jr. and Bobby Kennedy, the escalation of the war in Vietnam, and the prospect of the draft, I had lost my desire to focus on tennis. I chose to attend Stanford in Italy. When I returned, I was not prepared to commit to the team. We mutually decided that it would be best if I did not participate any longer as a team member. I am forever grateful that Coach showed me compassion, understanding, and support. He conveyed to me the message that my welfare as an individual was paramount, and that he would support whatever I needed to do in my personal life. Not every coach would do that."

When Rob returned to school the following fall, he literally begged me to reinstate him to the squad. I was not going to do this, but he persisted in his request. Finally, after several days and a lot of soul searching on my part, Rob convinced me he *really* wanted to recommit to the team, and I relented. He responded by playing his heart out and having just a great year.

Rob ended up with the best win–loss record on the team and reached the NCAA doubles finals with Roscoe Tanner. *"Coach welcomed me as if a prodigal son,"* he said. *"He could have and perhaps should have denied me. Instead, he showed forgiveness, patience, and tolerance. Turned out that was the best year by far in my tennis career, playing number one doubles."*

As a token of appreciation for my faith in Rob, for years afterward, Rob's father would show up at every match at UCLA—adjacent to the town where the Rippner family lived—simply to say, *"Coach, Alan Rippner—just wanted to wish you well!"* It taught me to never be too quick to judge a player and to give them as much latitude and chance to grow as possible—as long as it didn't have a negative effect on the attitude of others on the team.

My third player, Ron Kahn, '70, was also really affected by all that was going on outside the world of tennis. Here's his recollection of the time:

"Coach's first years at Stanford coincided with the escalation of the war in Vietnam and then the assassinations of Martin Luther King, Jr. and Bobby Kennedy. Tennis had been the most important thing in my life in high school. Now it was, shall we say, diminished in importance. At the time, it seemed that Coach was blissfully unaware, but that's probably unfair. It's more likely he was just making the best out of a bad situation. My life had changed irrevocably, but his treatment of me, and I suspect of everyone else on the team, remained the same: relentlessly upbeat and encouraging."

The main lesson I was lucky to learn early on from these great young men was that tennis was not necessarily the most important aspect of my players' lives. From that time on, I had extra sensitivity and patience when dealing with challenging situations, as well as with players who did not seem to be measuring up to what I had expected. This absolutely made me a better coach!

TRAGEDY STRIKES

When I was a freshman, Mike Falberg, a former US Open Junior Tennis champion, had returned to school. He had been struggling for a few years, having dropped out of school in the middle of his sophomore year.

I remember him practicing with the team a few times when he returned the next year. One late afternoon, still very early in the fall, Coach took us out to Angel Field to do some interval training. Mike wasn't with the rest of us that day. Those were difficult workouts, and perhaps in anticipation of the sure-to-be discomfort from the running to come, someone asked, "Where's Falberg?"

—Jim Grabb, '86

We often don't know what is actually going on in the heads of others on a team, no matter how close to that person we might be. This was the case with Mike Falberg, who was the United States Open Junior Tennis champion and one of the best players and athletes I have ever had the pleasure to coach at Stanford. His first year he played in the top four and helped lead our team to the NCAA championship. Given what eventually happened, it's hard to believe that during a changeover in the NCAA final match at Georgia, I was so mad at his casual play and playing "not to lose," that I grabbed him from behind as he was sitting on the bench in a headlock and yelled in his ear to "get going!" or else. He did and won a key match for us.

I felt Mike was destined to become a top international player. Increasingly, there were multiple indications Mike was struggling with important things in his life. Eventually, I tragically learned things were not right.

"I remember Coach handling that situation in a very firm way," says Jim Grabb, '86, who was one of Mike's teammates, *"although I don't remember the exact words. The message was roughly as follows: 'Mike is battling extreme personal problems. Each one of you is unique, different. I will treat everyone fairly, but perhaps differently when the situation calls for it. Are there any more questions about Mike?'*

"While there may have been a bit more that I can't remember, that seemed to do the trick. Differently, but fairly. That is a good lesson, and quite realistic as well. In retrospect, there must have been a dynamic that was operating on at least three levels. We had a bunch of freshmen that year, all probably with dreams of breaking through and making it into the top group. They all probably feared that they wouldn't get a fair shake.[3] Second, Coach had a situation that he just didn't have control over, and knowing his personality, that was probably difficult. Lastly, at a personal level, knowing Mike's situation more closely (we didn't, but coach obviously did) must have been hard for Coach, who at a certain level probably felt responsible and was obviously concerned about Mike's well-being.

"I don't think Mike finished that fall quarter . . . If he did, he wasn't out to practice much. I don't think I saw him much after that."

Jim is right that he was not privy to the whole story. What Jim didn't know was that things were bad enough for Mike that after returning for the fall quarter he soon dropped out of school. When he finally decided to return the following year, the housing

---

3   This team ended up winning the national championship with five freshmen in the top seven.

deadline had passed. There was no longer university on-campus housing available. Although it was illegal, I welcomed Mike into my home rather than have him live off campus by himself at this crucial time in his life.

He was eventually finally able to move back into an on-campus dormitory, but shortly thereafter, he concluded it was not going to work and dropped out again. Not much later, Mike was institutionalized. Finally, after his release, he took his own life. I had to tell the team. *"A year and a half later,"* says Jim Grabb, '86, *"Coach told us that Mike had taken his own life. It was right before a big match (I think), and I don't remember much more, although Coach was obviously affected."*

This was especially hard on me—I loved Mike—just a great young man with an incredible future ahead. I honestly felt I did all I could do, including arranging for school counseling, but it proved to not be enough. Mike's teammates also loved him, and, as one might guess, were deeply affected by his suicide. They each contributed $500 to name a $5,000 chair in our stadium's "Rows of Champions" in Mike's honor with all their names engraved on it. How sad it was a few years later to look up in the stands after practice and see a gentleman seated in "Mike's Chair." I went up to see who it was, and it was Mike's father just sitting there and remembering. When I realized who it was, we both had a big cry together. Another painful life lesson: sometimes, no matter how hard you try and how much you care—and I truly did—it may not be enough.

DEATHS

Coach doesn't know this, but the Goose (a local family pub) sessions he insisted on made the biggest difference in my world. Really, really a big deal. This is the genuine Coach, and, therefore, even at a young college age, we all wanted to play as hard as we could for his program and keep the Stanford men's tennis tradition going.

—Misha Palecek, '98

Misha remembered the note I sent him when his brother died, which was well after Misha's graduation.

When someone in a player's family, or even a close friend, passes away, it obviously affects that person greatly. In this circumstance, team matters naturally take a back seat because young people need to take time to try to really understand how they feel, and if appropriate, to reach out. These are always private occasions, and oftentimes the team may not know what a teammate is going through. A coach/leader may offer extra leeway to someone experiencing difficulties, whether or not the team is aware of the situation. Hopefully, the coach/leader has built up enough rapport with their team that such actions are not questioned, and in turn, do not affect the team itself negatively.

Another time we had a parent die unexpectedly. Scott Lipsky's father was very fit and training for a triathlon. He had just finished one-third of the practice course, paused by his car to change into clothing for his next segment, and dropped over in his tracks.

When news reached us, it was understandably extremely difficult for Scott to be three thousand miles away.

"I think that the loss of Scott Lipsky's dad illustrated a fairly special issue," All-American and NCAA singles semifinalist Ryan Haviland, '03, recalls. *"I certainly respected the way that Coach seemed to take him under his wing and really just tried to be a substitute father figure for him in his time of need. I thought that was mighty important for him at the time, and very classy of Coach."*

DIVORCE

My sophomore year I struggled a bit personally (with my parent's divorce) and academically. Coach turned out to be my strongest supporter, helping me navigate through a very difficult time. Since graduation and over the decades, Coach has amazed me with his loyalty.

—Geordie McKee, '86

Divorce is far more common than deaths, particularly after the kids leave home for college. Both Anne and I had experienced parental divorces when we were away at Stanford as students. I too went through a divorce when my oldest was sixteen. This is not an easy time for anyone, especially the young people involved. Because of my personal experiences, I was especially empathetic when it happened to any of my players.

COMING OUT

I would say Coach handled an unidenti-
fied player "coming out" to him in private
just prior to the NCAAs in '90 incredi-
bly well. In hindsight, I know this player
was distraught, and the team was a bit in
shambles as a result. I was disappointed
because I didn't know what was going on
and thought I had earned the right to play
ahead of this player that year. Not doing
so probably cost me an invitation to the in-
dividual tournament, but Coach called me
when I didn't make it to pat me on the back.
I appreciated that.

—Glenn Solomon, '91

Spring break following winter quarter final exams was always a natural respite in the competitive tennis season. These breaks/ lulls are not uncommon in the cycles of a business. For me, it was a time where I could step back a little to evaluate and reflect on how we were playing and provide a good time to make lineup changes. This often occurred in doubles, where I would change the combinations of teams.

At our first team meeting before the start of spring practice one season, I gave a scathing review of our winter quarter play. I was particularly unhappy with the play of our doubles teams, and I announced new partners for two of them. One of my players called me that night to let me know he could not play as a doubles partner with the teammate with whom I was going to pair him. I replied by asking, "Why not?" And I proceeded to restate why I wanted to try them together—basically because I thought their tennis skills complimented each other's game so well.

He responded, *"Because I am attracted to him."*

I said, "So what?"

"Because I'm gay!" he replied. This was a new situation for me at the time. People were just starting to "come out." I asked him to repeat what he had just said and moved the phone over to where my wife was so she could hear for herself. She was totally empathetic.

I had a dilemma to face. I really felt the team would be supportive, so I asked him if he would be receptive to me calling a team meeting to let him share this with his teammates. We had a team of particularly good guys, and I felt they would understand, and I did not want this to be a distraction later on in the season. I thought he could do this. He replied that he had to do it on his own time—that he had not even told his girlfriend yet—that's when I realized this was not to be.

He did tell a couple other of his teammates during the spring, but it was not yet general knowledge. For example, we were in line for breakfast one morning a few days later at an IHOP in Arizona before a team match. One of our freshmen who happened to be rooming with him on this trip, rushed up to me, pulled me aside and said, *"Coach, _____ is gay!"*

I calmly answered, "So what?"

He responded, *"But he's gay!"*

I asked if he was okay. He hesitated, then answered in the affirmative. I asked if he wanted to change roommates for that night, the last of our two-day trip. He thought for a moment, and replied, *"No, I guess not."*

PREGNANCY

Today you will meet my son.

—*Anonymous*

Although we never talked about it, cell phones never were a problem at practice until one fall when one of my guys always seemed to be taking calls or making them. His teammates spoke up about this, and I made a general comment to the player to "ease off it."

We were leaving for a tournament near where he lived months later that spring when he told the team during a meeting in preparation for the trip that he had something to tell us, and he did. He told us that we would be meeting his newborn son on this trip. It caught us all, especially me, by surprise. He was not married, and in retrospect, one could only wonder how he had been able to handle all of this internally, and yet keep up with his studies and his tennis. Obviously, phone accessibility was a big help to him!

This lesson is easy: it's important for the leader to get the full story before rushing to conclusions.

General Challenges

How Coach and Coach Whit handled this one senior when he had many crises and was wrestling with inner demons stands out. As a player on the team when it was happening, I didn't understand it.

When I learned what really happened and how Coach was struggling with how to

*manage it, it made perfect sense. Someone
else with less empathy could have easily
cut him loose, and who knows what might
have happened to him. Coach helped navigate him through a difficult chapter and
somehow managed not to lose the rest of
the team in the process.*

—Dan Turbow, '91

Here's a further example the 1990 team hasn't known about until
now. We were warming up to play an undefeated 35–0 Tennessee
in the 1990 NCAA team finals. About fifteen minutes before the
match was to start, one of my players' fathers walked right onto
the court to see me during the final warm-up. He was ashen, and
when I asked if I could help, he asked me to try to get his son's
room key out of his tennis bag. He said he thought his son might
be planning to take his own life and wanted to check out his hotel
room to be sure there was nothing there he could use to facilitate
this action. He found nothing, and I was able to return the key to
the bag undiscovered.

While my player was an emotional wreck and did not play well,
the team recorded a big upset by defeating Tennessee to win the
title! Even though it was the final match, I must admit I had to
really work hard to get myself to concentrate on the job at hand.

The biggest takeaway? As the leader of your team, *always* be empathetic *and* do your best to focus on what is most relevant when
all seems to be falling apart around you.

ONE I MISSED

I never liked the sport, and I always dreaded the competition. Growing up, winning was everything. I put too much pressure on myself to ever allow myself to breathe or to play anywhere near my full potential. Tight, tense, and full of dread, that was me. But I still always wanted to be an All-American and get my picture on the clubhouse wall.

—*Eric Rosenfeld, '86*

It really hurts to see one of my players suffer, especially when I might have been able to do something to help them. I pride myself in not putting too much pressure on my players. But here is one I missed and really regret. Eric Rosenfeld, '86, responded to my request for help with this book, but only after more than a year had passed from when I'd sent out my original twenty questions. I always considered him one of my best competitors. He generally played around numbers five and six, places in the lineup where we always have had one of our best chances for a win. His parents never interfered, and each Christmas, I would receive from them a thoughtful gift of thanks.

Until I received this note with Eric's answers to the questionnaire, I had absolutely no idea how much stress the pressure of competing had caused him all those years ago:

"Just for cathartic-sake, I've gotta say, Coach, that I really hated tennis—well, not so much tennis, but my experience with it, and

*all the regret and shame that I surprisingly still sometimes suffer
through at not ever making it.*

*"To add insult to injury, I was one easy smash away, up 5–4 in
the third set against Tom Fontana [of the University of Texas] in
Athens to move into the quarters and seal my All-American status. I didn't put that easy shot away, and I lost the match. To this
day, I sometimes wake up in the middle of the night smashing my
fist into the mattress, hating myself for missing that one shot that
would give me some sense of self-achievement in that sport. All
the guys I came in with are on that wall but me. But I came up
short. So I have a sore spot when it comes to tennis. I avoid it and
all mention of it like the plague. . . . I am a drug counselor in Malibu, I have three amazing kids, and an ex-wife who has become a
buddy of mine now."*

As the team leader, it is my responsibility to be aware of things
like this and to address them appropriately and always with compassion. Obviously, in this instance, I missed it. I am deeply grateful for Eric's enlightening response.

Day-to-day life presents immediate and unexpected challenges.
Often, they are serious ones. As leaders, we must realize that the
best developed plans will be disrupted. Things rarely go exactly
as planned. The best laid game plan may not work for a variety
of reasons. Just when things seem poised for great success, it is
again Murphy's Law that an unexpected challenge, such as an
injury or extreme personal problem of a key performer, will arise.
Every team—not to mention every era—presents different challenges. The bottom line for the team or group leader is that in
times of crisis: *listen!* In times when there is no apparent crisis:
listen! Always *listen!*

Summary to Dealing with Special Issues

In our personal and professional lives, little remains static. Challenges are constantly arising that test our patience and our charac-

ter. Above all, we cannot ignore them by simply hoping they will go away. Often, we fail to confront what seems like a small issue. But then it grows and becomes a much larger and more difficult one to address, even to the point of affecting others not initially involved. As leaders of our teams, we must be proactive and learn to look for signs of hidden or potential problems. As this chapter title suggests, I have missed many signals. Perhaps the most important thing is to listen—really listen. In our sport or workplace, it is critical to "feel" the pulse of those around us, which can best be achieved by listening.

Once a potential problem is identified and defined, we always have a choice about how to face it. The choice we make defines us as a person and our effectiveness as a leader. It will vary depending on the situation. In most cases, I personally am extremely tolerant and trusting, but I am still able to make my point. However, I have no empathy when it comes to lack of effort, procrastination, or alibis—just read of examples in the "Trust Violated: Coach at His Angriest" section of this book.

Above all, one must not lose the connection with their team! A recurring theme of this book has been that you must be true to yourself and your own values—that you must lead by example. It is not imperative you have all the answers, and often you must make a decision by only your gut! But recognize your shortcomings and work hard to improve on them. In the overall process, listening and being decisive are key. Your door must always remain open *and* inviting. Bringing a team together to talk through a problem with you and even eliciting suggestions can be helpful. Remember, you are all in this together. Every issue is a special issue, and how you deal with it is reflected in team morale, and in turn, results!

Chapter Twelve

SUSTAINING SUCCESS

CONFIDENCE

Coach allowed us to be who we were, not something we were not. He created an environment at practice that made us want to get better. The competition at practice was relentless. It was getting us to believe in ourselves and that we were good enough to handle anything and anyone, no matter what.

—Pat DuPré, '76

BELIEF IN ONESELF

There had been some top players at Stan-
ford, but as a team, Stanford perennially
finished no better than third in its confer-
ence, the Pac-8, behind USC and UCLA.
Bob Lutz had been enrolled the previous
fall, but he lasted exactly one quarter be-
fore transferring to USC. So Coach was
left with some decent but not overly serious
players. He may have been frustrated, ex-
asperated even, but he never once showed
it. In the face of overwhelming evidence,
to the contrary, he was confident he could
build a team that would compete at the
highest levels of intercollegiate tennis.

—Ron Kahn, '70

When we were starting out, we were good, but not great. We had no real tradition of team success. This confidence in both myself as the true leader of my team and in the team itself took time to develop. Yet I always tried to show my confidence in them and in where I felt we were headed.

As the years went by and as I saw more and more successes, I gained much more confidence in what I was saying and in my methods. I learned that it's critical the players never fear losing a point or a match. It was not only critical to never portray a personal fear of my team failing to succeed, but in fact, to portray that success is assumed because it is impossible to sustain success without an inner confidence and belief in the organization itself. Jim Miller, '82, sees it this way:

"Coach was a force of nature. The combination of an expectation of winning, and a lack of fear of laying it all out and losing, created 'bold and fearless' players. In a game where a little tightness or tentativeness can ruin a player, this is a huge deal. Not everyone was bold and fearless all the time. But boldness and fearlessness dominated the team during the time I was there. Coach was also a bundle of contradictions. Low-key approach but intensely driven. Expecting to win, but gracefully accepting loss. ('We'll get them next time!') The combination of expecting to win, and not fearing losing as long as you gave it your best shot, made Stanford teams get better in a pressure cooker when most teams got worse. And Stanford expected to win nationals! Coach kept experimenting and adapting over the course of the season and somehow helped the players do the same."

I also learned that a leader can't inspire confidence in others unless they personify complete confidence in themself. *"Coach thought of himself as a winner and thought of us as winners,"* says Chico Hagey, '75. *"The confidence was contagious. One result, for me at least, is I played better on key points."*

This is conveyed by how they speak (tone of voice, looking directly into the eyes of the one(s) being addressed, references used) and even how they walk (stride with a purpose; head up) because it is true that a major part of communication is nonverbal. *"Coach Gould was tremendously self-aware,"* Gene Mayer, '76, writes, *"and he knew his strengths and weaknesses, His people skills were arguably the best I have ever seen. Coach understood his role as an enabler in the best sense of the word. He created an atmosphere of excellence without supercharged pressure."*

Confidence in One's Team

Success in tennis, as in most things, is based on execution and the confidence to execute! The ability to execute well, especially in big competitions, can be a challenge. Sustaining success starts with confidence in oneself and in one's teammates. Confidence helps one to overcome many immediate challenges.

How does a coach/leader prepare a team or individual with the confidence to perform best when much is at stake? And not just on one occasion, but time and again, year after year, especially when what may have seemed easy in practice becomes harder to do when mental pressures are added to the equation. This is compounded when the outcome of the entire team directly relates to one's own performance.

In my business, confidence is gained through repetition of the parts, which are then incorporated into the whole. Gradually, the coach introduces repetitions in practices that are more game-like and adds as many pressure situations to practice as possible. In time, it all fits together and the results can be spectacular.

The best competitor is the one who can make the most of what they have or the conditions they are given at any certain time! Rarely will these be ideal. This also is not the person who plays their best—this will never happen because one can always play better!

For Pat DuPré, '76, this was largely based in believing he didn't have to play "out of his mind" to be successful. Pat was the national junior champion but had sustained an extremely serious wrist injury at the end of his senior year. Yet he came back to reach the Wimbledon semifinals and achieved a world singles ranking of number fourteen. *"Coach got players to believe in themselves. We were all great players, but he got us to know it,"* says Pat. *"Also, that how I played the game was good enough to beat anyone, I didn't need to be someone I wasn't. In addition, I didn't need to play out of my mind to deal with anyone. That's*

*something that really served me well on the pro tour. I often won-
der what I would have done if I hadn't hurt my wrist so badly."*

This can come in different ways to different people. As Vimal Patel, '94, puts it, *"Coach always made me believe I could win. He
gave me confidence, even when I was a pain in the ass for him. He
treated me like he treated our number one player on the team, and
it made me feel just as important as the top player on our team."*

Scott Lipsky, '03, was a top competitor on the team, having arrived
as one of the best junior players in the nation. But he too needed
boosts to his confidence just like the lesser-heralded players: *"I
think the biggest thing that Coach gave to most of us players was
belief in our abilities. All tennis players have doubts sometimes
about being able to beat our opponents, but he was always really
good at giving a great motivational speech before the matches.
He always had a game plan for us, and as long as we executed
that game plan, we felt like we were able to be at our best. More
often than not, that helped make the difference and allowed us to
play at our best."*

Icing and ibuprofen and taping were good for Pat DuPré's injured
wrist, but there is no stronger medicine than a firm belief in oneself and what one can do! It is not about what one is doing wrong,
but how that person (or team) is getting better! And it's up to the
coach/leader to help them do this. A historical background of success helps, but everyday actions from day one are most important.

This confident attitude must then be reinforced by specific actions
and behaviors: the way a coach looks into the players' eyes when
conversing with them; how they emphasize the good things—
even in defeat; in tennis, the timing of any intersquad (challenge)
matches, which can destroy players or make them tougher; what
they say in public; how they subtly display/present past successes;
how calmly they faces challenges (outwardly, at least); how they
reflect on improvement; how they look ahead rather than back;
and on and on.

Jeff Salzenstein, '96, explains: *"I was a little kid from Colorado who grew into his game under Coach. That was really, really special to grow into my game at Stanford. To get bigger. To get stronger. To develop that big serve. To become a serve and volley player—he really helped me with that. He helped me believe the kid from Colorado could become an All-American who could play number one. He basically looked to me and said, 'You're a leader of this team.' That felt good. Coach helped me become a leader. He helped me believe in myself."*

Here is a situation with Jared Palmer, '93, in which I said something in a casual setting, but without making a big deal out of it, saw it turn into a very big deal indeed! Jared picks up the story:

"Coach led by example in the way that he seemed to remain unflappable in the face of adversity. All his players could see that he brought a 'let's get this done' attitude to the table day in day out, and he had a very thick skin, and that gave us the confidence to believe that when crunch time came, he would make the right decisions. When I was playing in the NCAA singles tournament as a sophomore, I was playing number three for our team behind Jonathan Stark and Alex O'Brien. My year up to that point had been up and down, with a few good wins and some pretty bad matches as well. I had struggled with my game and with confidence throughout the season. I remember the four of us were in the car about to drive back from practice at the NCAA championships and Coach turned around and said, 'Remember guys, we've got three guys in this car who can win this whole tournament; don't forget it.' Whether he was or not, I felt like he was talking directly to me."

All three of these players went on to singles rankings on the pro tour in the world's top forty, and all three reached the #1 world ranking in doubles (with different partners), but on that day, this casual comment resonated with Jared. A few days later, he reached the 1991 NCAA singles finals against Patricio Arnold of Georgia on his home courts. Before a large Georgia crowd, Jared played what I would consider a nearly perfect match—patient, but applying relentless pressure—to win 6–2, 6–0. He claimed that I made my comment about three of us guys having the ability to win the tournament *"with such conviction and sincerity that I totally believed him. I think that really set the tone for me to go on and win the title."*

Michael Flanagan, '94, also remembers how this atmosphere of confidence helped him cope all season with playing number one. *"I remember a few times feeling overwhelmed by playing number one singles for Stanford or competing in the finals of the NCAA team championships or singles championships, but Coach Gould never seemed overwhelmed by the moment, I guess because he had experienced so many similar moments before I got there. I remember thinking that even if I didn't think I could do something, the number one player for Stanford could and had many times before, and I better get off my ass and get the job done or else there would be someone else playing number one for Stanford the next time around. This motivation helped me to achieve way more than I ever thought was possible."*

The moral? Never sell individuals nor your team short.

I learned that everything I said or did should be meant to project and instill confidence—first, in myself, and second, in my team. When I first started coaching, I made the mistake in my pre-match meeting against the SoCal powerhouses in saying something like, "Okay guys, if we play our best, maybe we can win a match or two."

There were two major fallacies in this statement. First, it implied we had to play our best. This is a reference we often hear when engaging in a competition or performance. We tell our own kids: "Do your best!" This is essentially an impossible feat to achieve— our best is constantly outdistancing us—we never really know what our best can be, but we can constantly strive to get better!

Second, I showed a lack of confidence (although well-founded) early on with my team. I was admitting I didn't think we could win. One of my players, Rick Fisher, '73, responded by saying in a pre-match team meeting, *"What are you talking about, Coach? We're going to kick their butts!"* I was embarrassed that my players had more confidence in what they could do than I did.

I offer four further examples, two individuals and two teams, which clearly indicate my lack of confidence and belief in my players and teams then and what they could accomplish:

1. Gene Mayer, '73, enrolled at Stanford when we arguably had our best and deepest team ever. Although he was a top junior player, he was stuck well in the second six his first year or so in the lineup. He had one of the best forehands I have to this day ever seen (a two-hander), but his dad was converting him to a one-handed backhand, which in the end, probably slowed down his development in college. At the end of his last and junior year, Gene frankly surprised me by barely making it to the top four on the team. A few years later, and when his dad had returned him to his two-handed backhand, he became #4 in the world, my second highest-ranked player ever behind John McEnroe!

2. Jim Gurfein, '81, another New Yorker, began as a solid number ten in the team lineup and stayed there for much of his freshman year. I wondered if he would ever make the starting lineup. But he was steadily improving! By the end of his freshman year, he'd earned the right to start, and for the first time, played as a starter in the number six lineup position in the NCAA championships. His key wins helped lead us to the title. His second and final year, he played a solid number three on the team and reached the NCAA singles finals, where he lost in three close sets to teammate Tim Mayotte.

3. As for team championships, we were playing in the NCAA finals in 1980. It had been moved indoors because of the rain. We were matched against a great team from the University of California at Berkeley.

The coach, Bill Wright, was a contemporary and longtime friend of mine. Bill was such a good guy that everyone, including me, was almost always pulling for his teams. This was obviously going to be his best (and possibly only) chance to ever win a national championship. We were getting beaten so badly in the singles that I began to get the feeling we had no chance to win the match. (Cal had great doubles as well, which were played after the singles in those days.)

I hate to admit this, but I lost my focus and started thinking what I was going to do to congratulate my friend when he won. I was so excited for him. I was trying to decide between ordering him some bottles of champagne or to get a couple of cases of beer with which to celebrate. While my mind was elsewhere, all of a sudden, my guys—one by one—started coming back. Finally, sparked by a big win at number six by Jim Gurfein, we came back and won the championship! This was an unforgivable lack of faith and loss of focus in the heat of battle I exhibited!

4. In the second team example, we won the event in 1981, but in 1982, we lost four underclassmen who were slated to be our starters: NCAA singles finalists Tim Mayotte and Jim Gurfein and future top one hundred player David Siegler to the pros, and Mike Falberg to personal challenges. Predictably, we struggled and finished ranked at #14 nationally. My team for the 1983 season had five freshmen in the top seven nationally. In the preseason, people asked me what I expected with this young team. My reply was that we would be pretty good in a year or so, but that this was definitely a rebuilding year. Needless to say, these guys defied all odds and won the 1983 championship.

I never made the mistake of underestimating an individual or my team again!

DETERMINATION TO SUCCEED

Coach had represented persistence, clarity of vision, and institutional pride from our first sixty seconds together. It did not waiver once over the four years I spent at Stanford. I think that is a big part of the "why" we were so successful.

—Peter Rennert, '80

To accomplish great things and reach goals, an individual or team must have a fierce determination to succeed, as well as exhibit an unyielding persistence and tenaciousness to accompany this determination. The coach or leader of any team sets the bar in this regard. As for my tennis teams, we certainly needed it at the beginning.

Of my early teams in which moderately talented players had to labor under my ambition for a national championship, Ron Kahn, '70, says, *"Any sane person in his position probably would have been thinking, 'Oh my, what have I gotten myself into!' But I don't think that thought ever crossed Gould's mind. Gould's singular vision was in part forged by the lessons he learned in his first few years. That he pulled it off in a time of student rebellion and campus unrest is a testament to his enthusiasm, determination, and unflagging positive energy."*

Eventually, through determination, we turned it around. *"Dick managed to recruit some of the best players ever in the game and created a team culture that still exists today,"* is how Scott Love, '79, describes our time then.

I believe that a team culture of determination, persistence, and tenacity is almost as important as the players themselves in reaching team goals. I believe my players absorbed those qualities almost by osmosis. Peter Rennert, '80, NCAA singles finals and doubles finalist, as well as world singles #40 and world doubles #9, is a great example not only of belief in oneself, but of determination and persistence and where that can lead. Peter rotated at the bottom of the lineup his freshman year, but he was one of these especially determined individuals! This doesn't just happen year in and year out. As Peter describes it, *"Technically I came in as a walk on—there were no scholarships available. Title IX had happened that year, and national scholarship limits went down from eight to five. When I graduated four years later, I was the number one college player in the country. I rose to number forty in the world during the first half of my senior year getting to the quarterfinals of the Australian Open."*

Robert Devens, '94, also picks up on my implied lesson of accepting no other outcome than success. *"I remember I asked Coach one time how he got the Stanford tennis coaching job as a young man with little experience. He said, 'I didn't allow them to give it to anyone else.' I love that answer and the tenacity and aggressiveness within it. If you see something you want, go get it. Coach's in-match coaching style was the same—attack your opponent with aggression, get to net, and make him pass you for three straight sets."*

As a team leader, never be satisfied! Never let discouragement be a part of the equation, and remember that frustration must only be expressed in extreme teaching moments. One can *always* get better. It is important to *never* bend in providing an example of persistent and tenacious positivity. Or, as Scott Moody, '87, writes, *"I believe Albert Einstein once said, 'I'm not any smarter than anyone else, I just stay with the problem longer.' I think Coach embodied the philosophy that as an athlete you need to 'stay with the problem longer.' To me, that means tenacity. There were never any shortcuts in Coach's program. If there was a drizzle at lunch*

*time, I know some players would hope for a rain out that after-
noon. Instead, Coach would wait out the weather or have us play
on half a court that was dry. Maintaining a routine was important, and preparation was key."*

A leader must remember that part of being relentlessly determined
is to constantly keep in mind and believe that one can continue
to get better. *"Coach was willing to stick his nose into things to
make them better,"* is how Jim Miller, '82, remembers his time
with the team. *"Even if he got smacked in the face for it. And
it worked!"*

There is no place for complacency, especially at the leadership
level, nor at the team level. This is critical because all your competitors are gunning for you, particularly if you are on top. It is
important to be proud of well-earned achievement and give credit
where credit is due, but the coach must always remember that
good things rarely happen as quickly as he or she wants. Patience
can be such a great virtue. The patience in the process of improvement encourages the persistence to keep pushing the team's
determination to improve no matter how long it takes.

Greg Tusher, '93, understands this approach well. *"Coach had
a burning desire to search for constant improvement. He never
stood still. Players, alumni, boosters, etc. picked up on the energy. While he was never satisfied, it came from a positive energy.
There was never a letdown. He would say, 'Always leave the court
cleaner than you found it.' Perhaps it was a microcosm for his
burning desire to make Stanford tennis and the Stanford community better than when he found it."*

Be tenacious, relentless in your drive to get better, and never
be satisfied—great life lessons, which by example, rub off on
your team.

THE ULTIMATE KEY TO SUCCESS IS "TEAM FIRST"

Taking care of your teammates, trusting your coaches and your teammates. And always "team first." Tennis is an individual sport, but we always approached it as team first. It was always about the team and culture of the team, not individual players. It was not graduating player A or B who won last year's NCAA, it was the TEAM.

—*Eduardo Cardoso, '04*

Everything I've said so far is of absolutely no use without one final ingredient: everyone must believe that team success also leads to greater individual success. This simply means TEAM FIRST! Sometimes working with an individual became a great teaching opportunity to reinforce the importance of team.

"I remember coach telling me once," notes Dan Fowkes, '83, *"that 'if you're going to dwell on a loss you had or look for sympathy for your individual result, then you're saying, "this is about me" and not about the team.' A great lesson for any team. 'Team first.'"*

We succeed or fail on court, in the workplace, or in our personal lives together as a team. This stronger team makes all associated with it better. Continuing the tradition, sustaining the success, depends upon every player on the team. It is absolutely essential for a leader of a successful team to create a culture in which players develop a strong belief in each other.

Gene Mayer, '76, relates that *"Coach Gould was the glue. We were directed to values and concepts that were bigger than any individual. Confidence fit with the model, but selfishness did not."* One way we did this was by making everyone involved with the team feel as valued as possible. Geoff Abrams, '00, has his own take on this chemistry. *"Everyone was important to the success of the team, from team manager to the number one player. It made people want to sacrifice for the good of the program and team."*

The Coach's Ego

Once again, it all starts with the team leader providing the example, so task number one involves managing one's own ego! I define ego as "belief in self," and a leader of any great team must have a strong belief in themself. This does not mean that the leader has all the answers. Rather, it means the leader has confidence, through trial and error or by assessment and reflection on the challenge ahead or even together in consultation with their team, that they will be able to find the right answer.

At the same time, a coach has to continually remember that the execution of the participants on the team, not him or her, is what is winning the games or matches. The leader rarely can or should take credit for such! My players are the ones who won seventeen championships, not I. Former world singles #126 and Colombian Davis Cup player Alejandro Cortes, '77, emphasizes that *"it was about the team, about tennis, and about Stanford. Coach never made things about Dick Gould."*

How a coach or leader conveys all this—a strong self-belief combined with humility—is critical. But despite all the best actions and behaviors, and even despite years of national championships, challenges to building confidence still constantly arose for us at Stanford.

Most problems occur when a leader feels challenged. The natural tendency is to get defensive and to fight back. This is where egotism can take over and hurt the team. One way I managed this and avoided unnecessary conflict was by trying to show that obvious personal challenges from players rolled off my back.

The know-it-all can be one of the biggest challenges for a coach. Too many people, including athletes, think they can get by on their innate ability alone! They stop listening to coaching advice.

"I personally liked Matt Mitchell a lot," says Jeff Jones, '81, speaking about the great local player who would later win the NCAA singles title. *"One day at practice, he was hitting volleys and Coach offered some unsolicited piece of advice, and to the surprise of many onlookers, he said, 'F**k you, Coach.' Coach just smiled and shook his head. His ability to let that kind of stuff roll off him was undoubtedly pretty central to managing so many top players."*

Bill Maze, '78, agrees saying, *"Coach was surrounded by egos, and he responded by having no ego. I think this was the perfect way to deal with all of us because he provided nothing for us to push back on."*

Or as US Davis Cup captain Patrick McEnroe, '88, who certainly faced some of the same challenges in terms of balancing strong leadership with deferring to the players puts it, *"The other side of the responsibility thing is deflecting the credit for success, and again, Coach*

Patrick McEnroe: Team Captain–Stanford, US Davis Cup, Olympic; World Singles #28, World Doubles #3

Jeff Tarango: Team Captain; All-American; World Singles #42, World Doubles #10

owned that attribute. There are ways to do that that actually call attention, but Coach was authentically deferential when it came to apportioning credit for any of the successes we had."

Managing Egos

Once a coach/leader has shelved their own ego, they must manage those of his team. The leader must set the tone, first, as in everything else, by personal action and example, and second, by how they treat what Jeff Jones, '81, called *"the fragile psyches of young 'high-octane' players."* Ego Management 101 is the primary tool to getting everyone to put the team first.

This isn't always easy with a team full of top players or an office full of high-end producers. But it is absolutely essential for a leader of a successful team to be able to effectively deal with large egos, to increase self-belief in others, and, most important, to foster a belief in each other. And there certainly is no one way to do this, as every player is different. Perhaps the quotes included within this section and the next on cockiness will give some ideas that fit well for you and can be applied to one of your own team members. I also emphasize that the nature and caliber of the students at Stanford itself was a big help in this regard.

"Coach made you feel like you mattered," reports Greg Tusher, '93. *"But he knew that each player needed to be treated differently. Managing egos was perhaps one of his biggest challenges as a coach. And responding to those egos was perhaps the biggest secret to his success."*

All-American and world singles #11 and world doubles #2 Scott Davis, '84, elaborates that *"Coach was, and still is, a master at getting the most out of ANY personality with as little drama as possible. Less ego, more results, and success. I firmly believe that Coach had the greatest management skills of all personality types. He could mold all of these different personalities toward success. I believe that he knew the true meaning of 'the sum of each part is greater than the whole.' Coach Gould's ability to take team after team to the championship is a credit to his skills at managing all egos. He was an absolute genius at balancing this."*

Nick Saviano, '77, world singles #48 and later USTA Director of Coaching and Coaching Education, cites his 1977 team, which had three players who would reach the top fifteen in the world and three more who would reach the top one hundred. *"We had numerous challenges with interpersonal rivalries and an intensely competitive group. Dick Gould was a younger coach then, and we were an extraordi-*

Scott Davis: All-American; World Singles #11, World Doubles #2

narily challenging group. Getting individuals to strive to achieve a team goal must be done within the context of each individual pushing themselves to be their best. Dick either consciously or intuitively understood this, and therefore was able to create a successful team with many high-performance individuals in an individual sport. . . . Not easy to do."

As Nick suggests, his was one of the best teams of all time and won the NCAAs by a substantial margin, but it was also one of the most challenging years in my entire career in terms of ego management.

Cockiness

A belief in oneself is critical to team success. But often this can lead to cockiness. The leader has to be able to develop and sustain confidence and yet manage this confidence to ensure that it does not destroy team morale and trust in one another. The actions of only one member of a team have the potential to bring the entire team performance down. But reining in destructive cockiness must stop short of quashing confidence. Overall, we seemed to be able to do this successfully, but it was not an easy problem for me to address.

It was my nature (and perhaps a shortfall) to resist giving even more praise to an overly cocky player. Cockiness was contrary to my personal belief, which valued humility. But if it involves putting down someone else, usually in order to build oneself up, it can create negative feelings that can be detrimental to the spirit of any team. It is the least secure team members trying to build a reputation or even convince themselves of their abilities who usually shoot themselves in the foot by self-promoting, often at the expense of the team. This is true in any organization, and I have no patience nor respect for such people. The really good, top-notch, and self-confident people don't have to tell others about what they have done or how good they are. I really don't think they care—inwardly, they know. They feel best when the *team* succeeds. John McEnroe is great example of this. Despite his fiery on-court attitude, John was one of the best team players we ever had.

Parents and even youth coaches can sometimes be the source of problems of this nature, especially in an individual sport, when they have spent years encouraging their child by reinforcing the concept that they are going to be the next big thing! Their praise has been continuous, perhaps for years, and the player never, even when it is unrealistic, is able to accept that the glass may be less than full. I have had players enter Stanford for whom this was the case. In a team environment where not every positive comment was directed at those individuals, they could really struggle! In addition, what an extraordinary amount of pressure it put on the player himself.

On the other hand, it is difficult to be a great competitor without a strong self-belief in what one can do, especially in a pressure situation. One must practice hard enough and with the right purpose to develop a naturally strong confidence in one's ability to perform in the most stressful of situations.

I had an advantage in dealing with inflated egos and cockiness while coaching at Stanford. Stanford University itself is a huge contributor in helping to deal with egos. With so many students truly excelling in so many areas (athletics being only one), it is hard to maintain an "I am better than everyone else" attitude— ones who do get shot down and find themselves friendless very quickly! *"I think a lot of our tennis team success can be attributed to the daily exposure to an extraordinary population of individuals who collectively make Stanford so outstanding,"* points out Rick Reed, '68. *"A big ego can be counterbalanced in the classroom. Our pride is our experience being surrounded by others with equally great abilities in thinking and learning."*

This broader campus environment of excellence was a big unspoken help to me as a leader in dealing with the fine line between helping to develop and sustain confidence and yet keep that confidence in players at a level that does not destroy team morale and trust in each other.

A belief in oneself and what one can do is also a must for a true champion and directly relates to team success, *but* it can also destroy a team and team morale if not carefully manifested. How a leader balances such is an absolute key to success. *"It really seemed like the 'secret sauce,'"* explains Aleem Choudhry, '99. *"There was no shortage of egos, but Coach's ability to rein those in with a unified goal was, in my opinion, one of the keys to success."*

Egos and cockiness are complicated, but the principle is simple: Team First! A championship team in any endeavor, not just an athletic team, must have or develop a team first attitude. The leader must set the tone, first by personal action and example, and second, by how they treat others. In the words of Mike Bryan, '00, *"Coach was masterful at helping everyone see the team as the priority. He helped the top players swallow their egos and push their individual goals to the back burner. When Bob and I came into Stanford, we were super cocky and thought we were invincible. I think this was one of the reasons that Coach called us both 'Rookie.' He wanted to let us know we were newbies, and there was a lot to learn. It was a subtle way to put us in our place and make sure we knew where we stood."*

Our Final Championship

The tournament was in Tulsa, Oklahoma in my final year of coaching, 2004. Our doubles team, KC Corkery and Sam Warburg, in the last match of the championship, won the individual doubles title. KC and Sam were exhibit A of two guys playing doubles together—being a team —who were certainly not best friends off the court, but whose skills complemented each other's on the court. I was really proud of their coming together as a true team to win this title, in this case, my last match ever as a college coach. Here's an account of that event by KC Corkery, '06, All-American and NCAA doubles champ:

"There seems to be a delicate balance of getting people to believe in a common goal while still allowing and even celebrating what makes individuals different.

"Coach was a master at finding that line. Coach gave us the confidence to perform when the pressure was on. I have no real sense for how he did it, but I'd like to share the story of how he prepared my doubles partner and me for the NCAA finals in 2004.

"We had just come off a tight win in the semis and we were flying high with confidence, knowing that we were playing really well. I was expecting Coach to give us a motivational speech about how great we were playing and how we could ride the momentum into the finals. Instead, he told us how many better teams he had seen and coaches who couldn't finish the deal once they got to this stage. He talked about all the players with pictures on the wall of the trophy room and what it would mean.

"I thought Coach was just messing with us (and maybe he was, but looking back, it was the best thing he could have done for us). He made us think about and address how big a deal winning a national championship was a day before we had to get on the court to do it. While neither of us slept great that night, by the time the match came around, the nerves had run their course and we were ready. Our opponents seemed to be the ones who were nervous on the big stage, and we were ready to take advantage, jumping on them early and holding on to win. I think Coach knew what we needed to hear rather than what we wanted to hear, and I'm forever grateful. While the team had a disappointing championships (breaking his streak), I hope he is able to take pride in the fact that he coached us to an individual title in the last match of the season in his last season."

SUCCESS BREEDS SUCCESS: THE ROLE OF TRADITION

I think quite obviously the longevity of the program's success is attributable to the tenure of Coach and Whit. The numbers speak for themselves. Coach and Whit were very good at emphasizing the traditions of success, great teams of the past and instilling a culture of winning. I think Coach was very good about talking about the larger goal and the tradition of winning at Stanford: 'Every player wins a ring during their tenure.' I remember coming to Stanford and feeling a great sense of pride in that tradition and incredible sense of responsibility and desire not to mess it up! And it also made all of us feel like we were a part of something bigger than our individual accomplishments—you were a part of something spanning multiple championships and decades. The culture of success and winning put the little things in perspective.

—Robert Devens, '94

I was always big on the importance of recognizing tradition. I believe this can be a major asset in the performance of any team. But first, the brand must be established. Even before we had successful teams, we recognized those who had come before me and done well individually. As an example, when I was at Stanford, two of my teammates played on the United States Davis Cup team—Jack Frost and Jon Douglas. As my teams started to have success, we made sure that the players who followed Jack and Jon felt a part of the tradition, and hopefully a responsibility to keep it going once we had established ourselves. I am convinced this reminder of our tradition was a key to preserving and continuing our success. The players felt a responsibility to keep it going!

How this tradition was projected really did seem to affect and motivate my players, as team captain Curtis Dunn, '89, affirms:

"I remember hearing more than once that perhaps Coach had a pact with the devil because we came out with victories under some pretty insane circumstance. I think it's a matter of recognizing, 'Okay, we've been in this situation before with our backs up against the wall, we're not going to panic, we are going to keep fighting for every point, every ball, we are going to leave it all on the court, remember who we are, remember who we represent.' When you have a whole winning tradition behind you, you feel you can overcome any odds."

Fortunately, we eventually had an established and top product to sell, and our guys exhibited a tradition of excellence over time. It extended beyond team success. Our program's culture emphasized development of confidence in oneself and a relentless effort to improve, and our college tradition of success carried over to these guys' tennis careers beyond college. In fact, many were spectacular in the world tennis arena. As examples, for a decade beginning with the early eighties, it was not unusual to have ten guys ranked in the world's top one hundred at some time during the year.

- Nine guys from the mid-1970s through the early nineties attained rankings in the top fifteen in the world in singles.

- Fourteen reached top ten in doubles, and seven of these players attained a world #1 doubles ranking.

- On one team in the mid-1970s, six players later achieved world top one hundred ranking

- In the early nineties on one team, there were three players who later achieved a #1 world ranking in doubles.

- In 1981, eight men reached at least the round of thirty-two at Wimbledon

- In 1983, four men reached at least the quarterfinals of Wimbledon: John McEnroe, Roscoe Tanner, Alex Mayer, and Tim Mayotte. A Stanford woman from Anne's and Stanford's first championship team—Kathy Jordan—achieved that as well, while her sister and teammate, Barbara, won the Australian Open singles title in 1979.

All-time world doubles champions, Mike and Bob Bryan, added tremendously to our championship tradition, partially because they appreciated tennis history and were knowledgeable about and inspired by the players who came before them. Mike Bryan, '00, who was awed by the Stanford tradition as described above, expresses his sense of obligation to have extended it:

"The players who were lucky enough to wear the Cardinal color would always rise to the occasion. Great players would always play to their full potential when it mattered most, and the lesser players would overachieve. There was always a sense of Stanford pride that radiated from all the players. It came from a deep respect for the history that had been created and the high bar of excellence that was expected to be maintained. It felt like the way you acted and the way you competed had to fit the Stanford tennis mold of class and greatness."

Getting a tradition started is always difficult. As mentioned previously, patience is critical and frustrations along the way must be kept to the leader. It is critical to remain upbeat and positive and to never lose sight of the vision. There will be countless challenges and ups and downs. A leader quickly learns so much about

themself! But once established, if one assumes the future will be a mirror of the successful past, the tradition continues, as it did with Mike Bryan, almost as a self-fulfilling prophecy. And as John Connolly, '90, adds, *"There was an overriding belief that if we made it to NCAAs, we would win. I don't think we ever questioned it. I think that was in the minds of the other teams as well whether they would like to admit it or not."*

Stanford men's tennis led the way in the seventies in the revitalization of Stanford athletics with four national team titles. The Stanford women, coached by my wife Anne, won Stanford's first women's national team championship in any sport in 1978 as well, and men's water polo added two NCAA titles—a total of seven for the decade! Stanford men's tennis won six more in the decade of the 1980s and also in the 1990s, followed by one more in 2000.

Once we got our program going in full gear and had established our credibility, we were on our way. In summary, here follow quotes from four decades representing the belief that "success breeds success."

Glenn Golden, '76: *"Success sets the tone for continued success. Establishing a culture of excellence, bringing in strong players, solid coaching, and the school's well-earned world-class reputation all contributed to an environment that attracted more strong players. NBA free agents wanted to play with the Chicago Bulls of Michael Jordan and more recently with Steph Curry or LeBron James—everybody likes being part of a winning tradition."*

Mark McKeen, '84: *"It is true that 'success breeds success' and I certainly see it in my now thirty-plus years of major law firm practice. As we know, life is often about positive momentum, and Coach was all about positive momentum."*

Dan Turbow, '91: *"Success breeds success. The chance to compete for a national team title every year and be surrounded by high-caliber academic and athletic talent distinguished Stanford from every other program."*

Ryan Haviland, '03: *"I chose to play tennis at Stanford mostly due to the history of the program. More big-name pro tennis players had come out of there than pretty much all of the other colleges combined. And then the fact that they were number one in the country and had won four straight NCAA titles didn't hurt either. Success breeds success. Once the success started happening it made it a lot easier for it to keep happening as the very best kids from all over the country knew about Stanford tennis and wanted to have the honor of being a part of it. One generation inspired and brought along the next."*

Vijay Sekhon, '00, perhaps best summarizes how these principles apply far beyond the tennis court, the world of sport, into business, and honestly, any arena of human endeavor. *"It is interesting to see the similarities between successful and enduring corporations and Stanford tennis (also a successful and enduring program). There have been organizations that have great years, but only a few can accomplish long-lasting success."*

Chapter Thirteen

STAYING RELEVANT

What struck me the most about Stanford tennis was the level of innovation in marketing the college game. Dick was way ahead of everyone in building the modern game of college tennis. It was visionary, and it was audacious beyond imagination. He is a role model for rugged individualism with vision. I worked for Steve Jobs twice, but Dick Gould is the other person in my life who has walked the talk. Amazing that a kid from Yakima, WA would end up at Stanford during a tennis revolution and a technology revolution. Unreal.

—Scott Love, '79

VISION/CREATIVITY

Sustaining success requires many traits I feel are critical to our or any organization's longevity. But there was another key I wish to address separately—that of staying relevant.

Other than active participation in helping to further my profession, I especially want to highlight the topic of creativity. Creativity implies that we are always moving forward, establishing an image of a progressive program or company/department that is not satisfied to rest on past successes. I firmly believe this was a major factor in separating our program from others. To me, it was critical to envision ideas that portrayed we were actively staying relevant by being entrepreneurial, and in fact, leading the way!

Most universities pride themselves on their innovation. But Stanford and Stanford athletics were really good at it! If my coaching was my cake, the freedom the athletic department gave me to innovate was my frosting! I absolutely loved the challenge presented by the opportunity to continually innovate, which I wanted to do because I felt it was important in order to keep the program fresh and fun for my players. It was also important from a recruiting and community relations standpoint to project this aura to our recruits and our public. For all these reasons, I made certain that innovation was a clear trademark of Stanford tennis and my leadership style.

"I can't forget Coach's entrepreneurship," explains Bob Cookson, '70. *"Whether it was shown in the publishing of* Tennis, Anyone?[4] *(I think I still have a copy), the tennis clinics, or organizing the famous—some say infamous—'Champagne'ships,' it was always on display. For a young and impressionable person, these were wonderful examples of what could be achieved with vision, creativity, and effort, all of which I tried to practice as I pursued my business career."*

The challenge in all this is that it takes vision to be creative! Without a vision for the future, for success, for the next idea and the one after that, innovation is impossible. I never wanted anyone to be able to say, "His teams have won a lot of championships, but now he's just coasting." But that required constant and active "visioning" in order to come up with new ideas. *"From the 'Champagne'ships' to indoor matches at Maples Pavilion, Coach crafted new ways for people to enjoy the game as students, players, and fans,"* notes Mac Irvin, '80.

How well I remember a quote in the sports section of the *San Francisco Chronicle* many years ago. The Oakland Raiders had

---

4   Six editions in three languages

won the Super Bowl the year before (1976), and at the press conference to start the next season, the owner, Al Davis, was asked if he thought the Raiders could repeat. He responded, *"We'll see— it is like the Red Queen told Alice in* Alice in Wonderland—*you have to run as fast as you can to get somewhere, but once you get there, you must run twice as fast to stay there!"*

This has been my motto ever since our first championship. Entrepreneurship is part of staying ahead. In addition, the longer I coached, the more important I felt it was to convey that I was staying relevant. I tried to do something every four or five years that had never been done before. *And* to do it well! I have spoken about the Junior Davis Cup training camps, but the indoor matches were one of a kind.

INDOOR MATCHES

Dick was one of the most important innovators in our sport. I think the indoor matches in Maples were a tipping point. He took the sport to the next level, which had to happen. Tennis has never been a well-managed sport, but he somehow modernized the college program to a level of excellence that will never be forgotten with MAPLES! Dick was way ahead of everyone, and by the time I got there, matches in Maples Pavilion were being covered on TV and written up in Sports Illustrated. *I think Maples is still the crowning event. Nothing will ever compare in my mind. It was one of a kind.*

—Scott Love, '79

Maples Pavilion vs. UCLA before over 7,000 fans. Jim Delaney serving, far side: Team Captain; NCAA Doubles Champion (twice); World Singles #59

Here is how it all got started. It really is a leadership lesson: take advantage of all that is available and create even more opportunities.

Foothill College '64, '65, '66

To capitalize on tennis's rapidly growing popularity and to contribute to it locally, I approached the Los Altos Tennis Patrons, which I had cofounded, to see if there was interest in undertaking a major exhibition on the wood floor of the beautiful Foothill College gymnasium to raise some of our funds. This endeavor was quickly approved, and our first exhibition in 1964 included Wimbledon doubles champs Rafael Osuna and Dennis Ralston of USC. Both were amateurs and still playing college tennis. All expenses such as plane fare, hotel, and meals were covered, but in this "shamateur" world characterized by under-the-table payments in the era preceding pro tennis as we know it today, they also received an agreed-upon cash remuneration for "additional expenses." Neighboring Stanford University had a couple of top ten American women enrolled—Janie Albert and Julie Heldman—and they joined up as well. This event was a great success and enjoyed by a sold-out crowd of three thousand enthusiastic fans, a gigantic number of spectators for tennis in those days!

We held another exhibition in the gym the following year, 1965, featuring Chuck McKinley (world singles #2), Rafael Osuna (USC world singles top five), Arthur Ashe (UCLA world singles top fifteen), and Tom Edlefsen (USC US singles top ten from NorCal).

Our 1966 exhibition featured Rod Laver and Pancho Segura, two of the greatest pros ever. Another local pro and I split up with "The Rocket" and "Segoo" to round out a team for a doubles match. It was yet another unqualified success. In addition, our expenses were much less because ironically the professionals were less costly to secure than the amateurs. Fortunately, "shamateurism" became a thing of the past when open tennis began in 1968.

As an aside, later that same year I played on the wood floor at San

Jose State University in singles against Pancho Segura. In doubles, Segura and I played against another local pro and Pancho Gonzales. It was not much fun trying to return the Gonzales serve (acknowledged as the biggest of the day) on the lightning-fast wood surface. Segura and I later also teamed up as partners in the California state professional championships at the Monterey County Fairgrounds. Neither of us had great serves, but we both had great returns of serve. We lost a close match in the finals, something like 7–5, 8–6, and we held serve just twice!

Stanford Maples Pavilion—1974

A lot of amazing things were happening in the late fifties and sixties in Northern California, specifically in the local Palo Alto area, to kick-start the "tennis boom." Even when I was teaching at Fremont Hills Country Club in Los Altos Hills, there were approximately twenty-five private family clubs with tennis courts within seven miles of Stanford. Most of these were new. Courts at homes in the area were being installed almost weekly. Community tennis centers were being built, and I was lucky to be at the forefront of all this as a local teaching pro.

When I went to Stanford as coach in the fall of 1966, we fully capitalized on this momentum by focusing from the get-go on building tremendous community involvement. I believe this is relevant to the public acceptance, and in turn, success of most all businesses and organizations. When our program started gaining national prominence in the early 1970s by attracting players like Roscoe Tanner and then Sandy Mayer, it coincided with the thirst Stanford fans had for success in any sport, as evidenced by the fact that we could not even begin to accommodate all the fans who wanted to support us in big matches in our old 1,500-seat outdoor stadium.

I knew from the three years of indoor exhibitions at Foothill College averaging almost three thousand fans each time that spectator interest in tennis was there *if* promoted well. As our team got better and our crowds reached the outdoor seating maximum for our main matches, I proposed the idea to my superiors to stage matches with our traditional rivals, USC and UCLA, as combination outdoor/indoor events. The indoor competition would be held in the 7,500-seat Maples Pavilion, the home of Stanford basketball. This arena was built largely by a gift from the estate of Roscoe Maples, who I found out later was a past president of the Northern California Tennis Association.

But playing tennis on a wood floor in a countable dual match was not something anyone would elect to do—as I already had learned first-hand from my exhibition adventures with the two "Panchos" at San Jose State and Rod Laver at Foothill College a few years before! I was looking for a solution when I heard that May Company, a large department store chain in Southern California, was discontinuing sponsorship of a major indoor pro tennis event in Los Angeles. After a few phone calls, I learned that the Sports Face carpet the tourney had used was available and was being stored in a warehouse in LA. The higher ball-bounce off the carpet was much more comparable to an asphalt or cement court than the almost impossibly fast low skid that would come off the wood floor of a basketball court. I told one of our early supporters, Joe Burris, about my idea, and he said he would pay for the carpet. I asked one of my team members, Nick Saviano, to fly down with me to help check out its condition. We reviewed it section by section, and thought all looked good, so I had it shipped to Stanford.

I wanted to inaugurate this concept at our annual USC/UCLA home matches but needed Coach Toley (USC) and Coach Bassett (UCLA) to agree—actually a big concession on their part, especially since whomever we played until late on Friday night would have to travel to Berkeley to play a 1:00 p.m. match at Cal the next day. All credit is due to them that for the good of our sport and for college tennis, they readily agreed to give it a try. The matches were to be split sessions: respective lineup positions number three through six singles followed by lineup positions two and three doubles, all to be played outdoors starting at noon.

The second and main session would move into Maples, with the respective position twos playing singles at 6:30 p.m. This would be followed by the number ones' singles, and finally by the number ones' doubles.

Indoor tennis of any kind was extremely rare in NorCal at the time, and hence a real *buzz* began to build around this unique event. In fairness, one should remember this was before Title IX, and the Stanford media relations department had only eight men's sports to cover throughout the year, so we were able to promote the heck out of this event via the press, as well as at the local clubs, public tennis facilities, and tennis shops. Our efforts paid off, and the usual 1,500 people packed the outdoor stadium each day for the afternoon matches. On Friday night indoors against USC though, 5,500 people attended, supported by the Stanford band, and the Dollies, which was the name for our female cheerleaders!

The next day against Glenn Bassett's Bruins, the outdoor stadium sold out again in the afternoon, and over seven thousand people showed up for the indoors that evening, many after pre-match tailgating parties held between the matches. The whole weekend was covered live by Stanford's student radio station, KZSU. The buzz was on, and the great sportswriter from *Sports Illustrated*, Joe Jares, was in attendance. The next issue included a full two-page feature article on the match and the electric atmosphere it created.

This was a rousing success as a total of over fifteen thousand fans attended the two days of matches—the largest two-day crowd to ever watch college tennis. I will never forget those who came forward to make something great for the advancement of college tennis possible—in this case, Coaches Toley and Bassett.

The players loved it more than anyone. *"Maples was brilliant,"* says Pat DuPré, '76. *"That took guts. It could have fallen flat had we not packed the indoor arena with over seven thousand spec-*

tators for a dual match. Tennis indoors in Maples Pavilion will never be forgotten nor be duplicated. The energy inside there still brings out a reaction in me more than forty years later. When asked about my greatest tennis experience, I still answer, 'It was my senior year playing in Maples,' even bigger than playing in the semifinals on Centre Court at Wimbledon!"

**Pat DuPré: All-American;
World Singles #14**

As Pat suggests, the historic and successful matches in Maples Pavilion were an innovation— perhaps our most famous one— that put tennis competition in a different light. Everyone wanted to play in Maples!

These matches continued for thirteen years until the first phase of our new outdoor stadium was completed. The anchor event of the year was always the Stanford vs. USC/UCLA men's weekend, but also later included dual women's matches against USC (1978) and UCLA (1979) and several mixed matches—a two-day outdoor/indoor mixed extravaganza against Trinity University (1976, '80), regular World TeamTennis style mixed matches with USC (1977), Cal-Berkeley (1982, '83, '84, '87, '88), and even a couple of matches against the Bay Area World TeamTennis (WTT) franchise named the Golden Gaters (1977, '78).

"I would be remiss," says Perry Wright, '78, *"if I didn't emphasize the indoor matches against UCLA and USC and Golden Gaters in Maples and other places (I played in three of those) with my favorite my sophomore year when Matt Mitchell and I beat two of the world's top doubles players, Tom Okker and Frew McMillan of the Golden Gaters of WTT. Matt and I came*

*back from 1–4 to win 6–4, and the crowd went crazy. Those
indoor matches were so great for the players. It was so cool."*

Regarding the World TeamTennis format, I have often felt that
before a school dropped tennis from their sports offerings because of the expense of having both a men's and women's team,
they should first explore the possibility of having a smaller team
using the WTT format. This would involve as few as three male
and three female players (if the players only played one event),
so squad size could be reduced from ten to twelve players each
to approximately six to eight players total, and coaching staff
sizes/costs could be halved. In addition, spectators love the
shortened format.

Some Fun Maples Memories

1975: Equipment Time-Out!

John Whitlinger was playing Billy Martin of UCLA (soon to become UCLA's coach) before some seven thousand people packed
into Maples Pavilion. John was at the baseline and about ready
to serve. He hesitated just before doing so, looked over at the
umpire, and asked if he could speak with me—he said it was
an emergency. The ump said OK, so Whit came to the bench. I
had no idea what to expect. John said his jock strap had broken,
and he wanted to know what to do. Then I looked at the umpire,
Norman Brooks—a good friend—and explained what had happened. He graciously gave Whit an equipment time-out. I'm not
even sure there is such a thing in tennis! Whit went to the locker
room and exchanged his broken jock for another one. Someone
in the stands must have overheard my request, which was quickly
passed on to the infamous Stanford band. When Whit returned to
the court a couple of minutes later, the band began playing "Yel-
low River," a popular song at the time. Word had traveled fast,
and all of Maples was applauding and laughing. Sometimes it is
better to keep conversations private. ☺

1976: Lost Match, Regained Perspective

At the risk of an overload of tennis information, this story includes such an important message about competition in any situation that it must be told in full.

In 1976, we had just an incredible match between the two top ranked teams in the country—one of the most exciting in which I have ever had the privilege to participate. We went into Maples against UCLA after a great outdoor battle involving lineup positions numbers three through six singles and positions two and three doubles with the score tied at 3–3. We were using no-ad scoring (the first one to win four points wins the game), the norm in those days. I had just moved Bill Maze arbitrarily from the number one slot to number two. He was *not* happy with me. He was soooo mad that he was determined to show me I was wrong. He went out and beat a future world top ten player, Brian Teacher, 7–6, 6–2. Pat DuPré followed at number one, losing a tight match to Peter Fleming, also a soon-to-be world top ten player, 7–6, 6–4.

The score was then tied at four matches all going into the final match of the night, the number one doubles. DuPré and Maze were playing Fleming (soon to be a world doubles #1 with John McEnroe) and Teacher. The teams split the first two sets 7–5, 6–7, and stayed on serve with no service breaks in the third set up to 4–4. The pro-Stanford crowd was going crazy—it was almost 12:30 a.m., and no one had left the pavilion. At that point, there were four successive 3–3 sudden deaths, meaning the next point wins the game. In the first with Stanford serving, UCLA won the point for the first service break of the third set and was now serving for the match and the entire team match at 5–4.

The next game on a 3–3 point, we broke them back to even the score at 5–5. At 3–3 yet again, UCLA broke us for the second time in succession to take at 6–5 game lead. The atmosphere was electric! On their serve, the score reached 3–3 for the fourth game in a row. It was 12:45 in the morning and match point for UCLA for a match that had started at noon in the outdoor stadium. It was also break point for us, which would have put us into a nine-point tie break for the overall match. Just a *great* point followed and ended with all four players at the net in a rapid-fire volley exchange. UCLA won the point and the match, 7–5 in the third set, and thus the overall team match, 5–4. We were absolutely devastated!

I didn't sleep at all that night, but as I lay awake feeling sorry for myself and my team, I suddenly realized how lucky we were to have participated in such a contest and extended it to the last strike! I could not fault my players—it was one of those competitions with two great rivals in which no one deserved to lose. It was a perfect setting for tennis in the intercollegiate sports world, and the tennis world in general.

The guys dragged in to practice on Monday, still devastated by the loss. As the team leader, I sat them down on the court and started to describe how lucky they were to have participated in one of our sport's greatest moments. They actually started to listen. I reminded them of a saying by the famous football coach, Vince Lombardi, which epitomized how I felt: "IN GREAT ATTEMPTS, IT CAN BE GLORIOUS EVEN TO FAIL!" This could never have been more true than in this situation. This is just a great statement for us all to remember! This loss, in perspective, is one of my favorite memories of my time coaching. It was a *great* day for college tennis, and a great life lesson for me and for my guys!

As a sidelight to this match, it also provided one of the most embarrassing moments in my coaching career. I mentioned that Bill Maze was really mad at me for "demoting" him one spot in the lineup to play number two. Instead of sitting with me on the bench on changeovers every two games to receive my coaching advice, he—in front of seven thousand people—deliberately avoided me and any suggestions I might offer by walking around the far side of the net and just standing on the baseline to serve or return as the case might have been. In the meantime, his opponent Brian Teacher was having congenial conversations with his great coach, my good friend Glenn Bassett. Brian then would calmly walk back onto the court to resume play. Talk about wanting to shrink into an invisible state. That being said, Bill and I remain great friends to this day. He has been a successful college coach for years, but I doubt he's ever been embarrassed as much as I was on that evening. Suggestion: try to put yourself in the shoes of your player. You can often gain more empathy for how they feel about something.

Chapter Fourteen

FUNDRAISING: THE NECESSARY EVIL

Dick Gould had remarkable vision for the tennis dynasty he wanted to build. His vision of what was possible plus his sheer force of will, energy, enthusiasm, talent, and personal magnetism. The capital improvements alone make the place almost unrecognizable. In every way, what he accomplished at Stanford was a monumental achievement.

—Jim Healy, '73

Any business or even nonprofit needs money to operate. The same holds true for youth groups, and certainly this is true of what are often thought of as minor sports in comparison to football and basketball. Usually in any endeavor, the team leader is responsible for this. It may be their personal responsibility, or if they're lucky enough to have a development officer, or of course a finance team responsible for rounds of funding. This is the lifeblood of a team, and so I include memorable examples here.

I actually started raising money during my tenure as coach at Foothill College during the midsixties, which was truly the beginning of the tennis boom. As an example of great tennis interest in the area at that time, my oldest daughter, Sue, and top NorCal junior friend Charlene Murphy, played a short exhibition on grass on the fifty-yard line at halftime of a San Francisco 49ers NFL football game versus the Detroit Lions in front of forty-five thousand fans in 1975.

We needed extra funds to help expose our youngsters participating in the nonprofit Los Altos Tennis Patrons area (later, the Mid-Peninsula Tennis Patrons) to special and interest-stimulating events. An example of one of these was an annual plane trip in team jackets for our area Junior All-Stars to SoCal to play the juniors of the Jack Kramer Tennis Club, where a good friend of mine, Vic Braden, was the teaching professional. This included a side trip to Disneyland.

Of course, innovation implementation usually requires money. One must realize that the most important ingredient to raising funds for a sport, as well as for many other causes, is through community involvement. It is imperative to have oneself and one's team personally exposed to and involved in the community as much as possible. This cannot be overemphasized! People are more likely to support a program in which they have had personal contact with the players/team members and have experienced and appreciated their outreach.

Scholarship Endowment

Our first attempt to raise monies at Stanford was for a scholarship endowment. Summer camp earnings for a couple of years contributed to this effort. It helped us to get started. This was soon augmented by special team participation.

So many of our former players were having great success on the pro tour that it seemed like a logical idea to ask them to give back by returning to campus to play a one-day exhibition to raise money for a men's tennis scholarship. The first was in 1981. Apple was secured as a sponsor of the event, and *every* player asked committed to participate: Roscoe Tanner, Sandy Mayer, Gene

Mayer, John McEnroe, Pat DuPré, Nick Saviano, Tim Mayotte, and Scott Davis—this at their own expense (travel, etc.). Well over $100,000 was raised for the scholarship endowment fund by this first "Courtside with the Stars" event in our old stadium. It was like a garden party—entering spectators were greeted by a champagne fountain, a string quartet, and so on.

The second such event was held in 1982 indoors in Maples Pavilion and included the aforementioned and a dozen other established Stanford pros. This was also where we first publicly presented our vision of a renovated outdoor facility.

Courtside with the Stars Endowed Scholarship Fundraiser with all of the former Stanford greats returning to participate in Maples Pavilion.

In the meantime, a former teammate of mine, Bob Bowden, began hosting the team for a meet and greet reception in his home during our annual trip to La Jolla for the USTA Pacific Coast Men's Doubles Championship at the beautiful La Jolla Beach & Tennis Club. He invited La Jolla and other San Diego area friends to attend and meet the team. Of course they were asked to donate to the La Jolla Tennis Scholarship Fund. It was an instant success, and it continues today with a variety of host families who lend financial support for this endowment.

At this time, this is among the nine named scholarships that provide adequate funding to support more than the amount needed for our NCAA- allowable four and a half scholarships for men's tennis.

STADIUM RENOVATION

*Coach embodied the entrepreneurial cul-
ture that had been at the heart of Stanford
and the West for a long time. When I was
visiting various East Coast schools, all the
coaches grumbled about their aging, mediocre facilities. They would all say with a
shrug that they had asked their athletic departments for funding but had been turned
down, so this is what they have to work
with. Coach said the same thing when I
toured the green shed that housed the tennis program in 1983.*

*Except, instead of taking "no" for an an-
swer from the AD, he went to Nike and private donors and began building the Stanford tennis complex on his own. Coach
Gould created his own job description,
which was part coach, part CEO. He invented the job as is it done today by most
other top schools.*

—Scott Moody, '87

Our original stadium was built in 1926. With the addition of some
old bleachers from our rugby field, 1,500 spectators could crowd
in on bench-style seating. However, the main structure was full
of dry rot and termites. Our program was becoming very popular with fans as we continued to build lasting and loyal relationships within the local tennis community. It was time to address
the stadium issue and do something that could functionally add

to the players' well-being and better represent and portray the program's success.

First Phase (1983)

The Ralph Rodriguez Clubhouse kicked off our stadium renovation to replace my office of seventeen years—the "old shack"! Thanks to the generosity of tennis fan Ralph Rodriguez and his family, it was completed in 1983. It provided a rooftop deck, which immediately proved to be a great location from which to film the number one court matches. We conceived of a way to feed these matches live to our local Palo Alto cable station, which had an unused channel we could plug into directly. Russ Cohan, Chris Bradley, and Todd Lewis, three of our former Recreation Tennis, Inc. instructors, were able to take time off from their day jobs. They proved to be outstanding broadcasters in the 1990s for these matches, which were picked up across campus as well as by the adjacent city of Palo Alto. The Mike Orsak Family Heritage Room was the focal point of the clubhouse. In addition to a meeting room, it contained beautiful display areas for our championship team trophies (thank you Bill Closs and Adidas) and the Heritage Wall, which includes a mural of all individual national collegiate champions. Thanks to the support of the Tom Ford family, we added a twelfth court to the previously existing eleven. And the nation's first electronic scoreboard for college tennis was designed and installed. It was a great start!

Second Phase (1986)

One of my good friends, Stanford University Associate Director of Athletics Alan Cummings, actually suggested I do something to improve the rest of the stadium, but he said that there would be no athletic department or university funding available. So in 1986, exactly forty years after the original stadium was completed, we announced an ambitious campaign to raise funds for 1,500 individual seats, including a section of about four hundred shaded box seats. These were built in an L shape, with our new clubhouse at the center point of the L. We now had assistant coaches, so the second floor added two more offices and the Craig Johnson Family Player's Lounge, a small meeting room for the men's and women's teams. On the first floor, we added public restrooms as well as the John Hoisch Family Men's Locker Room and Bob McGlinchey Women's Locker Room. In addition, we were able to construct an almost full-sized practice court under the main seating area, which provided a welcome workout range during inclement weather.

To spearhead our fundraising efforts, we asked the seating company to reduce the size of the seat number on each seat plate. This gave us room to add four to five lines of three or four words to be able to personalize and sell each seat. In the box seat area, one could buy a box of eight seats, which gave those eight seats access to an immediately adjacent refrigerator to keep soft drinks, water, beer and wine, as well as hors d'oeuvres. A personalized plaque could be placed on top of each fridge to identify the box seat owner. These boxes ranged from $50,000 to $250,000, based on location. In essence, a single box seat cost a minimum of $6,250 for life. These four hundred seats sold out quickly, but seats outside the shaded box seat area could be purchased for $5,000. I would be remiss if I didn't mention the uncommon financial support given to this project by the Jack Gifford Family, the Herb Dwight Family, Bob and Sue Boniface, Peter and Helen Bing, and John and Fran Arrillaga.

In fact, we also offered a special commemorative seat area just behind our center court called "Rows of Champions." To have a personalized seat in this area, patrons must have participated as a tennis team member at Stanford.

Not only have former players helped build the stadium by donations subsequently recognized in this special area, but families of players have continued to give support by donating a commemorative chair in their child's honor.

Well over 150 men's and women's players are recognized in this special and ever-expanding area.

The donation of a chair (or box) to Stanford gave the donor use of that chair for life—a valuable commodity for securing the best stadium seats not only for Stanford events, but also for stadium special events after paying the listed ticket prices, such as the Bank of the West women's professional tour matches.

A good friend and a lead sports columnist for the *San Francisco Chronicle*, Glenn Dickey, ran an article saying the Phoenix Cardinals' football stadium was the first sports franchise to have used proceeds from what then became known as "personal seat licensing" to help build a stadium. This was near the time we began our own stadium rebuild fundraising. I called the Cardinal front office to check when their funding efforts began. As it turned out, their announced campaign was begun approximately six months *after* ours had been announced at Stanford! Stanford had therefore probably initiated the first personal seat licensing program in the US to help build an athletic facility!

The project was completed in 1989, and in conjunction with local charity, the Peninsula Center of the Blind (for which I served as a board member), a tented on-court evening benefit celebration was held. This included a gala dinner and a great dance band. An incredible auction of major tennis-related items (trips to Grand Slam tourneys, tennis-oriented cruises, etc.) was successfully held and raised another $250,000, split equally between Stanford tennis and the charity.

The indoor dual matches at Maples were discontinued shortly after the completion of this portion of the stadium, and the last indoor match was held in 1991.

Third Phase (1997)

The implementation of this second phase of the stadium was extremely successful, but plans were already afoot to complete

the other side of the stadium. The plans included additional restrooms, major space under the seating including classrooms, a
kitchen, two conference rooms, and an office, as well as a sunken,
full-sized championship court. This was a much more ambitious
project of approximately $6 million. Thanks largely to the gen-
erosity of the Tad Taube family and the Koret Foundation, this
became a reality in 1997. Our three-court stadium seating now
totaled 2,500 individual stadium seats.

Stadium Interior Build-Out and Lighting

East Palo Alto Tennis and Tutoring (EPATT), for which I served
as a founding board member, was looking for space on campus to
conduct their incredible tennis and tutoring program founded by
one of my former players, Jeff Arons. EPATT had lost use of their
classrooms at an underserved middle school in East Palo Alto that
were destroyed by a fire. Simultaneously, the eight tennis courts
we funded and built on school property were largely eliminated
by school classroom expansion needs. I approached Stanford
University about moving this great program to Stanford's Taube
Tennis Stadium. It immediately passed approval from the athletic
department, the provost's office, and the president's office and
was brought onto the campus and into the just-completed Taube
Stadium facility in 1997—never had I been more proud to work
for Stanford University!

We convened an evening meeting in Jimmy V's Sports Café in
our athletic department with EPATT and Stanford tennis boosters
in attendance to discuss and present ideas. That singular meeting
raised $1 million to (a) build out the underside of the stadium
with over five thousand square feet of classroom and conference
space (completed in 2000), and (b) provide lighting for all eleven
stadium courts (also completed in 2000). This court lighting was a
first for Stanford tennis, and we also were able to provide lighting
for the Taube South complex (completed in 2002) immediately
across the street. Now not only could EPATT kids practice after
our teams got off the courts in the winter when it got dark earlier,

but now our teams could extend playing time, as well as offer more recreational playing time for our general Stanford community—a win-win for both EPATT and Stanford tennis. These endeavors were largely aided by lead gifts from the Rick and Donna Fluegel family for meeting space, Victor and Gwen Riches for classroom space to be used by the East Palo Alto Tennis and Tutoring Program, and by Paul and Andy Koontz for a kitchenette and office space for the EPATT staff.

Completion of the Taube Tennis Center Complex (2003–2004)

I had long envisioned hosting the NCAA championships, but to do so required upgrading a set of six courts across the street (2002) as well as improving seating for our back courts (2005). In addition, I did *not* want to host while I was coaching—to do so in the manner I envisioned would have seriously detracted from my effectiveness as a coach, my primary responsibility.

In my mind, I was going to retire from coaching after forty years *or* after I went four years without a player winning a team championship ring. We failed to win a ring in 2001, 2002, and 2003, and the chances dropped remarkably for the 2004 season. Thus, I approached athletic director Ted Leland before the start of the season to say I intended to resign at the end of the 2004 season but

wanted to stay on as director of tennis and accomplish some of the things I had not been able to devote enough time to while serving as a full-time coach. I handed him my suggested job description, and he accepted it.

Coach Gould retirement celebration

I immediately told my good friend and mentor Tad Taube. Tad asked what I was going to do for a retirement party. I replied I honestly did not want such. He answered, "But Dick, we can make a lot of money to complete our facility if you have one." I was hooked. The athletic department really got behind this and finally settled on the four-hundred-seat Arrillaga Alumni Center as the venue. But the reservations kept pouring in, and it was finally decided that it would be held on the floor of Maples Pavilion. Over nine-hundred people paid a premium price to attend. The event resulted in a great "Roast Coach" evening by former coaches and players. Even more significant, it netted over $1 million. It allowed us to finish the repositioning and rebuilding of the courts across the street with bleachers and finally the bleachers behind the back stadium courts in 2005.

Tad Taube

Few coaches in a sport like mine can do well without strong community support. This can come in many forms. It usually is partly the result of the ingenuity and community building efforts of the coach. We had established a solid donor base over the years, and

it included not only former team members, but several six-figure donors to special projects. A few totaled over seven-figures, leading to several scholarship endowments and men's coaching positions.

Tad Taube presents Coach Paul Goldstein, the Taube Family director of men's tennis, with his award commemorating induction into the Northern California Jewish Sports Hall of Fame. (Paul was Team Captain, NCAA Singles Finalist and World Singles #58)

But every once in a while, we get lucky, and a special benefactor appears.

I was the beneficiary of such good fortune when I started to fund-raise for the last major phase of our tennis stadium—an approximate $6 million effort. I made a general appeal for help, and a gentleman I did not know well from our booster list asked for a meeting to further discuss things.

Tad Taube and I met in Woodside at a famous venture capitalist hangout, Buck's Café. We hit it off immediately, and from that meeting on, we have enjoyed a special and trusted relationship. Tad funded this part of the stadium project to the extent that it now bears the name the Taube Family Tennis Stadium. After additional help, notably from the philanthropic Koret Foundation at the encouragement of board member Tad Taube, the entire complex became known as the Taube Tennis Center.

In addition, and among many other things for which he always seemed to be available to help, Tad completed our program endowment by pledging to endow the Taube Family Director of Men's Tennis Coaching Position. This endowment was completed in 2020. I shall be eternally thankful to my incredible friend and his wife, Dianne, for their generosity in these and so many other countless ways. It is no wonder this incredible philanthropist, because of his generosity in the tennis and sports world, has been recognized by his induction into the USTA Northern California Tennis Hall of Fame and the Northern California Jewish Sports Hall of Fame.

Special Pro Events: Bank of the West (1997–2017), Fed Cup (1999), Siebel Senior Championships (2000–01)

The completion of the Taube Family Tennis Stadium represented the prime outdoor facility in Northern California for special outdoor tennis events. The first major event held in now Northern California's most incredible tennis venue was the Bank of the West women's tour event—the longest running women's only event in the US. It was looking for a home. A good friend, Erik van Dillen,

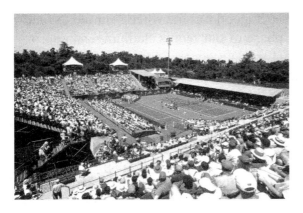

**Bank of the West Women's Championships
in the newly completed Taube Family
Tennis Stadium**

then head of the IMG San Francisco office, approached me about holding this event at our new Taube facility. Stanford accepted this proposal, and it began its run of twenty-two glorious years on the mid-Peninsula. I probably sold an additional four to six box seats annually to benefit our tennis program because people wanted guaranteed best seats to the women's event, which featured essentially all the world's top female players over the years.

Word got out about our ability to draw fans, and in 1999, the USTA approached me with the idea of the Taube Family Tennis Stadium serving as host for the Fed Cup finals. I went to my superiors, and they agreed this would be a good thing for Stanford. The US had reached the finals and was to play Russia for the title. The team was coached by Billie Jean King, and for the first time both Williams sisters competed together in an international team competition. EPATT students were the official "ball kids" team. The US won, and it was a win-win for all.

The next year, we were approached to host two senior men's events. In 2000 and 2001, the Siebel Senior Champions event, a part of the Association of Tennis Professionals (ATP) Champions Tour, was held in Taube Stadium, with EPATT as the designated charity. McEnroe, Connors, Borg, and Wilander headlined those sold-out events.

More Technology and Other Stadium Improvements

The core facility was now complete, but to cap it off, we wanted to develop state-of-the-art technology, which continued to evolve in the following years. We had earlier dabbled with this by developing two versions of electronic scoreboards. To increase and facilitate spectator interest for the 1983 season, we worked with Fair-Play scoreboards to develop the first electronic scoreboard specifically designed for tennis. The board showed all six competition courts and provided for doubles and singles results. The umpire in each chair used a specially designed consul to reflect on the scoreboard both the point and game score for the match on their court.

An improved version was added several years later in 1999—the Phil and Penny Knight Scoreboard. The scores were fed live onto our tennis athletic website for live public viewing. Phil founded Nike, our team equipment provider, and we had established a respectful relationship. This board also included a message center announcing upcoming matches and events.

Streaming 24-7 Web Accessibility with Audio and Web Scoring

As we prepared for the possibility of now hosting the NCAA championship, I wanted a way to actively bring the matches to those who could not attend in person. It was very difficult to find and view live tennis on the web, and the experience left something to be desired. The technology allowing one to watch live video with audio while simultaneously viewing synchronized scores and overall match scoreboard was nowhere to be found.

Enter Gerald "J. R." Keenan, to whom I will be forever grateful. He is a combination of a visionary and artist, and a true professional in all ways! I could not have asked for more. We installed cameras in both facilities in 2005 in preparation for the expected

NCAA event on seventeen courts in all. We developed and moved to our own website presence, with a video player, and created a synchronized scoring module, as well as an "always live" streaming offering. This was a tremendous bonus to the team and community, and now our matches and special events could be accessed for free *at any time* by all web browsers from any computer worldwide.

This made it possible for any Stanford tennis player on the courts at any time, as well as club and camp players, to share their play with viewers at home. Up to this point, only intermittent scheduled broadcasts of live tennis were available. Now, smaller matches and tournaments, and even EPATT players practicing and playing, could be watched by their families and friends from home or at work when their child was on the court.

We engaged Daktronics to design a scoreboard that could show the scores of every match simultaneously on the twelve competition courts, all controlled wirelessly by the umpire in the chair on each respective court. Our prototype was perfected during the season and was ready to go. This streaming may have been a first for any NCAA championship (2006) in any sport.

Other Technological Additions Related to Streaming

A mobile app was created by J. R. and publicly released in 2011. It enabled access to all our streaming. This was for fans, and especially for parents of our players living out of the area and even in foreign countries—they never miss their child's match! This could be accessed not only on one's computer, but on one's iPad or cell phone.

High-definition cameras were added for the six competition courts, which upgraded our streams to broadcast quality. In 2016, a coaching app was developed whereby the coach on court can access the last point or two, or last couple of shots for immediate review with the player via iPhone or tablet on any court—

this short sequence can be replayed as desired or paused or shown frame-by-frame.

A PlaySight station was added by a gift from Bob and Mary Siebert.

Historical Kiosk (2010)

I'm a big believer of the history of tennis, and more particularly, Stanford tennis. I wanted not only my current team, but my recruits to see what former greats had accomplished. Many stars were aligned at about the time of my first season: 1966–67. Open tennis started in 1968. More matches and events were appearing on television. Home video recorders such as Betamax were being introduced. And my ex-players were starting to make a mark on the pro tour. I had a seven-foot satellite dish at home, and every time I knew one of my players was playing in a final, if at all possible, I tried to record the match. The result is hours upon hours of home video, from Tanner and Mayer to McEnroe and Mayotte, to the Bryans and many in between. But the lifespan of videotapes is limited, so I engaged one of my grandsons to convert these videotapes to DVDs.

This was completed about the same time I'd met J. R. I asked him if we could we develop a "jukebox" of sorts for these thousands of hours of video. He said it could be done, and that in fact he could design an outdoor all-weather kiosk to house such with a touch screen call up. And in 2010, we completed it, thanks to the incredible support from Stanford tennis fan Lawrence Korn, who proudly dedicated it to Coach John Whitlinger! It currently houses three general areas of videos: (a) Stanford in the Pros; (b) Collegiate Events (team indoors, dual matches, NCAAs, etc.); and (c) Special Events (Bank of the West matches, instructional videos by our coaches, etc.). This is located at the entrance to the stadium, below the large-sized outdoor HDTV monitors, which themselves can also be used to show movies, the kiosk materials, DVDs, or a match in progress on any court inside the stadium.

Thanks to a gift from longtime donor Jackie Thompson, these are now reformatted and stored in the cloud and accessible by demand to a preselected private group of boosters, players, our SID office, and a few others.

Video Board (2016)

Among the special video board qualities developed with J. R. and Daktronics is the capability to show:

- Scores from each of six singles matches from two court complexes simultaneously, each on one half of the scoreboard.

- One match—singles on one side of the scoreboard, doubles on the other.

- Video of any selected court on one side of the board and the matches singles or doubles scores on the other.

- The entire board to show a movie, a videotape, a DVD, a telecast, or a live broadcast/interview from courtside.

- Its content broadcast at venues throughout campus, including the actual broadcast of matches.

Broadcast System (2016)

J. R. developed essentially a one-man broadcast system. With permanent cameras on all courts, the broadcaster with the push of a button can take the viewer from court to court, depending on the score and where the action is. They also have a second camera at this booth in order to zoom in on close-ups of the server or receiver. The viewer has the option of selecting any of the other six courts to watch, or to stay with the broadcaster and be taken from court to court where the broadcaster deems the most excitement is.

The total match score appears as a scroll down on the computer or mobile device, and the score of that particular court appears point by point at the top of each screen as it is recorded by the umpire.

We established a portal so that the match could be received live directly into the Pac-12 studio. This would make it simple for our conference to then send this broadcast out via their TV broadcast network if so desired. (I am not sure why, but they never chose to do this, especially since a normal TV broadcast of a tennis match costs approximately $40,000 to produce, and our stream is free and of very good quality.) The match may also be recorded internally for immediate or future viewing by coaches and players. I think I am most proud of this project, which was built from the development of the earlier video stages.

Summary

Forty Years of Generous Support

Here's a hypothetical example of how an endowment works:

A $100,000 gift is made to the nonprofit to use as an endowment.

It is invested, not spent, and earns approximately 10 percent annually ($10,000).

Half ($5,000) of this earned amount goes back into the principal, so that the next year the earnings are based on investing $105,000. This is to help keep up with inflation. The remaining 5 percent ($5,000) is the expendable amount that can actually be used for that year and legally must be used for the express purpose the donor has designated. One can quickly realize that endowing a program takes a tremendous amount of money.

Milestones

- The *building* of every piece of the Taube Tennis Center, including all furnishings and stadium improvements, most notably the incredible video system and video board/broadcast system. Beginning in 1982, we raised over $20 million to fund the Taube Tennis Center and its improvements. Frankly, I am very proud of this achievement, especially because endowment monies were not used for this purpose.

- An *endowment* covering 100 percent of the men's tennis budget, approximately $15 million in 2017, funded:

    a. Positions: The John L. Hinds Director of Tennis Position, The Taube Family Head Coaching Position, The Martha and Jim Poppy Assistant Coach Position.

    b. Scholarships: All four and a half (the limit allowed by the NCAA) with the John Arrillaga Family Scholarship, the William T. Closs Scholarship, the Irving Carlton Deal Family Scholarship Fund, the Matt Harris Scholarship, the La Jolla Scholarship, the Jim and Willy Mitchell Scholarship, the Ralph Rodriguez Scholarship, the Rixford K. Snyder Scholarship, and the Pat and Bill Wilson Scholarship.

    c. Operating Budgets: 100 percent at the level allowable by our department of athletics.

    d. Maintenance and Repairs: support from the Irving C. Deal Family generated approximately $100,000 in expendable funds annually. In addition, John Klotz and Bob and Frances Low provided a maintenance endowment specifically for our streaming equipment maintenance. Terry and Carol Eger provided a major cash gift for indoor court repairs, which were further augmented by rentals from outside facility use and internally from lesson and camp surcharges.

    e. Discretionary Expenses: The William. T. Atkins Men's Coach's Discretionary Fund, established by one of my first players, Bill Atkins, primarily intended for facility improvement.

We all must recognize the importance of fundraising to guarantee the continued existence of what some would call minor sports.

In addition to the thirty-five years of designing, fundraising, and building the new facility, I am equally proud that when I retired in 2018, our men's tennis program was completely endowed. Stanford men's tennis might have been the only athletic program in the country in any sport that was truly and completely endowed at that time. We—our former players and supporters—did essentially all of it! This totaled approximately $35 million, and the results included the complete stadium rebuild, as well as our complete men's tennis program endowment that ensures its future.

Special Donors (Non-Endowment Major Gifts for Stadium Construction and Improvements)

I would be remiss if I did not recognize several people for their uncommon support for the stadium renovation in addition to the ones previously named: Tim and Barbara Arnstein, John and Fran Arrillaga, Peter and Helen Bing, Bob and Sue Boniface, the Herb Dwight family, Terry and Carol Eger, Rick and Donna Fluegel, the Tom Ford family, Jack Gifford and family, the John Hoisch family, the Craig Johnson family, Phil and Penny Knight, Paul and Andy Koontz, the Koret Foundation, Lawrence Korn, Bob McGlinchey, Jerry and Phyllis Olefsky, the Mike Orsak family, Victor and Gwen Riches, Claude and Louise Rosenberg, Bob and Mary Sibert, and Jackie and Russ Thompson. Without their major lead support coupled with the help of hundreds of others, the stadium project could never have been completed.

In summary, being entrepreneurial is critical to staying relevant because one must stay ahead of the game. In addition, for many sports, including tennis, it may even be the assurance needed for survival in today's athletic world. And of course, the initiatives and actions of entrepreneurialism require funds, hence fundraising, which in turn depends on building an ongoing and enthusiastic constituency. Active community involvement is of critical importance to the success of these efforts. It is all related. It would be nice to be able to just recruit and coach, but to stay on top, it requires that which is much more complex, involved, and essential.

PARTING THOUGHTS:

COACHING IS A SACRED RESPONSIBILITY

Thanks to the extraordinary response and generosity of 83 percent (166) of my players, I'm confident now that I am much better prepared to provide some answers to original questions posed by Jack Gifford and Matt Knoll respectively:

How did we win so many championships, and why did we perform so well in the big moments?

I reread all of what the players had provided in order to select responses that might suggest a better answer than the one I had originally offered—simply, we had the best players. I was astounded to find so many different examples, detailed in this book, in which a player described what he felt was the key to our achievements.

My conclusion now is that there is no one single answer, but rather many ingredients that went into our success. The ingredients of our "secret sauce" centered largely around our recruiting and culture, and my particular style of leadership. Each of these ideas consisted of a wealth of satellite ideas, all of them important. The responses below seem to best summarize the most important answers to these two questions:

According to Mike Bryan, '00, who has won more Grand Slam doubles championships than anyone in the history of the game:

"I feel the unique culture of class and greatness helped create a magical atmosphere that produced remarkable results. It came from a deep respect for the history that had been created and the high bar of excellence that was expected to be maintained.

"There was also a no-bullshit mentality. Everyone was there to work hard and be successful. Since only a handpicked select few of the best players in the country were a part of the team, it was easy to fall into this mold. When you joined the team, you automatically felt like you were there to do your job and that was to help win an NCAA championship. Coach magnified this sense of pride and purpose each and every day.

"Coach Gould had an aura that demanded respect, and he had all the attributes that made it easy for players to put their faith in him. He was always prepared and knew what to say. You could see that he cared deeply about his role and was extremely driven to succeed. You could see that he knew the formula of what it took to be a championship team, so there was no reason to resist it. There was never doubt in his eyes, and he always confidently executed his plan. It was nice to be able to trust that this man could guide the team, and in turn help every member reach his full potential."

Nick Saviano, '73, a member of one of my first championship teams and today one of America's greatest coaches, sums it up from his vantage point of almost a half-century past:

"I think in reviewing Dick Gould's legacy, as with any person who has achieved truly great results, it is most important that people don't get blinded by the results. It is critical to understand that the results that Dick had are truly the by-product of his personal greatness. His pursuit of constant and relentless improvement. His pursuit of fulfilling and executing the value systems of work ethic, attention to detail, perseverance, determination, a willingness to take chances to do and be special, never letting his competitors see him down or discouraged, his amazing recruiting skills, optimism, can-do mentality, and his understanding of the poem he once showed me called, I believe, 'The Station,' which if

I may paraphrase, says that you never really arrive at the station and that life is really about the journey and the importance of making the absolute most of every day.

"If I were to summarize it all up, it would be that Dick had and has a profound understanding that life is about the journey and for God sakes make the most of it! This is the profound example that Dick Gould has passed on to me—

Nick Saviano: All-American; World Singles #48; USTA Director of Coaching and Coaching Education

of course I have learned it in other ways and through my own life experiences, but Dick's example has been so relentless and consistent that it has left an indelible impression on me in my life. Life is a journey, a blessing, an opportunity, so don't waste today. Make the most of it! The results are truly the by-products of an incredibly powerful and positive philosophy of life! That is a true legacy."

Coaching in any arena is a Sacred Responsibility! I cannot emphasize this enough. I think most of the people with whom I have had the opportunity to teach and coach would say the same thing. But there is something extra special about working intensively (three hours a day, six days per week throughout the school year for four years) with young people who are eighteen or so and away from home for the first time—who want to make their own choices and perhaps think they know it all, but in many ways, really have minimal life experience on which to base their decision-making. (In essence, just as I was when I started coaching.) The opportunity to serve as a mentor or role model at this critical age of independence carries with it a tremendous responsibility.

I have a responsibility to be certain that, in attempting to be the best, values and high standards are *never* sacrificed. We had our moments, but I was so very proud overall of how our teams represented themselves, their families, their teammates, our university, and our sport—both on the court and off. We set the bar high in showing how to win with humility and lose with grace. This to me was as important as any wins and losses, and I think my players understood this and became better people because of it. In the end, it was not the win nor the loss, but the process of it all that made the attempts worthwhile. I truly believe that our opposing players and coaches—although they wanted to beat the heck out of us, because frankly, we were the gold standard—had the utmost respect for how we competed.

As Scott Humphries, '98, describes, *"The coaching staff put the responsibility back on the players to hold each other accountable, which is one of the reasons I think the teams for decades were so strong. Unselfishness, respect for the program, sportsmanship. With all the guys who have come through the program, my feeling was that all of them were able to put the team goals over their own. I think this was just the culture. The sportsmanship piece is tied into the respect for the program because Coach stressed that we were representing the university, the team, and ourselves, and the teams always did it in a classy way."*

Achieving realistic goals is important, whether the goals are related to how one represents oneself or to performance itself. I am proud of what we accomplished in both areas, while rising from almost nowhere to winning seventeen national team championships in twenty-eight years!

After thirty-eight years at the men's coaching helm, and from the perspective of another fourteen years while serving as director of tennis in an administrative role, my advice to young coaches and young leaders of any type is to *never* lose sight of your dreams and *never* stop working to achieve them. There may be some pain and disappointment along the way, but that is life. Use those as opportunities to learn. The true measure of a person is how they rebound from these setbacks. If one approach doesn't work, try another. But above all, persevering for the right reasons and undertaking noble causes is a virtue, especially in this age of instant gratification!

Of course, it only took me thirty-eight years to learn all of this, and even now, it took the players to articulate it all. And this was only the foundation for other lessons I would also come to learn. Since day one, I was a work in progress, and for all great coaches I suspect this learning and striving to get better never stops.

Other leaders and coaches would have a different matrix of strategies and values, but these were mine. It always started with me setting a good example, by exhibiting class and integrity, and expressing enthusiasm and positivity. I felt I had to be organized, prepared, and listen to my players while communicating my own expectations and feelings. Then, putting the team first, we worked hard with a purpose and made no excuses. It wasn't always perfect, but it was pretty successful.

In looking back over the years, there is so much for which I have to be thankful—my health, my family, my friends, and my "hobby": the teaching profession! I take none of these for granted. I have been blessed to have had the incredible opportunity to serve well into the fifty-second year at my alma mater (the longest of any employee in the history of Stanford's department of athletics). But all good things at some time come to an end.

When I finally retire, I will be proud to have my tombstone read:

1. He had a great ride
2. He went for it
3. He got better
4. He had fun
5. He did it the right way
6. He had no regrets

Above all, I want to say, *"Thanks* to *all* my guys" for the time they took to express thoughts that were important to them. We had a great ride together. I am a better person for having had the opportunity to have been on this journey with them. They will always be a part of my *family*!

PS: I stand by my original answer to Jack: in all respects, I *did* have the best players—*and people*!

Dick Gould
Stanford, CA

Epilogue

RETIREMENT FROM COACHING AND TRANSITION TO DIRECTOR OF TENNIS

Final NCAA Team Championship (2000), spanning four decades

After just over thirty years of coaching, I decided I wouldn't coach more than forty years or if we went four years without a four-year player receiving a championship ring. (Every starting player for thirty-four years earned at least one.) We had great teams in 2001 and 2002 especially, but in both cases, my number one players Alex Kim and then K. J. Hippensteel, each respectively at the time ranked number one in the country, incurred season-ending injuries—Alex in the NCAA quarterfinals and K. J. the next year in our conference championships. In a sport where only about two-thirds of the starters have an athletic scholarship, a loss at the top of the lineup of this magnitude and at season's end that affected not only singles, but doubles as well, proved to be an insurmountable challenge.

We had the chance to win again in 2003 and ensure I would coach for my self-proclaimed "forty-year limit," but one of my top three players elected to leave the team, and we were not good enough without him to win a title. The chances of winning in 2004 were so remote that before the season started, I did what I had promised myself I would do—I went to my boss, AD Ted Leland, and told him I was going to retire at the end of the season, after thirty-eight years. I almost made it to forty years.

NCAA Men's and Women's Championships

In the same meeting with Ted when I resigned from coaching, I submitted a job description for "Director of Tennis," which Ted approved. Now I would be able to do some things I felt needed to be done that I could not do while I was coaching: hosting joint men's/women's NCAA championships, develop a state-of-the-art streaming/broadcast system, fully endow the men's tennis program, and so on.

Our facility by now was ready to host a championship. Immediately, with the backing of my athletic department and accompanied by Beth Goode, our assistant director of athletics (also a member of the NCAA tennis committee), I went to the NCAA headquarters in Indianapolis to propose that the 2005 NCAA championships be hosted by Stanford. I also proposed that it be held as a combined event for men and women. The women's NCAAs had been held at Stanford several times while I was coaching the men's teams. *If* we hosted in the manner I envisioned, I wanted to ensure it would be spectacular and nothing short of first class and innovative, which I hoped was becoming my trademark!

The NCAA men's tennis committee was caught off guard by this proposal to host a championship for both men and women at the same site. But they promised they would give it full consideration in upcoming talks with the women's tennis championship committee. The first-ever national championship with men and women playing simultaneously at the same site was approved for the 2006 NCAA championships. The number of participants doubled to over three hundred players, and the synergy created proved to be incredible!

It was meant to be a community celebration of tennis, college tennis in particular, and to be something the players would never forget. To this end, we raised approximately $1 million over and above our NCAA budget to make it truly special. We formed a blue-ribbon committee of volunteers, all devoted to hitting a home run.

Among the many special and unique features was a two-hour-long NCAA "Magic Moments" highlight film I contracted with ESPN to assemble that featured the NCAA finals over their twenty years of broadcasting the championships. This played continuously throughout the tournament on our monitor at the stadium entrance.

The mixed format was a resounding success, and crowds loved the event. Essentially the same format was repeated when the next NCAA championships were hosted at Stanford in 2011, though an improved streaming system was developed in time for that championship. Thanks to the efforts and dedication of hundreds of volunteers and the full support of our athletic department, it was "mission accomplished!"

Assistant Coach John Whitlinger

It was a big deal when assistant coaches were permitted to be hired for tennis. I had been coaching three teams simultaneously, each with about ten to twelve players. Even with the phaseout of freshman teams in 1972–73 and JV teams with the advent of Title IX in 1974–75, I still had ten to twelve guys to coach. I found it difficult to work with one individual at the expense of the rest of the team. Finally, after my first twenty years, Stanford was prepared to let me hire an assistant coach.

John Whitlinger: Team Captain; NCAA Singles and Doubles Champion; World Singles #75; Assistant and Associate Head Coach (18 years), Head Coach (10 years)

I knew in my mind what I wanted—someone I could as a parent entrust my own child to (morally, ethically, etc.). Someone who was technically sound, who understood the tactics of the game, who had achieved success on the pro tour, and who understood and respected Stanford. I wanted in essence another head coach. I think the main leadership takeaway is *always* look to hire up—*never* be threatened by hiring someone who makes the organization and culture better. John Whitlinger was just off the pro tour, where he was solidly in the world's top one hundred. He had been one of the top and most respected junior players in the country. As a college player at Stanford, he won a rare triple crown: NCAA singles, doubles, and team championships.

I recruited John Whitlinger, '76, hard to get him to attend Stanford as a player, but I had to work even harder to get him to return to Stanford as my assistant for the 1986–87 year. He subsequently became my associate head coach. John recounts:

"I wish I could remember all the stories, but I've forgotten a lot of them. I was in a unique position to play for Coach, and later to coach with him as well. It was a great time in my life. I just can't imagine how my life would have been different if I had gone to play at UCLA. All the letters from him to 810 Hewitt St. in Neenah, WI, and then the amazing time at the Junior Davis Cup camp made it an easy decision to go to Stanford. And finally, I thank him for his trust in making me his first assistant coach. I

didn't want to do it initially, but my dad said, 'Try it, you might like it.' Well, I did, and we made a great team for many years!"

For two years, John and his wife Jan, and their two little kids, lived not in a mobile home, but in a trailer, rent-free on the property of one of my high-school- days friends who happened to be Stanford athletics' biggest booster, John Arrillaga. In addition, one of my former college roommates, Bernie Magnussen, a reputable car dealer, helped him out with a courtesy car. John and Jan soon were able to save enough money to purchase their own home!

In 1991, in a cost-cutting move, the NCAA mandated that assistant coaches in many sports be designated as "restricted earnings" coaches to save money because athletic department expenses, largely caused by Title IX, were mounting. This meant assistants in both men's and women's sports, who had already been hired at a certain rate, were now restricted to $12,000 in earnings during the school year for their coaching duties and to $4,000 in earnings during the summer months. Whit could not afford to continue to serve as my assistant under these restrictions in the high-priced area around Palo Alto. But creative thinking can accomplish a lot. Fortunately, John was able to load up on teaching PE courses. Because this remuneration was coming from a different university source than our athletic department, he could accept this extra pay. In addition, some local clubs held events with Whit as tournament director and in which our team gladly participated, so he received compensation that way too. The restricted earnings rule was rescinded by a federal jury in 1998 as a violation of antitrust laws.

Whit made a difference! I could kind of be the bad guy and Whit could come in and cover up for me. Plus, being younger, he could still hit with the guys and feed balls much better than I could. He made a thousand little changes that paid huge dividends simply because he understood the game and his players. For example, he moved the grip over on Alex Kim's forehand, which made it an incredible weapon. This led directly to an NCAA singles title and a solid pro career. He got future NCAA doubles champ Sam Warburg to move closer to the baseline when playing from the backcourt.

I assigned him to be courtside for several national champion-ship individual matches, first with Alex O'Brien. Alex was on the verge of being the first player since Whit to win the triple crown of NCAA championships: singles, doubles, and team. And with Whit on court to guide him for his NCAA singles final, he did. The list goes on and on. John was at least as responsible for the championships we won after he arrived, as was I. We were a great pair. I was so proud when he was named to follow me as head coach.

GIVING BACK

First meeting of every year, Coach encour- aged us to give back to the program when- ever we left. We won the NCAA title one year in Athens. At the same time, there was a capital campaign to raise money to up- grade the Georgia facility. During Coach's acceptance speech for our team winning the NCAA championship, he pulled out a personal check made out to the Univer- sity of Georgia, handed it to Coach Dan Magill, and encouraged all the Georgia fans to give what they could ('Even ten bucks, which is just a couple of beers') on their way out so that we could all con- tinue to enjoy this beautiful venue. Such a class move!

Paul Goldstein, '98

This small check was the least I could do to let the great Geor- gia fans and supporters know how much we appreciated them and what they were constantly doing to improve their facil- ity. I think it was one of the first gifts to kick off their facility improvement campaign.

As coaches and leaders, we have an opportunity to teach appreci- ation for what one has. We have a responsibility to be sure this is not taken for granted. Further, we must teach that as our players are able, they have an obligation to give back the same way their tennis/athletic experience was given to them: by the work, sacri- fice, and efforts of their predecessors!

Collegiate tennis players, and college athletes in general, are given a lot of things, from clothing and equipment as junior players to scholarships, equipment, coaching, medical care, special meals, tutors, travel opportunities, and so on. They are used to receiving. In fact, too often they expect things to be given to them! Unfortunately, many times the more they get, the more they tend to want.

Being on a team is *not* an entitlement; it is a privilege. Most of my players felt a commitment beyond their individual participation. I actively tried to impart the message of the responsibility each team player has to give back to the program, as well as to the game in general.

I am especially proud that our men's tennis players have substantially led all other Stanford athletics teams in percentages of team members who have contributed financially to their respective sports programs/athletic departments. *"You have to give back!"* Joe Kao, '04, adds. *"That was the biggest lesson that Coach imparted in me."*

How great to see my guys giving back to tennis by serving in other ways as well. For instance:

Members of the USTA board of directors:

- David Wheaton, Martin Blackman, Patrick McEnroe, Jeff Tarango, Sam Warburg; Paul Goldstein also served on the USTA nominating committee

USTA coaching leaders:

- Nick Saviano (USTA Director of Coaching for Men's Tennis and Director of Coaching Education and Sports Science)
- Patrick McEnroe and Martin Blackman (USTA Player Development Heads)

TV announcers and journalists:

- John and Patrick McEnroe, Jeff Tarango, David Wheaton

College coaches:

- Rich Andrews, Mike Best, Paul Goldstein, Gery Groslimond, Bill Maze, and John Whitlinger.

Davis Cup coaches:

- John and Patrick McEnroe

Professional tennis teachers:

- Rich Andrews, Jeff Arons, Ricky Becker, Mike Best, Lloyd Bourne, Chris Bradley, Scott Davis, Pat DuPré, Rick Fisher, Glenn Golden, Greg Grover, Ryan Haviland, Ron Kahn, Daryl Lee, John Letts, Scott Lipsky, Marcos Manqueros, Alan Margot, Gene and Sandy Mayer, Tim Mayotte, Matt Mitchell, Carter Morris, Jim Gurfein, Jared Palmer, Greg Parker, Vimal Patel, Peter Rennert, Bill Rompf, Nick Saviano, Jeff Salzenstein, Jonathan Stark, Roscoe Tanner, and Jeff Tarango.

EAST PALO ALTO TENNIS AND TUTORING

There is no question that the biggest impact Coach made on me was indirectly through the EPATT tennis program. To see someone who was so successful and a legend in NCAA tennis, but yet not completely absorbed by it, and rather showed that he still had other even larger interests outside of the game, was incredibly inspiring to me. It shows that one can still have other interests (and I'm sure in a lot of ways distractions) that make a positive impact on society, while still being the very best in their profession. Coach proved that if you're good at what you do, you can succeed in many different ways all at the same time. I think the EPATT program really also added to his legacy and proved that there was more to him than just winning championships.

—Ryan Haviland, '03

I am especially proud of one of my players, Jeff Arons. After he retired from the pro tour, he told me he wanted to teach tennis, but to those less fortunate than most. East Palo Alto is a community adjacent to Stanford and located in the heart of Silicon Valley. In the late eighties, it was per capita the "Homicide Capital of the US." I introduced Jeff to the gentleman in charge of the East Palo Alto Recreation Department, and he was quick to hire Jeff. This began a program that Jeff personally created and directed for its first ten years. Thanks to Jeff and the continued excellent leadership under executive director and one of our former Stanford volunteer team coaches, Dave Higaki, it is still thriving well over thirty years later. (Former team member Dan Turbow is currently chairperson of the board of directors, and several other team members serve on its board.) It has received numerous national and Stanford Community Outreach awards for its success in combining tutoring and tennis for the underserved. It has functioned as a home away from home for these East Palo Alto youths, as they have met at Stanford University in our Taube Tennis Center since 1997. Approximately 150 Stanford students have annually volunteered to tutor the same child twice a week throughout the school year. Our teams are also actively involved. *"Coach set a powerful example of what it means to give back to the community,"* notes Scott Matheson, '75, *"as shown by his support of the EPATT program, which has inspired the establishment of tennis-and-tutoring programs around the country, including here in Salt Lake."* Adds Philip Sheng, '05, *"I was always impressed by Coach's willingness to work hard for the community and serve them in any way possible. In fact, his example is the reason I still go out on Fridays and hit with the EPATT kids."*

Teaching Teachers

First and foremost, I am privileged to be a teacher. My specialty is the teaching of tennis. When I started serving as a club professional in conjunction with being a high school teacher, I thoroughly enjoyed working with all ages from seven-year-olds to elderly adults, and from complete beginners to players who were age group champs.

While at Foothill College as the first coach of the men's tennis team, I taught physical education classes to all ability levels. For the first half of my tenure at Stanford, in addition to coaching the team, I taught one or two physical education tennis classes per year. One was usually for tournament-level players who were just not quite good enough to be on my team. This became especially relevant in affording playing time and some group coaching after the implementation of Title IX when the junior varsity program was discontinued. The other was always "Beginning Tennis." I loved teaching beginners—they improved so quickly and were truly anxious to learn. This was a thrill for me.

When I came to Stanford, one of the few perks I requested was to be able to use the courts outside of team hours for my private teaching to help supplement my coaching income of $10,500 per year. Every Saturday morning, I would teach maybe one hundred people on four courts—twenty-four pupils per hour. Obviously, I could not do this by myself, so I hired as my staff up to eight members of my team to be at the courts to help on Saturdays from 8:00 a.m. to noon. This also gave them the opportunity to earn a little extra spending money. Almost all my team volunteered to do this, and many from my earlier teams have mentioned this as one of their favorite noncompetitive activities. A number of my players, especially those further down in the lineup, ended up making teaching tennis their life's work. For instance, Greg Parker, '72, recalls: *"I had taken lessons from Dick Gould at his home court near Foothill Jr. College. Dick was great. I learned a great deal from him about the game, including teaching. He was a tremendous enabler, and I had the privilege of being his head private instructor for three years."*

In essence, I was teaching them to teach. This was also at the time my best friend, Tom Chivington, who replaced me as the Foothill College coach, joined with me to form our teaching company Recreation Tennis, Inc. We successfully ran this company together for twenty years bringing tennis to twenty-five Northern California communities as well as running six concessions at Lake Tahoe before I went into the camp business and before Tom began coaching his former team player, Brad Gilbert, on the pro tour.

Tyler Comann, '72, reflects on his teaching experience this way. *"I will always remember how nice Coach was in telling me that my team days were over, but I could teach private lessons for him instead. Somehow, Coach made me feel like it was a promotion into something that I could excel at. I had a blast doing that for the last two years at Stanford. I really learned a lot through the teaching I did for him during the summers. From the basics of time management to the psychology of teaching a difficult subject. One thing that stands out was his emphasis that students need to be actively engaged during each class—that no one learns anything from standing around. Taken as a life lesson, it taught me to reach out in every group situation and bring everyone into the activity and conversation."*

I take great pride in how many of these young people enjoyed it so much that they made teaching their profession after college. The list includes several of the world's best teaching pros. I loved teaching teachers to teach. *"Coach taught me how to teach tennis for his company Recreation Tennis,"* says Greg Grover, '71, who went on to become "Pro of the Year" in Georgia. *"I always enjoyed phone calls Saturday mornings asking me to teach at Stanford for Stanley Pasarell, Roscoe Tanner, or Billy Atkins because they couldn't make it. I also loved teaching so much so that I made it a career! And he strongly encouraged that I follow my passion."*

"In addition to playing on the team," adds Rod Koon, '74, *"I greatly enjoyed teaching in the Stanford Saturday morning Dick Gould Tennis Camps during the school year. Not only did it give me some spending money at school, but it also gave me an insight into Dick's skill and abilities at motivating and working with players of all levels. He also had drills and techniques for teaching a group of people, much of which I incorporated into my teaching style when I taught tennis for a few years back in Tacoma after graduation (I was a pro at the Tacoma Lawn Tennis Club, etc.). I learned a lot about playing tennis and teaching tennis from Dick Gould. But I also learned a lot about always giving my best, not giving up, and keeping a positive, energetic, and encouraging outlook on what I do. I think that shows through in my work style and personal life to this day."*

"Though Coach Gould made dramatic improvements in my tennis," says Mike Best, '76, a world-class coach, *"he most helped me become a tennis coach for most of my career. Great teachers, coaches, mentors, and business leaders have one common skillset: the art of conveying information. I didn't recognize it at the time, but now, over fifty years later, I can say without hesitation that Coach was the best ever at conveying information.*

"First, he used similes and comparisons, positive reinforcement, and physical demonstrations to get the point across. But just giving a verbal instruction isn't enough. There are three pathways that activate the brain into optimal receptivity and utilization. First, speak the instruction. Other coaches do that and do it well, but Coach Gould didn't stop there.

"Second, Coach always asked us questions to engage our minds and make us actively respond, such as, 'How was your balance?' or 'Did you get to the ball too early?' or 'Where should your follow-through be?'

"And third, Coach had us take notes after practice or tournaments and review them. Why? Because some students are more responsive to written cues than verbal ones. Coach Gould utilized all these pathways to the brain, making him the coach that he was, and frankly, no one was better."

I have personally trained well over one thousand tennis teachers. I started doing tennis camps at Stanford when Tom and I turned Recreation Tennis over to my new assistant coach, John Whitlinger. I hired about twenty-five college-age students annually from all over the country to work in this camp. For most, this was their first teaching experience. Again, it is so very gratifying to see so many of them move into teaching and even college coaching themselves. I derived great satisfaction from teaching others to teach. In addition, teaching a physical education class of beginning players provided a special experience for me and gave me a different satisfaction largely centered around how fast they learned and how much they enjoyed their progress. However, the challenges of coaching my team still provided the frosting on the cake.

"Coach's instruction was by the book—the book, in fact, that he wrote: Tennis, Anyone? *" points out Chris Chapin, '72, "For the several years post-graduation that I taught tennis full-time at Round Hill Country Club, I must have said 'hold your finish until the ball bounces on the other side' ten thousand times. Taking the time to explain in words and actions that can be understood is EVERYTHING. One cannot be casual about that on the court or in the boardroom or during the sales presentation. Hitting a ball IS communication, and the hitter must be clear about what his intentions are. One must be organized and focused, yet flexible to adapt when necessary. Sounds like tennis . . . sounds like life."*

Anne and I started Tennis Week at the Stanford Sierra Camp in 1977. This is a camp for Stanford alumni and families, but one week at the end of the summer was designated Tennis Week. This tradition has continued for thirty-three years. Fortunately, one of my guys, George Rutherford, '74, who had previously taught with us, was a camp guest and had graciously volunteered to help us on court for most of those years. *"How well I remember working with Coach during Tennis Weeks at the Stanford Sierra Camp,"* George says. *"The contact with adult players looking to improve their games, Coach's infinite patience, how he doled out praise, and his all-around positivity are really imprinted in my mind."*

APPENDIXES

Subject: Anatomy of a Champion

Date: Monday, January 30, 2023 at 8:30:35 AM Pacific Standard Time

From: rjoss@stanford.edu

To: Dick Gould

Hi Dick:

After your talk at the Palo Alto Club, I ordered the book and was able to read it during my 8 week stay in Australia in December-January. I just wanted to say how much I enjoyed it and how much it resonated with all I try to teach our MBAs in my "Leadership Demystified" course. It is a great contribution to the leadership literature! It was also great for me to reflect personally on the good times I had playing in the Champagne-ships, participating in Stanford team clinics at the Los Altos Country Club, and visiting John Gardiner's Ranch (where my daughter was head girl counselor).

Thanks so much for taking the time and effort to put all this together and get it published.

Best regards,

bob

Robert L Joss AC
Dean Emeritus, Graduate School of Business
Stanford University
W: 650-723-3951
M: 650-799-1599
rjoss@stanford.edu

APPENDIX I

OVER FIFTY YEARS OF STANFORD TENNIS

1966—Coach Bob Renker retires after sixteen seasons

1966—Coach Dick Gould is hired in September for 1966–67 season

1969–71—Host: United States National Junior Davis Cup Training Camp

1972—Win first NCAA championship: Men's doubles: Tanner and A. Mayer

- First annual team Thanksgiving week trip

1973—Win first NCAA team championship

- Alex Mayer becomes first Stanford player since Ted Schroeder in 1942 to win both the NCAA singles title and doubles title (with Jim Delaney) in the same year

1974—Hold first indoor dual matches in Maples Pavilion

1975—Anne Connelly Hill is hired as women's coach to implement Title IX tennis

1978—Anne Connelly Hill leads Stanford women's tennis to its first national team championship in any sport in the Title IX era

1980—Host United States Junior Wightman Cup Training Camp for girls

- Anne Connelly Gould retires
- Frank Brennan is hired as women's coach

1983—Ralph Rodriguez Club House and Heritage Room is dedicated, and the first stadium electronic tennis scoreboard of its kind is installed

- 1986—Begin personal seat licensing program to help fund stadium operations

1986–88—Host the National Junior Training Camp for nationally ranked players

1987—John Whitlinger is hired as assistant men's coach

1989—Stanford stadium seating is rebuilt and locker rooms, coach's offices, indoor practice ranges are added, and installation of stadium lights begins

1997—Taube Family Stadium is "named" upon completion of the expansion which includes adding:

- More seats to total of 2,500
- A championship indoor court
- Stadium court lighting is completed
- First of twenty-two WTA Bank of the West women's tour tournaments

1999—Fed Cup finals (US Women vs. Russia)

- The Phil and Penny Knight scoreboard is installed

2000—Last men's NCAA team championship under Coach Gould

- EPATT build-out is completed
- Frank Brennan retires as women's coach after winning ten national team championships in twenty-one years

- Lele Forood, Frank's longtime assistant, is hired as head coach and names Frank's son, Frank Brennan III, her assistant

2000–01—Host Siebel Men's Senior Tour championships

- Lighting for back courts is added
- Heritage Plaza is completed
- Lele Forood wins first of ten NCAA team championships, which leads into the 2021–22 season

2002—Taube South complex courts are upgraded and lights are added; entire tennis complex is renamed The Taube Tennis Center

The original Taube Family Tennis Stadium retains its name

2003—Taube South seating is added

2004—Last NCAA individual championship under Coach Gould: doubles Corkery and Warburg

- Dick Gould retires from coaching to become director of tennis
- John Whitlinger is named head coach for the 2004–05 season
- Brandon Coupe is appointed assistant coach

2005—Seating for Taube Family Tennis Stadium back courts is completed

- Streaming capabilities for all seventeen courts is initiated
- Student attendance is enhanced with novel ID scanning system by Paciolan
- CourtKeeper, a court reservation system for the campus community, is designed and implemented

2006—Host the first NCAA combined men's and women's tennis championships

2010—Install the Historical Video Kiosk at the entrance to the Taube Family Tennis Stadium.

2011—Host the second NCAA combined men's and women's tennis championships

2014—Stadium streaming is upgraded to HD

- John Whitlinger retires as Head Coach
- Paul Goldstein is named the Taube Family Director of Men's Tennis
- Brandon Coupe continues as the Jim and Martha Poppy Assistant Coach

2016—Video scoreboard is debuted

- Broadcast system is implemented
- Back court scoreboard is added

2018—Men's tennis program completes endowment funding

- Dick Gould retires from Stanford athletics in his fifty-second year

APPENDIX II

SOME SPECIAL INNOVATIONS

There were a few additional items related to the evolution of our program briefly listed below that were not associated with fundraising.

STUDENT TECHNOLOGY ENHANCEMENTS

Paciolan ID Scanning (2005)

I wanted to develop a system to track student attendance at matches and to encourage them to come to more. A unique system was designed with great input from my granddaughter, Amy Brown, who served four years as team manager for Coach John Whitlinger, and later eight years as director of Stanford Women's Volleyball Operations.

A student ID was scanned upon stadium entry. The scanned cards immediately appeared on a spreadsheet with each attendee's email address. The system kept a running total of which/how many matches each student attended, as well as records of overall student attendance.

I worked with Nike, our team equipment provider, to design fifty long-sleeved, Dri-Fit "Court Club" tees. The first fifty students to attend five matches received a T-shirt. Since I had email addresses of every attendee, every week I would send out a personalized email to each student with all current point totals based on match attendance. The system was designed to highlight those in RED who had four points and would be eligible to pick up their tee at the next match.

To keep things going after a student received their shirt, we kept the point totals accumulating all season. At the end of the season, the top thirty point earners would gather, ranked in order of points awarded, to claim an item of surplus team equipment: a pair of shoes, a tennis skirt, a warm-up, and so on. This was a *great* system and easy to administer.

CourtKeeper (2005)

We developed this web-based court reservation system from scratch, and it has performed flawlessly. A student or faculty member can sign up online to use any one of twenty-five courts at three locations, up to one week ahead of time, during an hour when no regular activities (team practice/matches, physical education classes, special event) are being conducted.

COACHING TECHNOLOGY ENHANCEMENTS

SyberVision (1979)

We became loosely associated early on with this offering developed by Stanford professor Steve Devore. The concept was different from the usual video analysis in that one would select the *best* clip of their weakest shot and program it to repeat, rather than the usual viewing of video to see what they were doing wrong. If one had a backhand volley that needed work, the best example of this player hitting it correctly or as a successful shot was selected. It would then play over and over to music the player selected and in a controlled environment whereby it was impossible to focus on anything but the screen—drapes on either side of the player's viewing area helped focus their concentration straight to the over-sized monitor. The idea was to promote positive reinforcement through visualization.

CompuTennis (1981)

Our participation helped develop the great CompuTennis match statistics program, the brainchild of Bill Jacobson, the father of one of our players, Mark Jacobson. This was the forerunner of all instantaneously accessible match stats on TV today. Mark went on from our tennis team to later become Stanford's first environmental engineering professor.

Basically, Bill converted each key on the computer (CT120) keyboard to represent a shot—first serve, second serve, forehand (FH) serve return, backhand (BH) serve return, first volley, backcourt rally, FH or BH approach shot, lob, overhead, FH or BH pass shot, break point, and so on. A soft plastic overlay covered the keyboard with capitalized acronyms showing each shot for each key: FHP (forehand pass shot, etc.). One person could easily be self-taught to score a match either live or from a match replay videotape. Then the match stats could immediately be printed out, showing things like rates for first serve percentages rate, forehand serve return errors, backhand pass shot winners, break point winners, and on and on. This became a great scouting device on opponents. I could quickly tell by this printout what each of my players did well or poorly and what he needed to work on.

But the best part of this system was the fact that it was all encoded in a way that allowed me as coach, or the player himself, after reviewing the stat sheet to call up on the TV monitor the shots and situations needing work in succession (separated from all others) that could then be reviewed in our Jackie and Russ Thompson

Video Room: all backhand volleys errors; all wide forehand returns errors; all long backcourt point errors; all pass shots; all first volley winners; all approaches to the net; all breakpoints, and so on. It provided endless data for viewing by *shot* and by *point*! The players could come up to the video area outside my office immediately after their match or before the next day of practice, look over the stat sheets, and call up the relevant sequence(s) to review. *Incredible!* How proud my business and coaching partner Tom Chivington and I were to be the guinea pigs to test this great product and offer input and functional suggestions as CompuTennis was being developed!

John Yandell's *Tennisplayer* Magazine (Mideighties)

I am proud that our program was among John Yandell's first trial subjects as he developed his exceptional video analyses of the strokes of the top players and wrote his outstanding book *Visual Tennis*. His web platform has evolved into "Tennisplayer" video analysis lessons. John was one of the first instructors at the business Tom Chivington and I formed in 1967, Recreation Tennis, Inc.

APPENDIX III

STANFORD AND COLLEGE TENNIS (1967–2004)

Individual Titles

It is *extremely* difficult to win an individual championship title after winning the team title. There is absolutely no time to celebrate the team victory, and no time to mentally regroup! But many of my guys were able to achieve this. Below are some of my takeaways:

Best Played Singles Finals:

1. Dan Goldie def. Richey Reneberg (SMU, 1986) 6–2, 6–1

2. Jared Palmer def. Patricio Arnold (Georgia, 1991) 6–2, 6–0

3. Alex O'Brien def. Wade McGuire (Georgia, 1992) 6–3, 6–2

4. Alex Kim def. Carlos Drada (Kentucky, 2000) 6–1, 6–1

Three NCAA Singles Finals Featuring an All-Stanford Match:

1. John Whitlinger def. Chico Hagey (1974)

2. Tim Mayotte def. Jim Gurfein (1981)

3. Bob Bryan def. Paul Goldstein (1998)

Other Winners

Singles Champions:

1. Alex Mayer def. Raul Ramirez (USC, 1973)

2. Matt Mitchell def. Tony Graham (UCLA, 1977)

3. John McEnroe def. John Sadri (North Carolina State, 1978)

Doubles Champions:

1. Roscoe Tanner and Alex Mayer (1972)

2. Alex Mayer and Jim Delaney (1973)

3. Jim Delaney and John Whitlinger (1974)

4. Alex O'Brien and Chris Cocotos (1992)

5. Bob and Mike Bryan (1998)

6. Ryan Wolters and K.J. Hippensteel (1999)

7. KC Corkery and Sam Warburg (2004)

Triple Crown Winners: (NCAA Team, Singles and Doubles Titles)

1. Alex Mayer, 1973

2. John Whitlinger, 1974

3. Alex O'Brien, 1992

4. Bob Bryan, 1998

Team Results

NCAA Championships

1. 1973 (second place, USC)

2. 1974 (second place, USC)

3. 1977 (second place, Trinity Texas)

4. 1978 (second place, UCLA)

5. 1980 (second place, Cal-Berkeley)

6. 1981 (second place, UCLA)

7. 1983 (second place, SMU)

8. 1986 (second place, Pepperdine)

9. 1988 (second place, LSU)

10. 1989 (second place, Georgia)

11. 1990 (second place, Tennessee)

12. 1992 (second place, Notre Dame)

13. 1995 (second place, Mississippi)

14. 1996 (second place, UCLA)

15. 1997 (second place, Georgia)

16. 1998 (second place, Georgia)

17. 2000 (second place, VCU)

Toughest NCAA Team Losses

At the beginning of this book, I mentioned that one of my prompts for writing this was a question posed by the great Baylor coach Matt Knoll. Matt asked me how many times we had played in the NCAA team finals. I did not know, so I looked it up. We had appeared in seventeen NCAA team finals and had won fifteen of them. (Our first two titles in 1973 and 1974 were won in the old individual tournament format.) But the two team titles we lost really hurt. How well I remember both of those!

The first I have referred to earlier in the book. It was against UCLA in 1984 and was played in Athens, Georgia. With the original scoring system where doubles was played last and each doubles match (two of three sets) counted as one point, the score was tied at 4–4, and the deciding doubles match was tied at 4–4 in the third set. It was break point at 3–3 in the game, and Michael Kures in the "ad" court chose to take the return. John Letts and Jim Grabb had been struggling to hold serve, and getting the first serve in was critical. I thus called for a serve to the "Center T," where the net is lower. I also figured that, although Michael had a gigantic forehand, he would not be expecting the ball there. The result was that he hit the biggest forehand return I have ever seen, and we had no play on the first volley. Up a break, UCLA held serve for the match and a 5–4 victory! I still wake up at night thinking about my call and how I quite possibly cost my team the title.

The second was ten years later in 1994 at Notre Dame against USC. It was with the new format, and now doubles were played first—a school had to win the best of the three doubles matches to earn a single point now awarded for the doubles play. USC had beaten us three times that year—also, we had never won the doubles point in the second doubles competition with each team having won one of the other two matches—and were poised to win our first doubles point of the year against the Trojans. This was all-important since we had always split the singles matches. We needed the doubles point! We earned a match point. Bobby Devens ripped a return on a 3–3 no-ad point down the line to evidently win the match, but it turned out to be just barely wide, so the doubles match continued. And we eventually lost in a close battle. Rarely have I been prouder of a "losing" effort. Bobby didn't hold back. He went for it—aggressive with margin but a hair too little of the latter. USC went on to win the deciding doubles 9–7. This meant Stanford would have to win four of the singles matches to earn the title. Stanford had won three of these singles matches, and Jeff Salzenstein won the first set against Jon Leach but had lost the second set 6–3. In the final match and in the third set, everything went wrong that could: a broken shoe-lace, a slip and fall while going for a winning volley, and so on, and USC won the set 6–3 in the third, and the title. I felt so very, very bad for Jeff, who had had a great season and had played an outstanding match!

We had actually come extremely close to winning every time we reached the team finals! It is interesting to note that in the fifteen team titles we won, which began in 1977, we met eleven different schools in the finals.

Team Record Against Main Conference Rivals

1. UCLA: 53 Wins; 48 Losses

2. USC: 53 Wins; 46 Losses

3. University of California at Berkeley: 75 Wins; 12 Losses

4. Arizona: 52 Wins; 1 Loss

5. ASU: 48 Wins; 1 Loss

6. Washington: 27 Wins; 1 Loss

7. Oregon: 18 Wins; 0 Losses

8. Also, vs. Georgia: 14 Wins; 2 Losses

APPENDIX IV

STANFORD AND THE PROS

WORLD TOP 100
Singles, Highest Ranking

#1—John McEnroe ('80, '81, '82, '83, '84)

#4—Gene Mayer ('80)

#5—Roscoe Tanner ('79)

#7—Alex "Sandy" Mayer ('82)

#7—Tim Mayotte ('88)

#11—Scott Davis ('85)

#12—David Wheaton ('91)

#13—Derrick Rostagno ('91)

#14—Pat DuPré ('80)

#24—Jim Grabb ('90)

#27—Dan Goldie ('89)

#28—Patrick McEnroe ('95)

#30—Alex O'Brien ('97)

#35—Jared Palmer ('94)

#36—Jonathan Stark ('94)

#40—Peter Rennert ('80)

#42—Jeff Tarango ('92)

#48—Nick Saviano ('78)

#53—Matt Mitchell ('85)

#58—Paul Goldstein ('06)

#59—Jim Delaney ('76)

#73—Lloyd Bourne ('83)

#75—John Whitlinger ('75)

#96—Jim Gurfein ('83)

#100—Jeff Salzenstein ('96)

WORLD TOP 100
Doubles, Highest Ranking

#1—John McEnroe ('79, '80, '81, '82, '83, '84, '89)

#1—Jim Grabb ('89, '92, '93)

#1—Jonathan Stark ('94)

#1—Jared Palmer ('00, '02)

#1—Alex O'Brien ('00)

#1—Bob Bryan ('03–'16)

#1—Mike Bryan ('03–'16, '18, '19)

#2—Scott Davis ('91)

#3—Alex Mayer ('85)

#3—Patrick McEnroe ('93)

#7—Gene Mayer ('80)

#9—Peter Rennert ('83)

#10—Roscoe Tanner ('75)

#10—Jeff Tarango ('99)

APPENDIX V

FAVORITE PASSAGES

If I had to pick out two literary works to guide me in living my life, without question they would be Rudyard Kipling's "If—," circa 1895, and one that I first saw in a syndicated Ann Lander's column in 1981 called "The Station," written in 2003 by Robert Hastings, then editor of *The Illinois Baptist*.

I have referenced them both previously. They've had a big impact on my personal values and therefore on how I coach. Framed copies of both are in my home and work office. Each of my children and grandchildren have also received one as a gift upon high school graduation and the other upon college graduation.

I end every talk I give with one of these two pieces, whether it be to a group of campers, parents, coaches, or people in a company. Though I'd never really pointed either one out to my players, from the comments I received, many of them had taken them time to read one or the other posted on my office wall.

These are really my religion, my bible! I think you will agree, a leader could do a lot worse than aspire to live by these words from Kipling and Hastings.

IF—

by Rudyard Kipling

If you can keep your head when all about you
Are losing theirs and blaming it on you,
If you can trust yourself when all men doubt you,
But make allowance for their doubting too;
If you can wait and not be tired by waiting,
Or being lied about, don't deal in lies,
Or being hated, don't give way to hating,
And yet don't look too good, nor talk too wise:

If you can dream—and not make dreams your master;
If you can think—and not make thoughts your aim;
If you can meet with Triumph and Disaster
And treat those two impostors just the same;
If you can bear to hear the truth you've spoken
Twisted by knaves to make a trap for fools,
Or watch the things you gave your life to, broken,
And stoop and build 'em up with worn-out tools:

If you can make one heap of all your winnings
And risk it on one turn of pitch-and-toss,
And lose, and start again at your beginnings
And never breathe a word about your loss;
If you can force your heart and nerve and sinew
To serve your turn long after they are gone,
And so hold on when there is nothing in you
Except the Will which says to them: 'Hold on!'

If you can talk with crowds and keep your virtue,
Or walk with Kings—nor lose the common touch,
If neither foes nor loving friends can hurt you,
If all men count with you, but none too much;
If you can fill the unforgiving minute
With sixty seconds' worth of distance run,
Yours is the Earth and everything that's in it,
And—which is more—you'll be a Man, my son!

THE STATION
by Robert Hastings

Tucked away in our subconscious minds is an idyllic vision. We see ourselves on a long, long trip that almost spans the continent. We're traveling by passenger train, and out the windows we drink in the passing scene of cars on nearby highways, of children waving at a crossing, of cattle grazing on a distant hillside, of smoke pouring from a power plant, of row upon row of corn and wheat, of flatlands and valleys, of mountains and rolling hills, of biting winter and blazing summer and cavorting spring and docile fall.

But uppermost in our minds is the final destination. On a certain day at a certain hour we will pull into the station. There will be bands playing, and flags waving. And once we get there so many wonderful dreams will come true. So many wishes will be fulfilled and so many pieces of our lives finally will be neatly fitted together like a completed jigsaw puzzle. How restlessly we pace the aisles, damning the minutes for loitering ... waiting, waiting, waiting, for the station.

However, sooner or later we must realize there is no one station, no one place to arrive at once and for all. The true joy of life is the trip. The station is only a dream. It constantly outdistances us.

"When we reach the station that will be it!" we cry. Translated it means, "When I'm 18, that will be it! When I buy a new 450 SL Mercedes Benz, that will be it! When I put the last kid through college, that will be it! When I have paid off the mortgage, that will be it! When I win a promotion, that will be it! When I reach the age of retirement, that will be it! I shall live happily ever after!"

Unfortunately, once we get it, then it disappears. The station somehow hides itself at the end of an endless track.

"Relish the moment" is a good motto, especially when coupled with Psalm 118:24: "This is the day which the Lord hath made; we will rejoice and be glad in it." It isn't the burdens of today that drive men mad. Rather, it is regret over yesterday or fear of tomorrow. Regret and fear are twin thieves who would rob us of today.

So, stop pacing the aisles and counting the miles. Instead, climb more mountains, eat more ice cream, go barefoot oftener, swim more rivers, watch more sunsets, laugh more and cry less. Life must be lived as we go along. The station will come soon enough.

Copyright 2003 Tristan Publishing

APPENDIX VI

ORIGINAL TWENTY QUESTIONS SENT TO MY PLAYERS

1. Why did you choose to play tennis at Stanford (beyond the academics and beautiful campus)? What did you see and hear about our program (from me and/or others) that convinced you to join our team? Did what you hear live up to your expectations?

2. As a player, did you feel that Stanford tennis had a special culture? If so, what was it and how was it created? Any anecdotes related to this are welcome.

3. What are your biggest takeaways from your time as a member of the Stanford tennis team—lessons that you and others could benefit from with their own teams and companies?

4. Beyond the mechanics of the game, what did I do that helped you as a tennis player, person, and competitor that a coach or manager elsewhere could utilize? Examples are encouraged!

5. Do you feel we had clear team goals and core values? If so, what were they and how were they conveyed and achieved?

6. Are there any special *personal* values you feel a great team must have, and how did I help you attain them?

7. Tennis is basically an individual sport. Why do you think we seemed to be able to translate the talent and success of *individual* players, many with big egos, into *team* success? What lessons could be learned that others could use?

8. Looking back, what were my assets and strengths, as well as areas of needed improvement, with special focus on how I attempted to create a sense of unity and commitment to the teams? Examples?

9. What importance does *trust* (of teammates; of coaches) have to do in the development of a successful team, and was it developed within our teams?

10. Can you remember a story or two that illustrates examples of how I dealt with special issues in practice, during matches, or elsewhere?

11. During my tenure, we won seventeen NCAA championships. In fact, we won more total NCAA championships than conference championships. Why did we seem to play best when it mattered most? Are there any lessons here to impart to others in order to get peak performance when under the most pressure?

12. Our teams had a unique ability to bounce back from setbacks, disappointments, and distractions. We had *resilience*. Why? Examples.

13. How did I prepare you mentally and emotionally to handle both wins and losses?

14. Do you feel *all* players on the team felt relevant and took pride in being a part of the tennis program? If yes, why? If not, why?

15. How did I help you in your efforts to bring out your best?

16. If someone asked you to describe me both as a person and a coach, what would you tell them?

17. I tended to emphasize improvement of your individ-

ual weaknesses, perhaps at the expense of further developing your strengths. Was this productive?

18. In light of the fact that *new* players were coming in each season while others were leaving, to what do you attribute the *longevity* and *consistency* of the program's success? (For thirty-four years, every team starter earned at least one championship ring.)

19. What are some of your favorite individual or team off-court memories? (Team social events, Thanksgiving trips, etc.).

20. WILD CARD QUESTION: If you don't have the time or desire to answer the questions above, or if you have anything special to add, I would really appreciate it if you could offer your general thoughts below. Of special interest would be an interesting/funny/not-so-funny story or two from your experience as a part of our Stanford tennis program.

21. Added Question: When did you see me the maddest?

BACKSTORY

ABOUT DICK GOULD

Younger Days

I grew up during and after World War II on a small, thirteen-acre lemon orchard in Ventura, California, a farming community on the coast of Southern California. My father was a farmer, my mother was a teacher. I had two younger siblings, my sister Jean and my brother Bob. I loved school and developed lasting friendships dating from kindergarten. In fact, in high school I was elected student body president and was named by my senior class as "The Most Likely to Succeed."

Tennis wasn't on my radar as a child. I was raised with a horse and a .22 rifle, but I grew up loving sports. My dad had wrestled and played on the Stanford University JV football team known as the "Goofs" under legendary coach Pop Warner. My mom was very active in the Women's Recreation Association at Stanford, playing basketball and a variety of other sports. (There were no women's varsity sports in those days.) My granddad lived next door and loved baseball. We would spend hours playing catch in his oversized driveway. Our annual family drive to Northern California to visit my other grandparents in Watsonville and then attend the Stanford–Cal football game was a particular treat. In fact, as a youngster at a pregame event one evening, my folks introduced me to the university president, Dr. Wallace Sterling. He encouraged me by saying, "Richard, when you enroll at Stanford, we'll roll out the red carpet for you."

I was introduced to tennis when I was eleven years old, and my mom signed me up for a lesson. As a farm kid, I wasn't enthusiastic about anything involving wearing little white shorts, but Mom said that if I wanted to ride my horse that summer, I had to try at least one lesson. When I arrived at the court, my attitude changed when I saw two attractive fourteen-year-old twin girls just finishing their lesson. "Well," I thought, as I was just beginning to notice girls, "maybe I'll give this sport a try."

That day I met the first of several great teachers and coaches who would deeply influence me, both personally and in my later approach to coaching and teaching. Harold Chaffee was a great motivator and teacher who really drew me in. Because he made each ball I hit an exciting adventure and was able to equate it to other sports, I fell in love with tennis during that very first lesson. The brother of one of those twins at my first lesson later played on the Stanford team and had a daughter who also ended up playing at Stanford on the team that my wife, Anne, coached to Stanford's first national women's team championship in any sport in 1978. In fact, Caryn Hertel and her partner won the deciding doubles match.

In my first tournament, I lost 6–0, 6–1 in the first round. My mom, who knew really nothing about tennis, spent the hour drive home telling me everything I should have done better. I never let her watch me play again!

In junior high school I played football and basketball, but I also took a seventh grade tennis class where I met Tom Chivington. Tom would become my best friend, co-coach, and business partner. That spring, Tom and I played several school year USLTA[5] events in Los Angeles.

---

5   The organization was called the United States Lawn Tennis Association (USLTA) until the 1970s, when it dropped the word "lawn" and became just the United States Tennis Association (USTA).

When I entered high school in the early 1950s, I met another great coach, Arnie Saul, who had been an outstanding tennis player at USC. Truly a teacher's teacher, I learned a lot from Arnie. Whereas Harold was a larger-than-life personality, Arnie was more of a quiet leader and

Three coaches: Arnie Saul (Ventura High School Tennis and Basketball) surrounded by his high school pupils and doubles partners, Gould and Tom Chivington (former Foothill College State Championship coach; Partner with Gould—Recreation Tennis, Inc., a tennis teaching company)

very solid in his fundamentals. He was also my "B" basketball coach at school, and was always all about his players, not himself. That too was a valuable lesson, though I didn't realize it at the time.

In the summer of 1951, when I was fourteen, I started helping Harold Chaffee teach group lessons for the recreation department in Santa Paula, a neighboring community, in return for a pint of pineapple sherbet at the end of each workday. I thought this was a pretty good deal, especially after three hours in the hot sun! The second year, I was put on the Ventura rec department's payroll to help with Arnie's teaching program. By 1956, I was in charge of the program and also teaching swimming lessons and serving as a lifeguard at the Ventura community pool.

I also worked during the summers on the family farm. Between that and teaching tennis and working at the pool, I was never able to play in enough tennis tournaments to attain a ranking until the summer before college. However, that year I earned a #18 ranking in the Southern California eighteen-and-under age group. I was very proud of this.

Off to Stanford

I never wanted to go anywhere to college but Stanford because I literally had Stanford in my blood. Starting in the early 1900s, my dad's mom and my mom's dad had both attended Stanford. A generation later, my parents enrolled, and later my siblings would follow me. My sister, Jean, went all the way through to earn her PhD in history; my brother, Bob, was an engineering major and then a longtime pilot for Northwest Airlines. My stepbrother, Jim Hibbs, was an All-American baseball player at Stanford and played on the first US Olympic baseball team.

Unfortunately, I wasn't a shoo-in for admission. During the winter of my senior year in high school in 1955, I will never forget the postcard I received from Stanford's director of admissions, Dr. Rixford K. Snyder. The note said:

> Dear Richard,
>
> We are writing to inform you that the score you achieved on the Scholastic Aptitude Test is below that which generally indicates satisfactory success at Stanford. We are notifying you now in the event you wish to begin making alternate plans.
>
> Rixford K. Snyder
> Director of Freshman Admissions
> Stanford University

I was shattered! Alternate plans? I had no alternate plans! Stanford was the only school to which I had applied. In those days, SAT and ACT scores were not made available to the students, so I had no idea how far off the normal acceptance curve I was. I knew I didn't ordinarily test well, but I also knew that Stanford considered much more than test scores for admission. My high school grades were quite good, and I was heavily involved in student government and many other school activities, so I stayed the course and chose not to apply to any backup schools. I prayed I would somehow get admitted.

Fortunately, because I don't know what else I would have done, when April rolled around, I was accepted, and I enrolled in the fall of 1955. The good word Stanford tennis coach Bob Renker put in for me with the admissions office may have done the trick. Whatever happened, I was in! Years later, Dr. Snyder became a good friend and a big booster of our tennis program and endowed a men's tennis scholarship. I had the incredible honor to deliver one of the eulogies before a capacity crowd at Dr. Snyder's memorial service in Stanford's Memorial Church.

A Fledgling Coach

My plan had long been to major in political science, head for law school, and then become an attorney and maybe eventually enter the political arena. But I had so enjoyed teaching tennis and swimming and lifeguarding in Ventura during the summers and watching how the department of parks and recreation helped the community that almost immediately I dumped my major and my law school plans and aspired to become a community director of recreation like my summer boss, Thor Olson. Unfortunately, Stanford offered no major for recreation, so I signed up for a physical education major, a five-year program that would result not only in a bachelor's degree, but also in a master's and a general secondary teaching credential.

The physical education major was also beneficial for my tennis. As I was struggling to make the varsity early on, the five-year program allowed me to "redshirt" or sit out my junior year and then play my senior year and my fifth year while I was earning my master's degree. I finally earned a starting position as a senior. In my fifth year, 1959–60, I was #3 on the team and, as a bonus, was awarded the Buck Club Leadership Award for tennis. By the time I graduated, I was able to play close with, or even beat, guys with whom I could not even stand on the same court five or six years before. I was proud that I had started as a barely ranked junior player and ended up one of the better players in college tennis.

The extended time, extra degree, and teaching credential were also critical to my development as a coach. By the spring of my fifth year, when I was doing my student teaching at neighboring Los Altos High School, I knew I would soon be entering the coaching world, so I took special note of how coaches with whom we were competing against conducted themselves. My Stanford coach, Bob Renker, knew of my interest in coaching, and so in the summer of 1959, before my last year, he asked me to take his place on the Stanford coaching camp staff, headed by Stanford's director of athletics, Chuck Taylor. Sensing how well the tennis activity was being accepted, I conducted a survey at the end of camp. I was gratified that it showed tennis was the most popular sport offered.

I taught at the camp in the mornings, and then in the afternoons I served as an assistant at the Menlo Circus Club under Coach Renker, who was by now the club manager, and his director of tennis, George Kraft. I also started teaching lessons at private home courts in the neighborhoods adjacent to Stanford.

Through these initial teaching experiences, I drew heavily on what I had learned in my first lesson from Harold Chaffee—make it exciting for your pupils! My favorite example of this, and one that had a critical impact on me as a teacher, was best illustrated during one of my younger pupil's last lessons of the summer on a private court. She was a very small girl with a very big and heavy racket. After a lot of trial and error and a couple of lessons, she finally connected to hit a beautiful forehand. It is impossible to overstate how hard this girl and I had worked for this seemingly minuscule success, and how much it meant to her. I was clapping and celebrating, and she became so excited that she started jumping up and down as well. Abruptly, she stopped, seemingly in midair and looked down to be confronted by evidence of the mistake puppies sometimes make when they get too excited. Mortified, she took one final look at me, and then ran up the steps and out the front door. I never saw her again. I felt terrible for her embarrassment but was also grateful to her. She'd reinforced one of the great lessons I had learned and been validated for by Harold Chaffee: MAKE THE SUBJECT MATTER EXCITING! (Although maybe not *that* exciting!) If a teacher can make their subject—any subject—exciting, the rewards will be extraordinary for both their student and themself.

I believe my enthusiasm and commitment to making tennis exciting is largely why I enjoyed this early success. And, of course, that success only served to increase my love of coaching. My career was starting to take shape; it had almost become a calling. My first job after being a student at Stanford would cement it for me.

Coach and Teacher

I was hired at Mountain View High School in the fall of 1960, a few miles south of Stanford, to coach ninth and tenth grade JV football and boy's tennis, and teach driver training, social living (health education), and PE.

Coach Renker had encouraged me to find supplemental work to aid in take- home pay in addition to the stable income from teaching school. Fortunately, an older Stanford fraternity brother of mine, Bob Murphy, was the manager of a new nearby club, Fremont Hills Country Club. Bob hired me as the club's first tennis professional. I began teaching tennis there in the summer and on weekends to supplement my income while teaching and coaching at nearby Mountain View High School.

Coaching high school football had a profound effect on my coaching later on. I had about thirty fourteen- and fifteen-year-olds, and I coached both offense and defense with no assistant coaches. This was really my first time coaching a team, and I had visions of Vince Lombardi in my head, which meant that I thought I had to be a tough guy to be a successful football coach. I was cussing and swearing at these kids and being as gruff as I could. One day, one of these team members named Eddie Matias fell to the ground in an effort to avoid contact in a one-on-one tackling drill. As he was lying on his back, I ran up, glared down at him, and started giving him hell in the harshest way imaginable. He just lay there taking it all in. Finally, he looked up at me and yelled, "F**k you, Mr. Gould!"

I suddenly realized that the tough guy persona I had tried to adopt wasn't me at all. Thanks to Eddie and a couple of other kids in similar circumstances, I realized that I couldn't be Vince Lombardi. I had to be myself, simply Dick Gould. My approach changed pretty quickly. Henceforth I would just be me, for better or for worse.

Not many of these football players had ever played tennis and none belonged to tennis or country clubs, but they were pretty good athletes. I recruited a bunch of them to try out for the tennis team in the spring, when football season was over. In keeping with my philosophy to make the game exciting, we made it a big thing to be on the tennis team. I made scoreboards for each court, as well as an overall scoreboard, unusual in those days, to manually record all match scores. At each home match, we provided on-court towels, ice water, and sliced oranges for all players. We even filled two "rooter buses" with students to travel with us to give us extra support at our final match of the year against our crosstown rival school.

As a football team, we played most of our games against physically larger opponents. We were usually outclassed and lost every game until the last game of the season in my second year. I ended my football coaching career on a winning streak! As a tennis team, though, we came out of nowhere and got pretty good. We finished third in a large league my second year.

Foothill College (JC)

After two years at Fremont Hills Country Club, many of my students had earned USLTA Northern California junior rankings. I had established a solid reputation as a high school coach at Mountain View. I loved that job, but in 1962, I saw an opportunity at a brand new and neighboring school, Foothill Junior College in Los Altos Hills. As the tennis coach there, I would be involved with tennis full-time and could build a program from scratch, which had great appeal to me. And it was only about a mile from Fremont Hills Country Club, where I was still serving as the tennis professional.

This was the heyday of California junior colleges, which numbered about 120 statewide, all with great financial support and strong athletic programs. So I camped on Foothill College athletic director Bill Abbey's doorstep until he offered me the job of year-round tennis coach and physical education teacher.

All the coaches in Foothill's PE department were assigned to teach a "methods" class in their sport called "How to Teach." Mine covered tennis, as well as badminton, archery, and golf. This led me into a successful venture that I had not planned. I wrote an extensive syllabus for the tennis part of the course and titled it *Tennis, Anyone?* I had it bound and sold in the campus bookstore as a class resource book. To my surprise, a local publisher, Mayfield Publishing Company, saw it and proposed a publishing deal. Over the years, *Tennis Anyone?* sold more than five hundred thousand copies in six printings and three languages: English, Japanese, and French.

We developed a pretty good tennis team right away at Foothill College. In addition to many good local high school athletes, I was able to recruit top German player Horst Ritter, nationally ranked Hawaiian junior Rodney Kop, and top Mexican junior Raul Contreras. Foothill College tennis was on the sports map for good. Ritter and Kop each won a state JC singles championship, and Foothill won the first two of its many state JC tennis championships in 1964 and 1965.

Fremont Hills Country Club Teaching Professional

While at Foothill, I continued to enjoy my side job as the teaching pro at Fremont Hills Country Club, which I held for six years in all, from 1960 to 1966. Perhaps most important, the job gave me the opportunity to become entrenched in the Peninsula and Northern California professional tennis teaching world. My fellow pros became friends, and they would later identify with and support what we were doing at Stanford in the years to come.

It also taught me how to build something from scratch. Because Fremont Hills was a new club in 1960 and I was the first tennis pro, I had had to work hard to promote the game and attract people to take lessons. The work paid off when interest in tennis skyrocketed at the club. In 1961, we had to build two more courts for a total of four. By my fifth year, we had seven courts. The pro shop, which was inside the base of an old water tower, didn't exactly reflect our success, but I didn't mind—our tennis program was thriving.

Here and simultaneously at Foothill College, I learned the importance of community involvement. We formed an active and respected nonprofit tennis patron's organization—the Los Altos Tennis Patrons (later expanded and renamed The Mid-Peninsula Tennis Patrons Association). Its goal was to promote tennis activity in the area, especially for youth, including my teams at Foothill College, and for a while, even at Stanford.

One of my first big promotions was staging in 1962 an incredibly large novice tournament to interest area youngsters in tennis. The city of Los Altos proclaimed the week of the tourney Tennis Week. Right away we made it a truly special event with many side activities, such as visits from local professional sports stars and local high school homecoming queens, a barbecue steak dinner, free tickets to the local movie theater, and many other amenities. We attracted more than 350 participants who had a blast, all for a one-dollar entry fee. This was a huge number for an event in those days, but I was just trying, as Harold Chaffee had taught me, to attract young players by making the game exciting.

One of my future Stanford players, Jack Radin, '76, came to this tournament as a junior player and speaks to the kind of energy we put into the event:

"It always impressed me the way that Coach ran that tournament in contrast to the others. First, it was a novice tournament for players who were unranked, which was the case with me in my first couple of years of junior competition. Second, there was a consolation event, meaning that every entrant played at least two matches. Third, he gave very nice trophies. Fourth, there was a barbecue, swim party, and dance, as well as certificates of participation (all of which he printed by hand). This was grassroots tennis at its best."

We also staged sold-out exhibitions for three years indoors in the gym at Foothill College featuring the world's top players: Chuck McKinley, Dennis Ralston, Pancho Gonzales, Rod Laver, Pancho Segura, Rafael Osuna, and so on. We inaugurated a doubles and mixed doubles weekend tournament named the Champagne'ships on private home tennis courts, an event which grew to 1,200 participants and forty-four private courts in my final year as tournament director. The funds raised by these and other interfaces with the community provided financial help for the Tennis Patrons and the program at Foothill College, and for a short time at Stanford. They were among the things that tremendously increased tennis interest on the San Francisco Peninsula (Stanford area).

The tennis boom was on its way, and by my last year at Fremont Hills Country Club, which coincided with my final year at Foothill College, 1966, we had more than twenty juniors achieve rankings in Northern California tennis. I was already, apparently, inspiring others to become coaches, just as I had been inspired by coaches like Harold Chaffee, Arnie Saul, and Bob Renker. Among my Fremont Hills protégés I started with from scratch and who would later become top-flight and respected teaching pros, were

Nick Saviano, Steve Stefanki, Chris Anderson, Jeff Stewart, and Chris Bradley.

John Gardiner

Another early mentor was John Gardiner, a respected tennis promoter and founder of one of the nation's first and most respected summer youth tennis camps, at the renowned John Gardiner Tennis Ranch, a destination resort in Carmel Valley.

Promoting the game came naturally to me, but it was John who really taught me how to represent the sport. Even more important, he stressed the importance of treating people well, from superiors to peers to pupils to employees. With John, *everything* was first class, from the oversized towels in his tennis ranch guest cabanas to the quality of food for his guests to the immaculate dress of his teaching staff.

John also emphasized teacher education and formed Professional Tennis, Inc., or PTI, Northern California's first tennis teaching professional organization and the forerunner of the Northern California USPTA. John was elected its first president. I had the honor of serving on the founding board and succeeding him as president in 1967. Those were fun times because we brought the Northern California teaching community together. We developed a professional certification system, a series of great, albeit small, teaching pro prize money tournaments, and offered many other professional perks, such as insurance benefits and job endorsements.

I wanted to pursue this professionalization of tennis teaching further, and at the beginning of my fourth year at Foothill, I approached the dean of instruction about establishing a tennis teacher's education degree. I even submitted an outline for a course of study, including how to teach tennis, with an actual practicum at local clubs, community recreation departments, and so on. Today, Tyler Junior College, Ferris State, Berry College, and a handful of other great teaching professional education programs exist, and more professional tennis management programs are constantly being established to attract and train young pros. Ours would have been the first such program in the United States offered for academic credit, but life had other plans for me that would pull me away from Foothill before I could get this program started.

Back to the Farm

In the late spring of 1966, during my fourth year at Foothill, my Stanford coach and mentor, Bob Renker, announced his retirement after sixteen years at the helm as a part-time coach. During his tenure, and to his credit, Stanford never finished out of the top ten in the NCAA championships, and on average, finished about six or seven nationally.

I was extremely happy at Foothill College and Fremont Hills Country Club. I would not have left either to go anywhere but Stanford. At the time, Stanford athletics was not the juggernaut it is today. Stanford had eight varsity teams, all male, including tennis. Other than a couple of championships during World War II—men's basketball, and even men's tennis unofficially in 1942 (prior to official NCAA tennis team champions being named)—the last Stanford NCAA championship had been in men's golf thirteen years before in 1953. Stanford tennis had been reasonably successful but was still a long way from competing for an official national team championship.

Excuses for Stanford's athletic mediocrity were rampant, even among the coaching staff. "Top students and great athletes are not a mix," "We can't get enough blue-chip athletes admitted to Stanford," and so on. I disagreed and sincerely believed we could compete for the national championships in tennis despite the presence of the tennis giants to the south—USC and UCLA.

People who knew the collegiate tennis scene and the state of Stanford athletics at the time literally laughed at me. I had, however, learned two important lessons. The first, which I learned from the Stanford admissions office when I was nearly rejected eleven years before, was to go after what I wanted, regardless of the obstacles. The second, which had come through my subsequent experiences at Mountain View High School, Fremont Hills Country Club, and Foothill College, was about the importance of persistence when pursuing a job.

When I heard Coach Bob Renker was leaving, I immediately asked for a meeting with Stanford athletic director Chuck Taylor, whose camp I had worked at several summers earlier. I did not give Chuck the chance *not* to hire me! When we met, I told him I felt Stanford could win a national championship in tennis, and that I believed I was the guy to lead this effort. I was confident since I had coached Foothill to two state junior college championships and coached three players, Horst Ritter, Rodney Kop, and Raul Contreras, all of whom went on to be great NCAA college players and were about the same level as those I anticipated having at Stanford.

I told Chuck that to be successful, I needed to serve as a full-time coach, not part-time at $5,000 per year like Bob Renker. I asked Chuck to make me a full-time coach, match the salary I was receiving at Foothill College, approximately $10,500, and provide scholarship help to enable us to compete at the highest level. Finally, I asked his permission to use the Stanford courts for my personal lessons for additional income. This would financially allow me to leave my club pro job and devote my full efforts to Stanford.

My bold approach amounted to cockiness. I had no personal competitive experience or reputation outside of the immediate Stanford tennis area and teaching local pro tournaments. And although my reputation was growing in Northern California, it was still pretty limited in scope. I knew my dream would not be an easy sell. To my surprise, Chuck agreed to it all, and starting in the 1966–67 school year, I was hired to become Stanford's first full-time tennis coach. While I was certainly still a young man with modest accomplishments, I was not unprepared for the opportunity.

In retrospect, this background seemed adequate for the new job at Stanford. But despite these lessons learned, my education in how to coach and how to lead was only just beginning.

PLAYER INDEX

PLAYER NAMES, CLASS YEAR, SHORT BIOS

NAME. CLASS YEAR. TENNIS ACCOMPLISHMENTS; OCCUPATION

L Name	F Name	Yr	Bios
Abrams	Geoff	00	Captain; All-American; Pac-10 Player of the Year
175, 258			Assoc. Prof., Dir. of Athletics for Varsity Sports; Orthopedic Surgery Stanford Medicine
Alloo	Chuck	69	
xxiii			Retired: Former Tennis Pro and Real Estate Executive
Andrews	Rich	70	
21			Retired: Tennis Director; Academy Director; College Coach; Club Manager
Ansari	Ali	01	Captain
35, 85			President & CEO, FRESHBREW

Cornell	Brad	69	Captain
xxii			Emeritus Prof. of Finance: UCLA
Corse	John	82	
5, 14			Deceased: Formerly General Counsel, Baltimore Gas and Electric
Cortes	Alejandro	77	Pro #126; Colombia Davis Cup
258			Retired: Formerly an Investment Manager
Coull	Rod	86	
210			Retired: Orthopedic Surgeon; High School Teaching Assistant
Davis	Scott	84	All-American; Pro Singles #11, Doubles #2
260			Tennis Coach
Delaney	Jim	75	Captain; All-American; NCAA Doubles Champ; Pro #59
112, 212			Retired: Institutional Equity Sales
Devens	Bobby	94	
19, 20, 36, 41, 65, 77, 117, 166, 213, 222, 255, 266			Managing Director: Goldman Sachs (Private Wealth Management)
DeVincenzo	John	84	
54			MD: VP-Translational Virology, Enanta Pharmaceuticals; Pediatrics Prof., Univ. of Tenn.
Dey	Doug	70	
25			Research Scientist: Former Dir. Fish Ecology Division, Northwest Fisheries, NOAA
Dines	Bruce	76	
14			Senior Partner: Liberty Global Ventures
Dunn	Curtis	89	Captain; Represents US on Several International Teams
267			Software Developer/Solutions Architect

Golden	Glenn	76	Part of First Family to Earn Two Top-Ten Rankings in Same Year (Father/Son)
269			Tennis Coach: Midtown Athletic Club; Academies Tutor; Business Consultant
Goldie	Dan	86	All-American; NCAA Singles Champ; Pro #27
204			Wealth Adviser
Goldstein	Paul	98	Captain; All-American; NCAA Singles Finals; Pro #58; Stanford Coach
6, 10, 27, 58, 195, 317			Taube Family Director of Men's Tennis
Grabb	Jim	86	Captain; All-American; NCAA Singles Semifinals; Pro Singles #24, Doubles #1
7, 8, 73, 74, 128, 187, 231, 232, 233			Performance Coach/Meditation Instructor
Grover	Greg	71	
323			Retired: USPTA Master Teaching Professional
Gurfein	Jimmy	83	All-American; NCAA Singles Finals; Pro #96
49, 50, 88, 124, 135			Tennis Coach
Hagey	James "Chico"	75	All-American; NCAA Singles Finals; Pro #72
11, 13, 34, 247			Real Estate Developer; President: Red Leaf Village Company, San Diego
Hauser	David	00	
174			Senior VP, Software Engineering, BigCommerce
Haviland	Ryan	03	All-American; NCAA Singles Semifinals; Pro Tour
235, 270, 320			Owner & Director: Haviland Tennis Academy, Greenville, SC

Wright	Perry	78	Captain; All-American, NCAA Doubles Semifinalist
38, 279			Dir. of Construction: AMCAL Multi-Housing, Inc. (Developers & General Contractors)
Yee	Jason	91	Captain; All-American; NCAA Doubles Finals
64			Mergers & Acquisitions/ Corporate Development
Young	Rich	69	
26			Attorney/Partner: International Law Firm of Bryan Cave Leighton Paisner

* This list includes only those whose quotes were selected to use in this book.

ACKNOWLEDGMENTS

JACK GIFFORD: Whose persistent questioning provided the impetus to write this book.

MY GUYS: Who have taught me so much and have provided me with lifelong friendships *and* in addition thoughtful responses to questions I could not answer about their personal observations and experiences. *They* have become this book!

STANFORD UNIVERSITY and **ATHLETIC DEPART-MENT**: Whose belief in me gave me great freedom to develop as a coach and to create.

MY PARENTS: Who by example taught me so much about values, ethics, effort, and belief.

MY WIFE, ANNE: Also a championship coach and great teacher, who has taught me so much about patience and inclusion, let alone from her extremely valuable thoughts, insights, and countless hours of reading and editing this book, and for all else she has so unselfishly given me.

MY CHILDREN SUE, SHERI, KARIN, RICK, and **KIM**: For sticking with me as I pursued my passion and for showing me every day by how they live their lives and have raised their own families how much confidence we should all have in the generation that follows us. There could be no better examples.

MY TEACHAIDS CONCUSSION EDUCATION TEAM, IN PARTICULAR, CEO DR. PIYA SORCAR: Whose constant encouragement, work ethic, attention to detail, and "people" relationships have provided so much inspiration and taught me so much, let alone her editing skills of my book and allowing use of my office wall space on which to post thousands of player quotes. Special thanks also to TeachAids office teammates such as Christine Chen and Lisa Fu for their early on critical organizational support.

MY COLLABORATOR, TIM NOONAN: A valued member of our first two national championship teams and a top two hundred-ranked professional, who just happens to be the author of over thirty-five books. What a delight to work with Tim in an effort to make this book as strong and as helpful as possible to others, as well as a fun read.

OTHER WRITERS AND READERS: STEVE JAMISON, who from day one has so unselfishly given his valued input and advice; **PAUL FEIN**, an accomplished writer from whom I have learned so much about the importance of detail; **JERRY POR-RAS, PAUL ROETERT, JAKE WARDE, AMBER HEN-NINGER, BARBARA PUGLIESE, ROY GESSFORD, KIM** and **RYAN CALDBECK**, and **MAYA YUTSIS** for making time to read the manuscript and advise; and **JOEL DRUCKER, BILL SIMONS**, and **ED SCHEIN** for their constant inspiration, advice, and interest.

IMAGE CREDITS: Courtesy of Stanford Athletics, ISI Photos, David Gonzales/StanfordPhoto.com, Rod Searcey/Stanford Photo.com, Jan Null, Chuck Painter, Steve Lacey.

BILL GLADSTONE: CEO and founder of Waterside Productions, Inc. for his constant enthusiasm, encouragement, and out-of-the-box thinking regarding the publishing of this book. Special accolades and appreciation are due his incredible staff, including his most dedicated managing editor, Kenneth Kales; website designer, John Burke; outstanding layout designer, Joel Chamberlain; marketing staff led by Christopher Van Buren; and associate publisher Josh Freel. Thanks also for the work in the evolution of the cover design of Ken Fraser and especially Sheri Heckel. This truly has been a team effort led by a great leader, Bill Gladstone.

Made in the USA
Middletown, DE
03 August 2022

70421072R00235